Student Success in Community Colleges

Student Success in Community Colleges

A Practical Guide to
Developmental Education

Deborah Boroch, Laura Hope,
Bruce Smith, Robert Gabriner,
Pamela Mery, Rob Johnstone, Rose Asera

JOSSEY-BASS
A Wiley Imprint
www.josseybass.com

Published by Jossey-Bass
A Wiley Imprint
989 Market Street, San Francisco, CA 94103-1741—www.josseybass.com

Jossey-Bass books and products are available through most bookstores. To contact Jossey-Bass directly call our Customer Care Department within the U.S. at 800-956-7739, outside the U.S. at 317-572-3986, or fax 317-572-4002.

Jossey-Bass also publishes its books in a variety of electronic formats. Some content that appears in print may not be available in electronic books.

Library of Congress Cataloging-in-Publication Data

Student success in community colleges : a practical guide to developmental education/Deborah Boroch . . .
[et al.] ; foreword by John Nixon.—1st ed.
p.   cm.—(The Jossey-Bass higher and adult education series)
Includes bibliographical references and index.
ISBN 978-0-470-45555-5 (pbk.)
1. Community colleges.   2. Academic achievement.   I. Boroch, Deborah.
LB2328.S94 2010
306.4'830973—dc22

2009054079

Printed in the United States of America
FIRST EDITION

PB Printing   10   9   8   7   6   5   4   3   2   1

The Jossey-Bass Higher and Adult Education Series

Contents

**Dedicated to our dear friend and colleague
Debbie Boroch, who left us too soon
but left us richer for her leadership, wisdom, and inspiration.**

Foreword

Basic Skills as a Foundation for Institutional Transformation

As a community college president, I have found that opportunities to effect change that can lead to institutional transformation are rare. Community colleges are complex organizations, with competing interests and voices inside and outside the campus. Although all stakeholders may be committed to the goal of student success, their disparate priorities and approaches to achieving that goal function more often in organizational silos than in integrated unison.

A common example of organizational silos is the separation of instructional and student services units at community colleges, a separation that fragments faculty and staff, as well as students' integration into higher education. A primary challenge for community college presidents is recognizing and seizing the occasional catalyst that they can parlay into institutional transformation grounded in an agenda for student success. Such an opportunity came to light several years ago through a California program known as the Basic Skills Initiative.

When the State Academic Senate for the California Community Colleges proposed higher levels of math and English requirements for the AA degree, community college stakeholders, including the Senate, began discussing strategies for assisting students who may be unprepared to meet the new degree requirements. With 80% of students entering California community colleges placing in English and math courses below college level, the challenges facing colleges in meeting the basic skills needs of so many students are daunting. Ultimately, the discussions on basic skills and student success led to a significant and transformational state program to grow and improve teaching and learning in basic skills, named the California Community College Basic Skills Initiative (BSI).

My own engagement with the BSI began over dinner with the leader of the Research and Planning Group (RP Group) for California Community Colleges. My college had been selected to coordinate the initial activity of the BSI, developing a comprehensive review of the literature on effective practices in basic skills education. The RP Group took on the assignment and produced a document that has had the most significant and productive impact on teaching and learning at California Community Colleges that I have experienced during my 30 years in the profession. That document is the foundation for this book.

Faculty and administrators on my campus have engaged and embraced the review of the literature, not only to find rationale and research to support and question their own assumptions and practices, but to stimulate collaboration and exploration of new approaches and paths leading to student success in all disciplines. Campuswide dialogue, initiated through the shared experience of engaging the review of the literature, has brought down many of the silos that have inhibited past efforts to lead students to success. The BSI has been transformational for Mt. San Antonio College. When faculty and administrators respond to challenges with quality research, the resulting changes to policy and practice can change students' lives.

Basic skills, as defined and applied in this excellent text, can present such an opportunity, offering college leaders a path to a strategy, combining and directing effective practices, that can result in institutional transformation. *Student Success in Community Colleges: A Practical Guide to Developmental Education* frames basic skills as an institutional strategy for meeting the challenges of students who are unprepared for success in higher education—a comprehensive strategy, combining well-researched effective practices which promote student success. Implicit in the effective practices presented in the text is the fundamental notion that unprepared students must be able to identify, in a simple psychological sense, with a college and its mission, with faculty and staff, and with other students, as prerequisite to their discovery of motivation and purpose that will drive them to success in college and beyond. The application of effective practices in basic skills teaching and learning in bringing success to unprepared students carries with it the implication that many of the same effective practices can act as a foundation, or catalyst, for a comprehensive strategy for institutional transformation.

I would argue, using *Student Success in Community Colleges: A Practical Guide to Developmental Education* as support, that our success in assisting students to discover their unique motivations is dependent on our capacity to assist them in identifying with the culture of higher education, with learning itself, and with faculty, staff, and other students. Through such a process of identification, students can discover motivations that lead them to use learning to achieve present and future purposes and goals. The challenge of achieving identification is most effectively met at a college where programs and services are integrated across disciplines, as argued in this text most persuasively. Identification, achieved through integrated programs and services—as opposed to fragmented silos—with all faculty and staff focused on the mission of student success, leads to discovery of motivation, which leads to success in basic skills and to achievement in college and beyond.

As a community college president, I have the challenge and opportunity to create a campus environment that promotes the process of identification for students, which can lead to purposeful learning. My own discovery (but certainly not new knowledge to the profession) is that the path to student success described above is the same path that faculty and staff (and college presidents) must follow in order to create the learning environment necessary for student success, which in turn can become a path to institutional transformation.

Many of the effective practices presented in this guide can be combined and applied as a set of tactics, forming a strategy for institutional transformation. The desired transformation integrates mission, goals, resources, staff development, and programs and services into a focused, organic whole, as opposed to silos. Integrated organization can be achieved when the college president embraces and applies the same principles and practices that derive from the research on basic skills.

As a community college president, I embrace the research and findings put forward here. This volume is an essential tool and catalyst for institutional transformation, and I recommend it to all college leaders and practitioners whose mission and challenge are student success.

John S. Nixon, Ph.D.
President, Mt. San Antonio College

Acknowledgments

We would like to acknowledge the hard work and important contributions that specific individuals made to the original version of this document, once known as the "Poppy Copy" among California Community College practitioners. The original team of authors included Jim Fillpot, director of research at Chaffey College, who wrote significant portions of the self-assessment tool and also contributed to the cost analysis tool. Dr. Andreea Serban, president of Santa Barbara City College, contributed to the literature review. The project also benefited from its Faculty Review Panel, comprised of Dr. Jan Connal, Dr. Barbara Illowsky, Dr. Richard Mahon, and Ms. Nancy Ybarra. Finally, we would like to thank Elisa Rassen for her editing work on the Jossey-Bass edition of the "Poppy Copy."

The Authors

Dr. Rose Asera has been a senior scholar at the Carnegie Foundation for the Advancement of Teaching since 2000. She was the director of Strengthening Pre-collegiate Education in Community Colleges (SPECC), a four-year action research project that was supported by the William and Flora Hewlett Foundation. SPECC focused on developmental education in 11 California community colleges. Among the suite of SPECC project reports and essays, Asera is the author of *Change and Sustain/Ability, A Program Director's Reflections on Institutional Learning*. Dr. Asera has been part of the program planning committee for the California Strengthening Student Success Conference since its beginning in 2006; she is currently a member of the California Basic Skills Initiative Steering and Advocacy Committee. From 1995 to 1999 she worked with Uri Treisman as director of research and evaluation at the Charles A. Dana Center at the University of Texas at Austin. In 1991–92 Asera was a Fulbright Scholar at the Institute of Teacher Education at Kyambogo in Kampala, Uganda.

Dr. Deborah Boroch (1956–2009) held a master's degree in biology and an Ed.D. in organizational leadership, and had over 25 years of experience in higher education. As a classroom teacher, she taught in K–12 schools, community colleges, and in both public and private universities. From 2007 to 2009, she was the dean of instructional services at Mt. San Antonio College, a public community college in Walnut, California, where she previously served as associate dean of math and science as well as professor and department chair of biology. Dr. Boroch was the basic skills coordinator for the college, and previously served as project coordinator for the college's

Title V grant targeting improved student success in developmental mathematics. Dr. Boroch was coauthor of two publications related to the Basic Skills Initiative in California: *Basic Skills as a Foundation for Student Success in California Community Colleges* (2007), and *Effective Practices for Promoting the Transition of High School Students to College* (2009).

Dr. Robert Gabriner holds an Ed.D. in Higher Education from University of California, Berkeley and is currently the director of the Doctoral Program in Education Leadership at San Francisco State University. Prior to coming to SFSU in January 2009, he worked in the California community colleges for 40 years serving as an instructor of American History in the Peralta Colleges in Oakland, California, dean of Research and Planning at City College of San Francisco and finally, vice chancellor for Advancement at CCSF. Dr. Gabriner is also the director of the Center for Student Success of the Research and Planning Group and has been the project coordinator for the original California edition of *Basic Skills as a Foundation for Success in California Community Colleges* as well as the Jossey-Bass edition.

Laura Hope has been a community college educator and leader at Chaffey College for the past 20 years. During that time, she has served students as a professor of English, teaching foundation, transfer, and honors courses. Outside of the classroom, Ms. Hope has worked in various leadership capacities. She has served as the English, ESL, modern languages, and reading coordinator, Puente English instructor and co-coordinator, student learning outcomes coordinator, and interim dean of language arts and currently serves as the dean of instructional support at Chaffey. In 2000, Ms. Hope was elected Chaffey College Faculty Lecturer of the Year, and in 2006 she was honored by Chaffey College President and NISOD as an outstanding educator and leader. The primary focus of her career has related to the Basic Skills Transformation at Chaffey College, which has garnered both statewide and national attention for its results on student achievement.

Dr. Rob Johnstone holds a Ph.D. in social psychology and the law from the University of Oregon, and is currently dean of planning, research, and institutional effectiveness at Skyline College. Since shifting from industry in 2002, he served as a college researcher and chief instructional officer at Foothill College and has recently refocused his work in the arena of research and planning with his 2008 move to Skyline College. Dr. Johnstone serves as a vice president of the Research & Planning (RP) Group of California and has worked on numerous Center for Student Success and RP projects. Dr. Johnstone served as project administrator for Phases II & III of the California Basic Skills Initiative, in which professional development utilizing the Phase I findings was provided to all 109 California Community Colleges.

Pamela Mery leads the Office of Research and Planning at City College of San Francisco (CCSF). She has written three in-depth reports on precollegiate basic skills at CCSF. In 2005, Ms. Mery received an award for achievement in research from the RP Group for California Community Colleges for her first report on basic skills. She is currently pursuing a doctorate in educational leadership at San Francisco State University.

Dr. Bruce Smith holds a Ph.D. in Higher Education and Adult Development from the University of California, Los Angeles, as well as advanced degrees in educational methodology from Catholic University of America and Dramatic Arts from the University of California, Santa Barbara. Currently he is dean of the School of Liberal Arts at City College of San Francisco (CCSF). Prior to joining the CCSF administration, he was dean of Academic Affairs at Santa Barbara City College and served on the faculty of Antelope Valley College for nineteen years, including six years as academic senate president. In addition, Dr. Smith served on the Accrediting Commission for Community and Junior Colleges of the Western Association of Schools and Colleges. He has published articles on the impact of student involvement on persistence and academic progress in community college environments.

The Research and Planning Group for California Community Colleges (RP Group) strengthens the ability of California community colleges to undertake high-quality research, planning, and assessments that improve evidence-based decision making, institutional effectiveness, and success for all students. It does so through three primary strategies. First, RP's Center for Student Success (CSS) conducts research and evaluation projects that utilize the skills and unique perspectives of California community college institutional researchers, faculty, and administrators. Second, the RP Group builds the skills of administrators, faculty, and staff through a broad range of professional development offerings and by disseminating effective practices. Finally, the RP Group develops strategic partnerships and provides leadership on statewide initiatives to help keep evidenced-based decision making, accountability, and student success at the forefront of California community college efforts.

Since 2000, CSS has led dozens of system-level research and evaluation projects that have resulted in significant changes to the California community college system, including the laying of the groundwork for the statewide accountability system (ARCC), the modification of admission requirements for the registered nursing programs, and the publication *Basic Skills as the Foundation for Success in the California Community Colleges*, which was instrumental in the development of the Basic Skills Initiative and provided the framework for evaluating college-level basic skills programs throughout the state. The success of CSS projects is rooted in their design. Each project is led by a unique team of community college staff, faculty, and administrators who have proven research skills and a direct understanding of the subject at hand. Projects culminate in audience-specific products that stimulate discussion, improve outcomes, and strengthen student success. You can find out more about CSS research and the RP Group at www.rpgroup.org.

Student Success in Community Colleges

Introduction

THE ORGANIZATION AND stated missions for community colleges vary considerably across the United States; however, they share a common bond—providing access to higher education for students who, for a variety of reasons, attend two-year institutions to accomplish a postsecondary educational goal. According to the Community College Research Center, half of all students in higher education attend community colleges and 70% of those students aspire to a bachelor's degree as their academic objective. But only a quarter of those community college students ever transfer and less than 10% actually attain a bachelor's degree (Bailey, 2003, p.1).

There are many factors that influence the success of students in community college environments, but preparation for college-level work is clearly a core issue. Many community colleges are "open access," ensuring admission to any student regardless of their previous educational attainment or academic preparation. This means that many community colleges do not require a threshold level of skills attainment to qualify for admission. In California, for example, 90% of first-time community college students test below college level in mathematics and 70% test below college-level reading and writing (Moore & Shulock, 2007). Nationally, 40% of two- and four-year college students end up taking at least one remedial course (Adelman, 2004). Clearly, if community colleges are going to serve these students successfully, they must develop effective strategies for transforming students' goals into outcomes.

In preparing this guide, the authors reviewed more than 300 literature references and considered effective practices and programs presently in operation across the United States and internationally. Based on a synthesis of effective practices that emerged from this review, the project team also prepared a self-assessment tool and a cost-revenue framework that colleges may use to evaluate existing programs and services as well as plan for new and revised basic skills initiatives.

This guide is an *integrative review of literature* in the field of developmental education as it relates to the community college setting. An integrative review:

> [P]ulls together the existing work on an educational topic and works to understand trends in that body of scholarship. In such a review, the author(s) describe how the issue is conceptualized within the literature, how research methods and theories have shaped the outcomes of scholarship, and what the strengths and weaknesses of the literature are (*American Educational Research Association, 2006*).

The effective practices identified throughout this study are based on a careful review and comparison of research conducted over the last 30 years by experts and practitioners. In order to be included in this study, theory and practice had to meet the test of producing evidence of improvements in student learning and success in college (or similar educational environments). The authors have attempted to include documentation of the success of the practices that are identified as effective, including quantitative and qualitative evidence, as well as conclusions drawn by noted experts in the field. In some cases, there is very limited or no quantifiable evidence available to verify the effectiveness of the practice. Description of those practices is included when there is a reasonable level of commonly accepted acknowledgment by experts and practitioners that these practices are effective, particularly in the areas of instructional methodology and staff development. These practices are included in the interest of providing comprehensive coverage of this broad field of study. When outcomes data were reported, we have so indicated. In some cases, the lack of citations of specific quantitative data and results of statistical tests may be a function of the sources failing to include specific data, or may result from the difficulty of aggregating measures from different studies using different measures across different institutions over time.

What makes a practice effective? Various outcome measures have been cited in the literature as evidence of effectiveness. These measurements are both quantitative and qualitative. Quantitative measurements typically include course success, course retention, success in subsequent courses, program persistence, progression through sequential levels of developmental courses, progression to college-level courses, and course or program grade point average. Qualitative measurements include student and faculty perceptions and satisfaction with various elements of the program presented in a format consistent with the principles of qualitative research.

A variety of terms appear in the literature to describe this field of practice. These include *remedial education, foundation courses, precollegiate,* and *adult literacy,* in addition to the terms *basic skills* and *developmental education.*

The National Literacy Act of 1991 defined literacy as

[A]n individual's ability to read, write, and speak in English, and compute and solve problems at levels of proficiency necessary to function on the job and in society to achieve one's goals, and develop one's knowledge and potential (National Literacy Act of 1991, Sec. 3).

Boylan describes developmental education as

[C]ourses or services provided for the purpose of helping underprepared college students attain their academic goals. The term underprepared students refers to any students who need to develop their cognitive or affective abilities in order to succeed in a postsecondary educational experience. (2002, 2003)

For this guide, the authors have adopted the following working definition for basic skills:

Basic skills are those foundation skills in reading, writing, mathematics, and English as a Second Language, as well as learning skills and study skills which are necessary for students to succeed in college-level work.

College-level coursework is defined as courses that are degree-applicable or meet college graduation requirements, or both. Some studies include any course that is transferable to a four-year institution as *college level.*

The inclusion of English as a Second Language in this definition recognizes that all ESL is not, by definition, subsumed under basic skills. However, to the extent that a student is unable to succeed in college-level coursework due to the inability to speak, read, write, or comprehend English, ESL skills may be considered as foundation skills in accordance with the definition.

Finally, in this guide the term *effective practice* refers to

Organizational, administrative, instructional, or support activities engaged in by highly successful programs, as validated by research and literature sources relating to developmental education.

California Community Colleges: A Context for This Study

This guide to effective practices in basic skills for community colleges was initially developed as a resource for a statewide Basic Skills Initiative (BSI) in California community colleges (CCC). It was developed by an experienced team of faculty and administrators from across the state of California, each having specific expertise and many years of practical experience in the field of basic skills assessment and practice.

One of the challenges that the researchers and writers faced while writing the original guide to effective practices in developmental education for California community colleges was the extraordinary diversity of the colleges within the system. We were not developing a "one-size-fits-all" document because the colleges come in so many sizes, structures, locations, and combinations of student, faculty, and staff demographic compositions. In fact, using the term "system" in relation to California community colleges may be a misnomer, although over the last two decades there has been a movement toward a more systematic organization with a somewhat more centralized governance structure. However, as the following overview demonstrates, there are still major differences among the 110 colleges. The original guide was written with those differences in mind; rather than contextualize each effective practice and the related tools within the confines of a specific college's organization, demographics, size, or location, we tried to present the research and analysis in a form that could be adapted to any one of the 110 colleges. Similarly, we believe this national edition can be adapted to the characteristics of community colleges in different systems across the United States.

Open Access and Academic Preparation

As in most states, the academic preparation of California high school students varies considerably from school district to school district and even within school districts. In addition, many students return to community colleges after extended periods away from formal educational environments. This means that students entering community colleges have extraordinary differences in their preparation for college-level work. At most CCCs, students can enroll in many or most courses without demonstrating reading, writing, mathematical, or critical-thinking skills. Although most CCCs require some form of placement testing for enrollment in English and mathematics courses, many colleges do not have skills prerequisites for other college-level courses. At most colleges, the imposition of skills prerequisites are at the discretion of academic departments and college curriculum committees.

In 1988, the Mexican-American Legal Defense and Educational Fund (MALDEF), a Latino advocacy group, threatened a lawsuit against one of the California community college districts over the use of prerequisites, claiming that some course prerequisites were arbitrary and unnecessarily inhibited the progress of students toward their educational goals. In response, the California Community Colleges Chancellors's Office (CCCCO) adopted policies and procedures for the establishment of prerequisites, stipulating that a prerequisite was justified when it was "highly unlikely the student would succeed" in the course without the skills or knowledge of the prerequisite requirement. However, many colleges simply dropped most their course prerequisites to minimize any legal liability they might encounter. Only English and mathematics courses commonly have skills or course prerequisites at most CCCs; discipline-based sequential course prerequisites vary considerably by college and frequently even within colleges (for example, at some colleges, science may have sequence prerequisites, but social sciences do not).

Recently, the imposition of skills prerequisites for courses has become a major issue within the system, with a number of constituencies within and outside of the system arguing that some type of "basic skills floor" should be imposed on college-level courses to ensure that they have an appropriate level of academic rigor. Others argue that prerequisites place unnecessary obstacles in the path of students attempting to achieve their academic goals and delays students' progress toward degrees, certificates, and transfer. Statewide data indicate that 80–85% of students enter CCCs with deficiencies in one or more basic skills; at some colleges, it is as high as 90%. Course success rates in developmental classes have been consistently around 69% for ESL, 60% for English, and 54% for mathematics (Board of Governors of the California Community Colleges, 2008). Yet, of the students who enrolled in a basic skills class in the 2001–02 academic year, only 29% of those students had earned an associate degree, a vocational certificate, or had transferred to a four-year institution by 2006–07 (CCCCO). Therefore the role of developmental education remains a major challenge for California community colleges.

The Basic Skills Initiative

Over the course of several years, three events led to the development and funding of the Basic Skills Initiative for California community colleges. First, the board of governors (BOG) adopted a new comprehensive strategic plan in January 2006. One of the specific goals of that plan is to strengthen student success and readiness for college-level courses. Second, in September 2006, the BOG approved raising of the statewide minimum English and mathematics graduation requirements for all students earning the AA or AS degree. Under the new standards, all students earning an associate's degree must demonstrate proficiency in freshman English composition and mathematics at the level of intermediate algebra (a course one to two levels below college algebra at most colleges). The new requirements took effect in fall 2009.

While the strategic plan and the new graduation standards were being developed, a coalition of statewide organizations collaborated on a plan to address the needs of developmental education in CCCs—the third event leading to the BSI. The Academic Senate for California Community Colleges, the chief instructional officers, the chief student services officers, and Research and Planning Group, the organization of institutional researchers, developed the Basic Skills Initiative with the objective of balancing a concerted effort to improve outcomes in developmental education with the increased requirements of the new graduation standards. This plan was embraced and funded by the CCC chancellor's office, initially with a planning grant and eventually with a combination of funding for statewide and local initiatives.

The first phase of the Basic Skills Initiative was led by the Research and Planning Group with guidance from each of the constituencies that formulated the BSI. The main product of this planning phase was a 150-page document, *Basic Skills as a Foundation for Student Success in California Community Colleges* that was nicknamed "The Poppy Copy" for its brightly colored cover. That text is the basis for *Student Success in Community Colleges: A Practical Guide to Developmental Education*. The original text was broken into three parts: a review of literature and effective practices, an assessment protocol for effective practices in basic skills, and a tool to estimate costs of program improvements and downstream revenue from higher rates of student persistence and success. The organization of the Poppy Copy was designed to provide a basis for subsequent phases of the BSI which would include statewide orientations to the initiative followed by extensive self-assessment, planning, and implementation of annual plans at each college in the state. The self-assessment tool in the Poppy Copy was piloted at 12 colleges and revisions were made.

The second phase of the Basic Skills Initiative focused on orienting colleges across the state to the literature review, the self-assessment and planning process, and the reporting requirements for the use of the categorical BSI funds appropriated to local districts. A statewide steering committee was formed consisting of California community college stakeholders to provide guidance to the BSI. The BSI conducted workshops and provided technical assistance to all community colleges within the system. By the spring of 2008, every college in the California system had conducted a self-assessment, developed major objectives, and submitted an annual action plan to the chancellor's office. Approximately $31 million in ongoing funding was allocated to individual colleges, based on a formula, to help fund the action plans.

In Phase III, the BSI focused on continued support for local activities while initiating several new statewide efforts. Additional literature reviews were commissioned focusing on three main areas: equity and diversity challenges and strategies, high school to college transition, the transition from noncredit to credit programs and services. In addition, regional workshops were offered on the integration of student services and counseling into the basic skills courses and programs; strategies and training for local BSI coordinators; and the use of outcomes assessment tools. Matrices were developed for identifying and classifying precollegiate course levels in mathematics and English.

Phase III also initiated a centralized data collection resource on effective practices, strategies, and programs. Housed on the California Community Colleges Chancellor's Office Web site, it includes in-state and out-of-state submissions. The database can be searched by any of the twenty-six effective practices from the 2007 literature review using key words, targeted populations, and college demographics. The database is designed to be a "living project"—constantly updated and expanded.

Phases I through III were all funded by one-year grants from the CCCCO. Although each phase was informed by the work on the previous phase, there was no long-range plan for institutionalizing the initiative as a core component of the state and local programs and services. In the spring of 2007, a small group of community college professionals began discussing the need for long-term, ongoing resources for identifying, evaluating, and sharing effective practices and professional development designed to prepare faculty and staff to implement those practices.

Under the umbrella of the Research and Planning Group (RP), grants were secured from the William and Flora Hewlett Foundation, the San Francisco Foundation, and the Walter S. Johnson Foundation, to support a planning process during the 2007–08 academic year that brought together representatives of the principal constituencies that originally had formulated the BSI. Representatives of the Academic Senate for California Community Colleges, the chief executive, chief instructional and chief student services officers organizations, the RP Group, the chancellor's office, and experts and experienced practitioners from the colleges developed a basic plan for a permanent infrastructure to support the BSI.

That plan called for a multiyear effort (at least three to five years) rather than the one-year programming of Phases I, II, and III. In the transition to the more permanent infrastructure, the BSI would continue to provide workshops, consultants for local initiatives, and complete the work initiated in the previous three phases. Simultaneously, a statewide network would be developed to collect resources on effective practices, provide professional development training, and build the capacity of local colleges to use research-based innovations to improve student outcomes.

The plan's highest priority was expanding individual colleges' capacity to provide productive, effective, student outcomes–oriented professional development opportunities for faculty, administrators, and staff. Given the size and complexity of California's community college system, both regional and online "virtual" networking structures were proposed to ensure that all colleges have access to resources. The regional networks would directly connect faculty and staff from different colleges and provide affordable programs within reasonable proximity to all colleges. Virtual networking would be used to link colleges with similar characteristics or similar initiatives across regional barriers. Mentoring and consultation services were proposed as another aspect of capacity building. Based on requests from participating colleges, experienced leaders and practitioners would be linked with colleges based on the specific needs and conditions of the college requesting support.

Another key function of the networking would be ongoing knowledge building and sharing. Phase III of the BSI had initiated the development of a comprehensive manual on effective practices and substantial electronic resources. Building on the previous phases, the permanent infrastructure would include the careful development and management of a *knowledge base* to provide practitioners with accessible and useful (that is, "implementation-friendly") information in a variety of formats. Colleges would have access to regional *in-person networks* of professionals at local colleges and online *virtual networks* that would promote the use of this knowledge base at individual colleges across the state and provide feedback on successful programs and services statewide. This *knowledge loop* would inform all aspects of the BSI.

As noted earlier, capacity for usable research varies considerably among the 110 California community colleges. Even when significant research resources are available at a college, there is frequently a gap between the data provided by the research staff and the ability of faculty and staff to understand the use of that research to improve teaching and student support programs and services. Therefore, an essential component of the knowledge-building process would be developing practitioners' ability to use quantitative and qualitative data as evidence of effectiveness. Training faculty "data coaches" and creating bridges between research offices and instructional programs and services would be crucial to success. This *culture of evidence* would demonstrate the effectiveness of local initiatives and document the overall progress of the basic skills initiative and its impact on student equity.

Finally, the plan called for the development of an annual summer leadership institute, based on the models of success demonstrated by programs such as the Kellogg Institute at Appalachian State University, the National Writing Project, and the Washington Center for Improving the Quality of Undergraduate Education. Each summer, a cohort of 30–40 faculty and administrators would receive intensive training in leadership skills, the use of data to improve programs and services, models of effective practices, and resources for professional development.

The guiding principle of the proposed basic skills network was that *all effective professional development is local*. Whereas statewide and regional activities can stimulate change, building the capacity of individual colleges to evaluate and implement change would be the core function of the network. Each college in the system has its own culture, human and fiscal resources, and differing student demographics. Therefore, the network would be prepared to provide *college-specific* resources to each institution. Equally important, the network would identify common needs among groups of colleges, create opportunities for regional and statewide training and collaborative efforts, provide peer-to-peer support, and limit the costs of professional development with an economy of scale.

To accomplish this, the BSI proposed a system of regional hubs, in which each hub would have a coordinator. Initially, the coordinators would be involved in an assessment of needs and available resources for each college in their region, identifying the types of support that would be most useful for each college and documenting the successful programs and services at each college with an eye toward expanding the knowledge base of the network. The development of virtual networking—using electronic resources—would allow colleges from different regions to collaborate on similar activities, or would provide colleges that have similar characteristics the opportunity to work together across regional boundaries.

A central office would be responsible for coordinating all activities. The project director would provide leadership for building the infrastructure, developing statewide activities, creating partnerships with external professional development resources, developing specific programs and services, overseeing the work of the regional coordinators, and developing the knowledge base. The statewide leadership and regional coordinators would also focus on creating and promoting a research agenda for the BSI using metrics on student outcomes and student equity that demonstrate the effectiveness of programs and services and that document the relationships of *individual* professional learning and *institutional* learning to *student* learning.

Early in the 2008–09 academic year, the CCC Chancellor's Office issued a request for proposals for next steps in the BSI to commence in January, 2009. That RFP stipulated that the BSI in 2009 and beyond would be guided by a five-year renewable grant designed to continue the work initiated in Phases I, II, and III while developing a statewide regional network. In December 2008, the Los Angeles Community College District was awarded the grant based on a proposal that included all of the elements identified by the planning group.

Beyond California

Although the circumstances of California community colleges may differ from colleges in other states, the experiences that led to the development of the Basic Skills Initiative are common to most community colleges. *More and more students are coming to community colleges less and less prepared for college-level studies.* There is an increasing recognition in the national political arena that community colleges can and should be on the front line of raising the preparation of our workers and educating our citizens. The diversity of California community colleges provides a useful context for this study of effective practices in developmental education.

Organization of This Study

This study has been organized as a manual for practitioners. While each element of this book can be used by community chief officers, trustees, and many other interested parties, the focus of this overview is to provide people on the front line of developmental education with a comprehensive overview of the research and a set of tools to assess and improve their programs and services. There are a number of books that assess and comment on the role of community colleges in higher education and the impact of community college developmental education on the economic and social well-being of our communities, states, and the nation. There are certainly implications that can be drawn from this study on the broader role and effectiveness of two-year institutions. But the primary objective of this book is to assist faculty, student development personnel, department chairs, and deans in evaluating their developmental education programs and adopting research-based effective practices to improve student outcomes.

Based on this practitioner focus, the book is divided into two parts. Part One provides an overview of the research of effective practice, synthesizing a broad range of research literature and expert analysis into a set of major effective practices. Under each effective practice, there is a detailed description of the practice, the research that demonstrates its effectiveness, and references to programs and services that utilize these practices. Categorizing the practices around the organization of community colleges, Part One starts with institutional practices, then programmatic practices, followed by instructional and student development practices, and finally, professional development—the key to organizational change.

Part Two is designed to assist institutions in evaluating their existing programs and services using the effective practices described in Part One and developing and supporting program improvements based on those institutional self-assessments. First, Part Two presents a self-assessment tool that colleges can use to inventory and assess the practices employed in their developmental and collegewide education programs and to create plans for implementing new and revised programs and services focused on data-based improvements in student outcomes.

Part Two also contains a cost-revenue model designed to help colleges determine the long-range financial impact of initiatives that improve student retention and persistence. Cost is probably the most common reason colleges cite for not implementing effective practices that have been demonstrated to improve student outcomes. Many (but not all) of the effective practices described in this book do require some additional fiscal resources from already stressed college budgets. However, the cost-revenue model presented in Part Two allows colleges to analyze and demonstrate the long-range revenue that can be gained when students succeed in developmental education and move on to successfully complete their academic goals. All too frequently colleges see recruitment as the primary tool for capturing enough enrollments to generate their revenue goals. The cost-revenue tool, and the commentary supporting it, argues that an investment in developmental education can be as productive in maintaining revenue as recruitment while more effectively fulfilling the mission of the community colleges: to provide real access to higher education by ensuring the success of all who can benefit.

Part One
Effective Practices

PART ONE OF this study provides a comprehensive integrated literature review of approaches to developmental education across the country. Based on the review of more than 300 sources, the research team has identified a specific set of effective practices used by community colleges to successfully develop students' basic skills and, ideally, transition students into college-level coursework.

The practices described in this section are *not* the *only* effective practices in developmental education. Clearly individual faculty and institutions have discovered ways to produce improved student outcomes that are not included in this review. However, the practices that are included in this review have emerged across institutions and have met the tests of quantitative or qualitative research and have demonstrated replicability.

These effective practices have been divided into five categories, each of which is discussed in Chapters One through Five:

1. *Organizational and Administrative Practices:* Policies, procedures, and values that take place at an institutional level that support the success of developmental education programs.

2. *Program Components:* Elements of effective developmental education programs—such as student orientations, counseling, and financial aid—that assist students' successful completion of coursework.

3. *Instructional Practices:* Teaching and learning strategies and methodologies that improve developmental education student outcomes.

4. *Student Support Services and Strategies:* Approaches to enhancing students' success through support services.

5. *Professional Learning and Development:* Principles and practices that will improve abilities of faculty and staff to meet the needs of developmental education students and improve the outcomes for students

in developmental, career and technical, and degree-applicable courses and programs.

These individual effective practices can contribute to a successful approach to developmental education at community colleges nationwide. However, it is only through the integration and coordination of practices within and across each of the five categories that colleges will be able to truly develop basic skills programs that promote student success and goal attainment.

For example, commitment at the institutional level is key to strengthening development education programs; however, this commitment means little if the institution does not promote, facilitate, and support the development of effective program components, using professional development as a tool for innovation at the program, classroom, and student service levels. Similarly, it will be extremely difficult for individual college faculty and staff to initiate and implement a program, instructional practice, or support service described in this study without support at the program and institutional levels. Therefore, the effective implementation of individual effective practices frequently requires interaction among the practices.

Chapter 1

Organizational and Administrative Practices

AS INSTITUTIONS SEEK to improve their efforts to provide effective developmental education, a common question is "What is most important? What shall we do first?" Although the answer to this inquiry depends to a great extent on the assessed strengths and weaknesses of the efforts on individual campuses, most institutions would do well to examine key elements of their administrative and organizational practices as a first step toward addressing overall effectiveness. How strong is the institutional commitment to developmental education and how is this commitment demonstrated? How does the institution determine its optimal organization of program components, and what steps are taken to ensure appropriate levels of integration and coordination? Is there, in fact, a developmental education program that is viewed holistically as a vital, mainstream mission of the college on a par with transfer or occupational preparation?

As one of many functions occurring within a college, developmental education must be examined within its wider institutional context. Institutional choices concerning program structure, organization, and management matter, and have been related to the overall effectiveness of developmental education programs. In many respects, these organizational and administrative practices provide a foundation on which to create the essential conditions that foster effective practices at the programmatic and instructional levels. These conditions are *enablers*: practices that, if strengthened, pave the way for positive outcomes across all segments of the developmental program. Similarly, the overall performance of developmental education programs is impaired when these elements are not given sufficient consideration.

Ideally, developmental education programs and services will have been implemented at the institutional level with great deliberation and careful consideration of many potential strategies. In many colleges, this level of meticulous planning may not be evident, with more organic, less directive approaches driving development. Over time, changes in institutional conditions (for example, student demographics, institutional culture, executive leadership, and so on) also result in fundamental shifts of organizational focus that may have an impact on the delivery of developmental education. Vigilance is needed to ensure that the impacts of such shifts are purposeful and intentional, and not simply the result of organizational drift. The following effective practices included in this chapter are supported by the published literature and provide a lens for examining organizational choices as they relate to delivery of developmental education.

1.1. Developmental education is a clearly stated institutional priority.

1.2. A clearly articulated mission based on a shared, overarching philosophy drives the developmental education program. Clearly specified goals and objectives are established for developmental courses and programs.

1.3. The developmental education program is centralized or is highly coordinated.

1.4. A comprehensive system of support services exists and is characterized by a high degree of integration among academic and student support services.

1.5. Institutional policies facilitate student completion of necessary developmental coursework as early as possible in the educational sequence.

1.6. Faculty who are both knowledgeable and enthusiastic about developmental education are recruited and hired to teach in the program.

1.7. Institutions manage faculty and student expectations regarding developmental education.

1.1. Developmental education is a clearly stated institutional priority.

An authentic institution-wide commitment to developmental education is widely cited in published literature as a characteristic of colleges with exemplary programs. Roueche and Roueche (1999) conclude that positive student outcomes in developmental programs are more likely to occur when institutional leaders establish high standards for success, expect everyone involved to work toward achieving program goals, and create appropriate supporting frameworks for program success. Based on analysis of a large volume of literature and research studies, Boylan and Saxon (2002) further noted that commitment at the institutional level is repeatedly cited as a key factor in successful remediation. In a study of 28 exemplary programs, developmental education was rated as "completely" or "extensively" important when assessing institutional priorities in all but one case (Boylan, 2002). A study of developmental education in Texas colleges and universities also found that programs with the highest student retention rates were located in institutions that considered developmental education to be a priority (Boylan & Saxon, 1998).

An institutional focus and acceptance of remediation as a mainstream activity of the college are communicated via public declaration of administrative support as well as through appropriate allocation of resources. McCabe (2000) makes an explicit recommendation that community colleges give remedial education higher priority and greater support, stating:

> *Institutional commitment to underprepared students is of greatest importance. Successful remediation occurs in direct proportion to priority given to the program by the college. Most important is a caring staff who believe in the students and in the importance of their work. Presidential leadership, in word and deed, is critical to success.* (p. 49)

In California, the Community College Board of Governors (the body that regulates the statewide implementation of legislation affecting the 110-college community college system) echoed this notion in a study characterizing "best-practice" institutions as those in which the success of underprepared students is a stated institution-wide priority accompanied by adequately staffed and funded developmental education programs (California Community College Board of Governors, 2002). Other evidence of institutional commitment includes publicizing program results, featuring developmental courses and services prominently in college publications, and including developmental educators in discussions and decisions with respect to broader campus planning and implementation of academic programs.

In recent years there has been an increase in the number of institutions that have begun earnestly examining student outcomes and identifying achievement gaps. This scrutiny has often provided momentum for campus leaders to establish broad-based initiatives to change the way developmental education is valued and delivered in their institutions. In 2004, 27 community colleges were selected by the Lumina Foundation to participate in the "Achieving the Dream" initiative to enhance student success, particularly among low-income students and students of color. This initiative requires that colleges undertake comprehensive activities with the goal of building a culture of evidence to transform their operations on a large scale. Twenty-one of the participating colleges chose to focus their projects specifically on developmental education, bringing this key function into the academic and social mainstream. Although these projects are still in the early stages of evaluation, the near-universal identification of developmental education as the focus of institutional commitment for these projects is promising (Brock et al., 2007).

An example of an institutional commitment to developmental education is illustrated by the comprehensive planning and assessment conducted by Davidson County College (DCC) in North Carolina. Beginning in 1999, DCC selected developmental education as a theme for its accreditation self-study. The institution then undertook a multiyear assessment, planning, and implementation process, employing external expert consultants as well as internal task teams charged with examining current practices in the context of research-based effective practices. Following extensive planning and review, these teams made recommendations for strengthening college functions in the areas of advisement, assessment, coordination and learner support, communications, evaluation, and curriculum development; these recommendations were formalized in the institution's 2001 strategic plan. In implementing the broad-based elements contained within its plan, DCC made a cultural shift in which the functions of developmental education were embraced across the college by stakeholders who had by then spent several years studying these issues in the context of their own college.

Although dedication on the part of executive leadership is unquestionably vital in promoting institutional focus and primacy of the developmental education program, a true institutional commitment relies on the broader buy-in on the part of faculty and staff. Kozeracki and Brooks (2006) argue that developmental education must be cast in a more inclusive way in which faculty outside of the traditional disciplines of reading, writing, mathematics, and ESL embrace their roles and responsibilities toward developmental students. If one primary role of developmental education is to facilitate students' transition from remedial to college-level courses, then developmental courses must be fully integrated into the curriculum. Moreover, the effects of underprepared students who enroll in subject area courses without any specific prerequisites are felt by faculty in these disciplines. These faculty "meet the students where they are," even if they do not officially teach a remedial course. According to Kozeracki and Brooks (2006), an institutional commitment exists when faculty in all areas cease to see developmental education as the singular purview of a few areas, and instead accept it as a shared purpose central to their work in the college.

The degree to which developmental programs and services are comprehensive and institutionalized are two key factors in evaluating the extent of institutional commitment and prioritization. A strong correlation has been repeatedly documented between the comprehensiveness of an institution's developmental education programs and positive impacts on student learning. Isolated basic skills courses have been shown to be the least likely to produce long-term gains in student achievement, whereas programs that incorporate an increasing sophistication of learner support and cross-disciplinary learning "systems" are the most effective (Kiemig, 1983). In order to create and maintain such systems, institutions must place a high value on basic skills programs and see them as fundamental to the institutional mission.

The level of institutional support and priority accorded to developmental education programs are also expressed in the sufficiency of course offerings and support services to meet student needs. Colleges that prioritize developmental education constantly monitor student placement and enrollment data, and make every effort to maintain sufficient access for students entering at all levels of the program. Because basic skills learners already require extended time frames to complete their educational goals, best-practice colleges strive to avoid further delays caused by insufficient course offerings or lack of other necessary services. To the extent that providing access involves extra efforts at recruiting and maintaining sufficient staff, purchasing additional materials, or enhancing administrative structures, these colleges accept this responsibility for achieving the desired level of functionality.

The commitment to embedding systematic, comprehensive systems for developmental education requires increased institutional investment, but doing so has been associated with increased short- and long-range program outcomes (McCabe & Day, 1998). In an analysis of twenty educationally effective institutions that consistently had higher than predicted graduation rates relative to matched peer institutions, Kuh et al. (2005) demonstrated a significant correlation between student success and institutional leadership that consistently made student success a priority message. These authors also indicate that financial and moral support provided by leaders was an essential component in institutional effectiveness, as well as the promotion of complementary academic and social programs accessed by large proportions of students (as opposed to "boutique" programs supporting smaller targeted groups).

Roueche and Roueche (1999) also confirm that a systemic approach offers the greatest potential for the success of developmental students, and that the developmental program should be "one part of an institution-wide commitment to success for all students" (p. 29). Practitioners and professional organizations in New York State have also offered policy recommendations emphasizing institutional commitment as a key component of successful programs (Neuberger, 1999; Ritze, 2005).

1.2. A clearly articulated mission based on a shared, overarching philosophy drives the developmental education program.

Subscribing to an overarching, articulated philosophy of developmental education that is shared among all institutional stakeholders is an acknowledged best practice according to a variety of literature sources (Boylan, 2002; California Community College Board of Governors, 2002; Roueche & Roueche, 1999; McCabe, 2000). Developing and adopting such a philosophy should be the result of a highly coordinated effort involving multiple stakeholders. Researchers have concluded that the success of community college developmental education programs depends on faculty having a clear understanding and commitment to the philosophy and objectives of developmental education that are espoused by the institution (Sheldon, 2002). "Best-practice" institutions are encouraged to assign faculty to developmental courses only after they have been oriented to this shared institutional philosophy and the associated institutional expectations for desired student outcomes (Boylan, 2002) (see also Practices 1.6 and 1.7 in this section).

In addition to having a unified mission and philosophy of practice, successful developmental education efforts feature clearly specified goals and objectives for all courses and programs. Roueche (1973) notes that clear-cut goals are essential, both to set student expectations and to influence the development of a cohesive course structure having solid alignment between exit and entry skills across sequential levels. Further, the National Study of Developmental Education (Boylan, Bonham, Claxton, & Bliss, 1992) found that developmental programs with written statements of mission, goals, and objectives had higher student pass rates in developmental courses than programs without such statements. Other studies connected mission, goals, and objectives with higher pass rates on state-mandated tests and higher year-to-year retention rates for developmental students (Boylan & Saxon, 1998). The National Association of Developmental Education recognizes the importance of this element in effective programs and requires all programs seeking its certification to describe their philosophy, goals, and objectives for developmental education.

1.3. The developmental education program is centralized or is highly coordinated.

A considerable body of research has examined the role of program organization as it relates to effectiveness of developmental education efforts.

The consensus view among researchers originally established that a centralized model of program and service delivery was superior to a more distributed "mainstreamed" model (Roueche & Baker, 1987; Boylan, Bonham, Claxton, & Bliss, 1992; Boylan, 2002).

A centralized organizational structure places the delivery of all remedial courses, programs, and services in a separate department, supervised by a dedicated department administrator, with its own identified line of budgetary and other resource support. Advantages cited for this model include more accessible, highly integrated support services, and greater likelihood that faculty teaching remedial courses will be highly motivated and have specific expertise regarding developmental learners (Perin, 2002). Various studies have connected the centralized model with higher student retention and course success, as well as with higher first-term and cumulative grade point average (GPA) (Roueche & Baker, 1987; Boylan, Bliss, & Bonham, 1997; McCabe & Day, 1998). Evidence further suggests that the centralized model is more effective for students with the lowest skill levels. Furthermore, when surveyed for their opinions concerning the most desirable structure, many faculty identified a centralized model as being most beneficial to the students (Perin, 2005).

Despite the finding that centralized programs lead to more positive student outcomes, only a minority of community colleges nationally operate from a centralized department. One source reports that this structure occurs in 38% of two-year colleges (Shults, 2000); a more recent study finds that 44% of sampled colleges reported having centralized developmental education programs (Gerlaugh, Thompson, Boylan, & Davis, 2007). The alternative model, referred to as mainstreaming, distributes the teaching of remedial courses among various academic departments, and those individual departments may teach both college-level and remedial courses. Advantages cited for this model include greater cost efficiency, better alignments between remedial and college-level courses, greater communication among faculty across levels (for a consistent transmission of college-level expectations), and reduced stigma attached to students who are not isolated in a separate department (Perin, 2005; Academic Senate for California Community Colleges, 2003).

In any intentional effort toward restructuring to provide for centralized delivery, concerns regarding the separation of developmental courses and programs need to be addressed. Grubb (1999) observes that separation can relegate developmental programs to "a low-status activity, the custodial or housekeeping department of college-level instruction" (p. 171). In 1991, the Academic Senate for California Community Colleges (2000) recommended against the centralization of basic skills into a stand-alone discipline, fearing that "the establishment of a separate basic skills discipline would lead to a two-tiered system, where basic skills students were regarded as inferior" (p. 7). While the preponderance of research-based evidence does favor the centralized model, colleges that choose to move in that direction must clearly be mindful of any negative perceptions or stigma and take purposeful steps to communicate the rationale for the structures adopted.

Further studies have concluded that the demonstrated superiority of student outcomes associated with the centralized model may not be due solely to the structural organization, but may instead arise from the higher level of communication and collaboration associated with centralization (Boylan, 2002). This interpretation suggests that decentralized programs might achieve the same benefits with respect to student achievement as centralized programs, provided that they are highly coordinated. Boylan (2002) argues that decentralized programs still demand "coordination of developmental programs and services by an administrator with primary responsibility for campus-wide developmental education" (p. 11). Additional traits of a highly coordinated decentralized effort include the following: regular meetings of all those involved in the delivery of developmental courses and services, articulation of common goals and objectives for all developmental courses and services, and the integration of developmental courses and academic support services.

A number of other factors have been identified that relate to the choice of developmental program organization. Some colleges may prefer to distribute developmental students across departments so that the whole college shares responsibility for their progress. Other factors involved in the choice of program structure include student placement policies, the size of the institution and its academic departments, and institutional politics. Appreciating the diversity of institutional contexts and local conditions, the research literature fails to arrive at a consensus recommendation for a single "best" structural model for the organization of developmental programs across institutions. However, a strong message concerning the need to collaborate and coordinate among program components emerges as a consistent finding reported by various published sources.

In an effort to strengthen coordination in an environment where developmental courses were distributed among academic departments, one Florida community college created a new associate dean position. This individual was given primary responsibility for coordinating the various services provided to underprepared students. She also worked closely with department leaders from English, math, and college success (Freshman study skills), each of whom was also given release time for curriculum development and evaluation of programs. This hybrid approach might be considered as one possible way to provide for centralized coordination while still maintaining the discipline-based knowledge and connections needed to achieve integration of the developmental program with college-level courses.

1.4. A comprehensive system of support services exists, and is characterized by a high degree of integration among academic and student support services.

The majority of studies of best practices in developmental education call for the offering of comprehensive support services for remedial students (McCabe & Day, 1998: Neuberger, 1999; Raftery, 2005; Boylan, 2002; Roueche & Roueche, 1999). A review of 51 developmental programs reported that the "programs that showed the greatest gain in scores, GPA improvement, and retention also tended to be comprehensive in scope, mission, and services" (Boylan, 1983, p. 32). The impact of fully integrated systems that engage faculty and staff across all segments of the institution are clearly documented in a recent study to determine which community college management practices were associated with increased student success. Jenkins (2006) concluded that comprehensive, well-integrated delivery structures were associated with improved student outcomes. He writes:

> *Our findings suggest that, to promote student success, not only do particular student support services . . . need to be in place, but they must be well-aligned and coordinated across the campus. While administrators may see different functional areas of the college as providing discrete services, students do not see, nor should they experience, such divisions. Seamless integration of services from the students' perspective and collaboration among faculty, staff and administration in providing these are the college characteristics that seem to contribute most to student success. (p. vi)*

Support systems have been described as existing at four "levels," representing increasing potential to produce positive program outcomes (Kiemig, 1983). At level one, remedial courses exist in isolation, with no additional outside support provided. Level two programs offer some additional learning assistance, such as generalized tutoring not connected to individual courses. Course-related learning assistance is provided at level three, in which trained personnel who have specific information about course content, assignments, and expectations engage with students either inside or outside of class. Level four is characterized by the presence of comprehensive learning systems (for example, learning community models) in which all participants share the responsibility for providing monitoring, advisement, and instructional support.

Roueche and Roueche (1999) have explicitly called for colleges to examine the comprehensiveness of support services available to developmental students, emphasizing that "colleges must increase the support and structure they offer at-risk students who need support and structure more than any other students in higher education" (p. 29). The essential services include mandatory orientation, assessment and placement, expanded preenrollment activities, establishment of peer and faculty mentors, and more comprehensive financial aid programs. Integrated services combined with developmental coursework are further cited as contributing to student retention in Heisserer and Parette's summary of several studies (2002).

Developmental students who have the services of a comprehensive learning assistance program available to them have been shown to make larger gains in academic performance than those who do not (Neuberger, 1999). One approach to offering integrated, comprehensive support for developmental students is the use of Learning Assistance Centers (LACs). Maxwell's (1997a) review of the literature concerning these centers concluded that effective LACs commonly contain the following functions:

1. Academic evaluation and diagnostic testing

2. Instruction in study skills and learning strategies

3. Peer tutoring or professional tutoring, or both

4. Supplemental instruction, or course-related, systematic, and highly structured group tutoring

5. Computer-assisted instruction and access to other educational technology

6. Credit and noncredit developmental courses

7. Faculty services, such as research opportunities, assistance in developing SI programs, cooperative learning demonstrations, and classroom support materials

8. Publication of LAC programs through newsletters and class and faculty visits

9. College administrators who are informed about LAC programs and services

10. Staff training and development activities

11. Referral services to other programs and services on campus

12. Close relations with offices that provide personal, financial, educational, and career counseling and providing training for peer counselors

13. Integration with advising departments and faculty advisers

14. Program evaluation

Self-contained programs, such as California's Extended Opportunity Programs and Services (EOPS), which provides academic and support services for low-income and educationally disadvantaged students, also model the integration of a variety of student support services with academic instruction. These one-stop programs typically include counseling and advising, direct financial assistance, health and child care services, directed tutorial and other academic support services, and assistance with university transfer. The challenge for colleges often becomes one of scale—how to expand the service model operating effectively for small groups to one that can be implemented across the institution. The pervasiveness of an integrated systems model can be regarded as a reflection of the institutional commitment to developmental education for all students.

1.5. Institutional policies facilitate student completion of necessary developmental coursework as early as possible in the educational sequence.

There are two schools of thought related to how students should complete developmental courses versus other college courses. If existing assessment procedures are presumed to be accurate indicators of a student's actual level of preparation (and to the extent that basic skills competence is actually required for success in college-level courses), it is logical to infer that students are best served by completing preparatory developmental coursework prior to enrolling in other nondevelopmental courses. On the other hand, mandatory completion of a comprehensive basic skills pathway prior to enrollment in other courses slows students' progress and may be seen as stigmatizing or restricting students' engagement with the overall college experience. Concurrent enrollment in carefully selected academic or vocational courses outside of basic skills areas may help in sustaining student motivation and providing early successes that will enhance persistence. Acknowledging that both views have merit, research overwhelmingly supports the notion that early assessment and completion of developmental coursework improves student achievement.

Weissman, Bulakowski, and Jumisko (1997) examined the timing of remediation in relation to overall program effectiveness. In a study of 2,028 college-ready students and 1,254 underprepared students entering in the same semester, researchers reported that completing developmental education courses during the first year of enrollment increased persistence, especially for those students least prepared for college-level courses. They also found that students who took developmental education courses during their first term of enrollment remediated at a much higher rate than students who did not attempt any developmental courses during their first semester. They concluded that their study supports a policy of requiring underprepared students to begin their developmental courses upon initial enrollment.

Similar findings have been reported in another nationwide study, the Achieving the Dream initiative. This study of 27 colleges found that students who successfully completed any developmental course in their first term of enrollment were more likely to persist and succeed from that point forward than those in any other student group, including those who attempted but did not complete developmental courses, and even those who did not require remediation in the first place (Community College Survey of Student Engagement, 2007).

The actual practices of colleges with respect to the simultaneous enrollment of students in developmental and regular college coursework vary. In 1996, about two-thirds of colleges placed some restrictions on the regular academic courses that students could take while enrolled in remedial coursework; only one-third had no such restrictions. At least one study has compared success among college-ready students, underprepared students who did not remediate, underprepared students who completed remediation, and underprepared students concurrently enrolled in college-level courses (Castator & Tollefson, 1996). These authors found that underprepared students who had remediated and underprepared students concurrently enrolled in developmental and college-level classes earned grades comparable to those of college-ready students, whereas underprepared students who did neither had lower grades. They conclude that colleges are justified in implementing policies requiring completion of remediation either prior to or concurrent with enrollment in college-level courses.

Some practitioners fear that relegating students to a core of developmental courses that must be completed prior to entering other course offerings may create a "two-tiered" system, singling out and perhaps marginalizing students in these programs. In arguing for concurrent enrollment, Maxwell (1997c) asserts that college skills programs have historically been hindered by "enduring faculty myths." One persisting myth is that underprepared students will learn more if taught in separate classes removed from the main body of students. The fact that students do sometimes succeed when simultaneously enrolled in both developmental and college-level courses is offered as an argument that prerequisite remediation is not needed. Grubb (1999) asserts that "the idea that remediation has to precede content learning creates a teaching problem" (p. 184), in that such actions may tend to reduce students' cognitive development activities to repetitive "skill and drill" exercises, disconnected from meaningful applications in content areas. To the extent that such practices characterize the usual methods employed in developmental courses, the point is well taken. However, if developmental courses are designed to develop enhanced critical thinking and to scaffold learning in ways that contribute to increased self-regulation and self-efficacy, such experiences may instead enhance student preparation for higher-level study.

Boylan (2002) observes that students are rarely exposed to instruction in critical thinking in high school; developmental students' particular lack of this key ability leads to increased failure for these students. As developmental instruction moves away from simple repetitive practice to a more fully developed focus on critical thinking and learning strategy development, the acquisition of these foundation skills has great potential for improving subsequent success in a variety of content disciplines. Boylan argues that this shift in approach during the earliest developmental courses may help students reduce the overall time spent in remediation.

1.6. Faculty who are both knowledgeable and enthusiastic about developmental education are recruited and hired to teach in the program.

The pivotal role of faculty in developmental programs underscores the need to ensure that these key personnel are knowledgeable, experienced, and motivated to work with developmental learners. Roueche and Roueche (1999) argue that success of developmental students is predicated on faculty attitude and competence, and they call for a mandate to recruit, develop, and hire the best faculty. These same authors note that instructors who choose to teach remedial classes as opposed to being assigned to them were characteristic of successful developmental programs. McCabe and Day (1998) also recommend the use of "instructors committed to the students and the field" (p. 22). O'Banion (cited in Cooper, 1979) goes so far as to recommend that remedial instructors' discipline should be developmental studies. Perin (2005) recommends hiring instructors with experience and training in developmental education who are sympathetic to the needs of at-risk students, and further notes that this recommendation is more likely to be achieved in a centralized departmental structure than in a mainstreamed model (see Practice 1.3). At the recommendation of its executive board, the New York College Learning Skills Association also advises the hiring of "appropriately credentialed, trained, educated, and experienced faculty and professional staff" (Neuberger, 1999).

Despite these and other numerous references identifying recruitment and hiring of eager, trained faculty as an exemplary practice, only 20% of institutions in a national study reported requiring full-time faculty to possess specific training for developmental education before teaching remedial courses (Shults, 2000). Furthermore, there is a noticeable gap in the research-based literature connecting these desired criteria with any documented increase in student achievement or any other student outcomes. In a related statement, however, Boylan (2002) does find a correlation between negative attitude of faculty toward developmental education and poor developmental program outcomes, but details of the specific effects are not noted.

Assuming that knowledgeable, well-prepared faculty with specific developmental expertise would contribute to successful students, what are the characteristics of such faculty? The Academic Senate for California Community Colleges (2003) suggests that the attributes of effective developmental educators include the following:

- Demonstrates content knowledge and the ability to deliver the content
- Varies instructional delivery methods
- Maintains organized and structured activities
- Possesses knowledge of learning styles and how to apply this information
- Provides critical-thinking activities
- Relates the curriculum to the real world and careers
- Actively engages students
- Maintains high academic standards
- Engages in classroom research
- Engages in professional development activities
- Chooses to teach underprepared students; demonstrates a passion for working with these students
- Enjoys and respects students
- Sees the whole student

- Creates a "classroom community" learning environment

- Motivates students

- Engages in "intrusive" (proactive) student activities

- Encourages students to use all available support services

- Maintains an innovative spirit

- Knows how to and enjoys working with teams (p. 12)

A similar list of attributes offered by Casazza (1996) adds consideration of the affective needs of learners, the ability to assess strengths and weaknesses and communicate them to the learner, the ability to assess individual development, and the ability to gradually release responsibility for learning and self-assessment to the learner.

A number of researchers mention the role of adjunct faculty in teaching remedial courses, but reports vary on the proportions of adjunct versus full-time faculty teaching developmental courses. A recent national study of developmental education at 45 two-year institutions reports that only 21% of developmental courses were taught by full-time faculty, but notes that this is an increase of 4% from data reported 10 years earlier in a similar study (Gerlaugh, Thompson, Boylan, & Davis, 2007). Data from a study conducted in 2000 (Shults, 2000) reported a much higher percentage of full-time faculty teaching remedial courses in two-year institutions nationwide (33%). However, when noncredit courses are included, the proportion of adjunct faculty in the national workforce would likely be considerably higher.

Community colleges rely heavily on an adjunct workforce to deliver the transfer, occupational, and basic skills curriculum. Many educators assume that reliance on part-time faculty compromises student learning and potentially erodes academic standards; however, little research has been conducted to analyze the specific effects of part-time instruction. Using the National Center for Educational Statistics data, Jacoby (2006) evaluated evidence regarding graduation, learning outcomes, and the use of adjunct faculty. He concludes that community college graduation rates decrease as the proportion of part-time faculty increases.

Other research probes the relationship between a reliance on part-time faculty and student engagement. Because part-time faculty are less likely to be integrated into the institution, they may also be less available to students, affecting student engagement and assimilation into the college culture. In a comparison of grading patterns between part-time faculty and full-time faculty (McArthur, 1999), part-time faculty had a tendency to record higher grades, perhaps due in part to decreased job security and concerns about student evaluation results.

Although the use of adjunct faculty has been mentioned as a potential concern for effective practice, research has documented no significant differences in student outcomes between full-time and adjunct professors who teach remedial courses (Boylan, Bonham, Claxton, & Bliss, 1992). Programmatic outcomes, however, have been lower for institutions in which 70% or more of the developmental courses were taught by adjunct faculty (Boylan & Saxon, 1998). Because full-time versus adjunct status has not been shown to have a significant impact on student achievement, it may be that the time commitment for coordination, planning, and program development suffers when institutions employ large contingents of adjunct faculty. Boylan (2002) also notes that best-practice institutions identified in his 2000 study had only about 50% of remedial courses taught by adjunct faculty, and further recommends that any adjunct hired be "fully integrated into the program and considered as valuable assets to the program" (p. 56).

1.7. Institutions manage faculty and student expectations regarding developmental education.

Communication of explicit expectations for students and program providers enhances the effectiveness of developmental programs. Increasingly, students are coming to college with uninformed expectations that are not initially aligned with those of the faculty and the institutions (Venezia, Kirst, & Antonio, 2003). This mismatch results from the increasing number of first-generation college students who lack role models to convey accurate expectations and from students' experiences with the prevailing expectations in their elementary and secondary schools.

Research indicates that today's high school students report studying only about six hours per week on average; as compared with students of a decade ago, they more frequently miss class or are bored in class; and many students matriculate into college "with an entitlement mentality" (Kuh et al., 2006a, p. 32). Kuh emphasizes the importance of clearly defined expectations "because so many traditional-age students appear to start college already 'disengaged' from the learning process, having acquired a cumulative deficit in terms of attitudes, study habits, and academic skills" (p. 33).

Early attention to correcting misinformation about what students can expect in college and what mechanisms exist to support them in the college environment should be formalized to ensure that students are able to set manageable, realistic goals. Institutional values and expectations should be clarified early and often to matriculating students, and such reinforcement should be a shared responsibility among faculty, staff, and administrators of developmental programs.

Of particular importance is the confusion that arises from the "open door" message transmitted by community colleges. This message is meant to convey the accessibility of the colleges, but it does not speak to the particular need to prepare for college-level coursework. Since many community colleges do not advertise their academic standards and placement procedures, it is important that an institution's promotional materials try to distinguish readiness from access in the interest of communicating realistic expectations.

The common perspective that "anyone can go to community college" puts many incoming students at a disadvantage. Admission to a community college does not necessarily guarantee that a student will be spared remediation before becoming eligible for credit-bearing courses. Unfortunately, the optimal time to correct misinformation about college readiness is while students are still enrolled in high school, when decisions can be made to select appropriately rigorous coursework and maintain a strong academic effort. This certainly has implications for effective practices in establishing vigorous preenrollment programs at both the state and local levels. Researchers have recommended that colleges consider assigning permanent or itinerant advisers to high school campuses to explain the institution's readiness standards and requirements that will make students eligible for college-level versus remedial tracks (Bottoms & Young, 2008).

Several states have developed initiatives aimed at assessing high school students' readiness for college and providing mechanisms to assist students with setting appropriate expectations. The Kentucky Department of Education and the Kentucky Community and Technical College system are working together to assess college readiness in the tenth grade and devising mechanisms to identify academically at-risk students earlier, so that they can use the junior and senior year to become college ready. Similarly, North Carolina has designed a specialized twelfth-grade math course for students identified in the Early Math Placement testing program, which administers college placement tests in high school. The Montana University system encourages high school juniors to take its Writing Assessment and provides a supplemental online course called Strategies for Improving High School Writing. Minnesota's "Get Ready" program, established by its Higher Education Services Office, encourages college preparation starting as early as fourth grade and sponsors a comprehensive Web site of online advising tools, college preparation and selection resources, and information about financial aid. Two other notable informational projects are Indiana's Career and Postsecondary Advancement Center (ICPAC) and Florida's College Reach Out Program (CROP), both of which have invested substantial resources in developing data and delivery systems to help students and parents access student records and information about college requirements.

At the local level, another key point in the chronology of effective advisement occurs just after the student arrives at college and undergoes his or her initial placement testing. At that juncture, the dissonance between the student's expected placement and the reality of the recommended placement (often much lower) may be overwhelming for the student. More than simply prescribing a remedial course sequence, advisers should seize this opportunity to help students manage expectations for both their academic and social integration into the college. Effective advising will facilitate an understanding of the various implications of the course placement, address the advantages in pursuing recommended courses, and acquaint students with the resources and services available to assist them.

In a benchmarking study of best-practice institutions for developmental education, Boylan found that these institutions go to substantial lengths to make sure that faculty, staff, and students each know what is expected of them to support the developmental education effort (Boylan, 2002). Upon hiring, institutional and programmatic expectations are communicated to faculty and staff via an orientation to the program, and they are provided with continuing in-service training to ensure that they have the resources needed and are meeting the institution's expectations. One community college in Florida developed a training manual for faculty to improve the consistency of information that is provided to new faculty members regarding their roles with respect to the institution's strategic focus on student retention and success (Jenkins, 2006).

Boylan (2002) further recommends that each program should agree upon a definition of "successful developmental education" in the context of the institution, and this definition should then be widely disseminated. The activities of the developmental education program should then be publicized via newsletters, program reports, or other means so that expectations are continually managed across the institution. Boylan further emphasizes the need to specifically include adjunct faculty as part of this process, and recommends that course and program expectations be included in any written manuals or other documents provided for adjunct faculty orientation.

Conclusions

The organizational and administrative practices of community colleges clearly have a profound effect on the quality of the colleges' efforts to provide effective developmental education for underprepared students. It is not uncommon for structures and policies to evolve incrementally over time in ways that may serve particular needs but lack deliberate planning and coordination focused toward a well-defined mission or set of institutional goals. From a strategic point of view, thoughtfully assessing the organization of developmental education at the institutional level can pay big dividends by engaging a wide cross section of stakeholders in dialogue about the importance of developmental education to the mission of the college and student success all levels. With acceptance of developmental education as a shared responsibility, institutions are in a much better position to participate in meaningful assessment of programmatic and instructional practices.

Chapter 2
Program Components

ALTHOUGH ORGANIZATIONAL AND administrative practices exert significant influence on developmental education at an institutional level, effective practices operating within specific programmatic components are also validated by research. These broad-based areas of college operations serve developmental as well as other students in the college, but the published literature reveals certain practices that particularly apply to effective developmental education. Many studies verify that policies relating to how colleges advise, assess, and place students into developmental courses have a direct impact on student success and progress in courses. The literature also supports the key role of counseling, emphasizing particular approaches and interventions that work with developmental students. Additionally, the link between student persistence and access to financial aid is well documented. Finally, programs that routinely collect and evaluate meaningful data to review and improve delivery of developmental education also produce better student outcomes.

According to the literature, specific programmatic components that characterize highly effective developmental education programs include the following:

2.1. Orientation, assessment, and placement are mandatory for all new students.

2.2. Counseling support provided is substantial, accessible, and integrated with academic courses and programs.

2.3. Financial aid is disseminated to support developmental students. Mechanisms exist to ensure that developmental students are aware of such opportunities, and are provided with assistance to apply for and acquire financial aid.

2.4. Regular program evaluations are conducted, results are disseminated widely, and data are used to improve practice.

2.1. Orientation, assessment, and placement are mandatory for all new students.

There is widespread agreement in the literature regarding the benefits of mandatory orientation, assessment, and placement for developmental students. This finding is widely supported in study after study comparing student outcomes in environments having mandatory assessment or placement with outcomes in environments where such practices are voluntary or do not exist. In addition, mandatory assessment and placement are repeatedly cited as best-practice recommendations for exemplary programs (Roueche & Roueche, 1999; Maxwell, 1997b; Casazza & Silverman, 1996; McCabe, 2000; Neuberger, 1999; Boylan, 2002). An analysis of four of the most often cited literature references for effective developmental education found that mandatory assessment and placement was one of only two programmatic features named by all four sources (California Community College Board of Governors, 2002).

Calls for mandatory assessment are supported by evidence of improved student outcomes. Roueche and Roueche (1999) report that "information from colleges that make assessment and placement mandatory, together with data reporting the performance of all students taking remedial work, suggests that remediation correlates with improved performance over the rest of the college experience" (p. 47). They further comment that colleges in states that require assessment and placement showed improved student retention and success levels when mandatory policies were enforced. In a study of nearly six thousand developmental students from 160 two- and four-year institutions, students who were subject to mandatory assessment were significantly more likely to pass developmental English or mathematics courses than those in programs where assessment was voluntary (Boylan, Bliss, & Bonham, 1997).

Although often touted as a "best-practice" criterion, mandatory course placement after initial assessment has been somewhat more controversial with respect to outcomes data. Although mandatory placement was found to be positively correlated with student retention in four-year colleges, a negative correlation was shown for two-year colleges (Boylan, Bliss, & Bonham, 1997). However, developmental course success rates were positively correlated with mandatory placement in both two- and four-year schools. These authors interpret this finding as positive support for both mandatory assessment and placement. They argue that under voluntary placement, the weakest students may not take the remedial courses at all, and so they are not counted. In this case, the stronger students filling remedial classes are more likely to be retained, compared to a situation of mandatory placement in which the service population would include students with both high and low ability or motivation, resulting in more course drops. Essentially, voluntary placement tends to prevent a large number of the weakest students from being included in the program's service population.

If, as Cross (1976) observed 30 years ago, that fewer than 10% of those needing remediation survive college without it, mandatory placement's loss to attrition is the lesser of the evils. Even if some students are lost to attrition due to mandatory placement, more would be expected to be retained than if they do not receive any remediation at all.

The higher education system in Ohio affords an interesting opportunity to examine the effects of enforced placement and remediation. The colleges and universities in this state have considerable autonomy in establishing their individual assessment and placement policies, resulting in variation among the various schools' placement standards. A recent study examined students of similar academic preparation (based on high school courses, grades, ACT scores, and so on) who received remediation at a college with a stringent standard for placement compared to those who attended colleges in the system where the placement standard did not prescribe remediation. After controlling for a range of other variables in the student populations, this study estimated that over a five-year period, math and English remediation reduced the likelihood of stopping out by 10% and increased the likelihood of baccalaureate degree completion by 9% (Long, 2005). Although the study population did not include students at the lowest levels who were placed into developmental levels at both colleges, these findings do demonstrate the value of taking developmental courses to improve outcomes for students who are assessed at slightly below college level.

The Academic Senate for California Community Colleges has engaged in a comprehensive analysis of assessment and placement in California community colleges. Supporting the importance of both assessment and placement for basic skills, the authors of this analysis note:

> *Basic skills and ESL courses are the foundations for the other work a student will do at a community college. When a student does not enroll in these courses, a student jeopardizes his/her ability to successfully pursue college-level work. While the (state university systems) both impose deadlines for addressing remediation in language and mathematics skills, the California Community Colleges do not. (Academic Senate for California Community Colleges, 2004, p. 13)*

The report goes on to emphasize the importance of multiple measures for assessment, careful alignment of placement instruments with course content and objectives, and ongoing research and program evaluation to document that remedies prescribed via recommended course placements are translating into successful student outcomes. The report also focuses on the lack of complete information related to assessment, placement, and measures of their effectiveness with respect to the system's 400,000 noncredit students (Academic Senate for the California Community Colleges, 2004).

Given the very strong support for mandatory assessment in the research-based literature, it is interesting to examine the wide diversity that exists at the state level in terms of policies for mandated assessment and placement. As of 2002, over 20 states required that community colleges assess all new students. Of these, 11 specified one or more tests that its colleges must use. Five states (Florida, Maryland, Minnesota, Oklahoma, and Texas) have gone so far as to standardize placement policies and cut-off scores used across all colleges in the system (Prince, 2005).

Requiring student participation in mandatory course placement raises certain issues. In California, mandatory placement has been the focus of legal challenges, such as the 1988 suit filed by the Mexican American Legal Defense and Educational Fund (MALDEF). MALDEF challenged the use of a single means of assessment for determining course placement, particularly with regard to lack of validation for students of specific groups that might be disadvantaged by the instrument used. These issues have largely been addressed in that state with the implementation of required multiple measures for assessment, requirements for local validation of cut scores, and other regulations. Although this approach addresses many concerns for equitable assessment of diverse students, it has also led to the approval of over 90 distinct instruments employed by various California community colleges, with the consequence that assessment results are often not portable and not tied to any unified standard within the state.

At this time, empirical evidence documenting the effects of state-mandated placement policies intended to improve student outcomes for developmental education is still scarce. An argument can be made that, on its own, mandatory placement just drives up the numbers of individuals who enroll in remediation without necessarily increasing their success. This concern is addressed when the institution employs other effective practices including alignment of course learning outcomes with testing standards, careful design of articulated course sequences, and effective instructional pedagogy with integrated learner support to support successful student progression.

To combat the negative effects on student retention that may accompany mandatory course placement, McCabe (2000) reminds colleges of their responsibility to encourage students and to counteract decreasing student motivation that may accompany placement into remedial coursework. He notes that many students do not understand why they are required to enroll in remedial coursework, and adds that colleges need to do more to help students see the value of such courses and programs.

The prevalence of mandatory assessment and placement practices for college developmental programs is not reported consistently. In 1994, survey results indicated that 76% of the nation's developmental programs required incoming students to undergo assessment (Boylan, Bonham, & Bliss, 1994). A more recent survey of 1,100 community colleges across the country reported 58% of institutions required mandatory assessment of all students, and that 75% of those requiring mandatory assessment also required mandatory placement (Shults, 2000). Even more recently, a nationwide survey of two-year colleges claimed that 92.4% of the colleges in the sample practiced mandatory assessment (Gerlaugh et al., 2007).

In California, it has been reported that more than one-third of students who were assessed as needing further work in basic skills mathematics and English did not enroll in basic skills courses (Academic Senate for California Community Colleges, 2004). If, as Cross suggests, only 10% of these students are likely to succeed in college without such remediation, a serious loss of individual and institutional potential exists in the absence of prescriptive assessment and placement policies.

Recent literature has highlighted an additional factor regarding assessment and placement. Perin (2006) found that both colleges and states soften their own placement mandates by permitting subjective assessment procedures as an override to more formal assessment criteria. In one college, students could avoid required placement by signing a waiver; in another, lack of sufficient developmental sections resulted in the college allowing low-scoring students to take selected college-credit classes instead. These policy adaptations respond to threats of low enrollment and facilitate access to college curriculum for students eager to earn a degree. In addition, the very significant issues of validating assessment instruments and documenting successful outcomes of prescribed remedial coursework make the landscape of mandatory assessment less black-and-white. It seems that colleges recognize the "value" of universal assessment, but actual practice often reflects the challenges of consistent implementation.

Roueche and Roueche (1999) call for required student orientation, pointing out that universities are far better at this than community colleges, and further suggesting that new students be matched with experienced student mentors. In addition to advising students of college protocols and resources, orientation sessions can be used to encourage entering students to address their recommended English and mathematics remediation at an early stage. Research has demonstrated that those who participate in new student orientations are more likely to be retained in community college than those who do not receive orientation (Boylan & Saxon, 2002).

Despite the noted benefits of mandatory orientation, many community college students may not be receiving it. For example, of the 2.4 million credit students enrolled in California's community colleges in 2002–03, 1.5 million were directed to mandatory orientation, whereas over 37% were exempt. Of those required to attend under the state's matriculation guidelines, only 1 million actually did so. Of the 393,322 noncredit students enrolled in that year, less than 7% received directed orientation (California Community College System data, as reported by the Academic Senate for California Community Colleges, 2004).

2.2. Counseling support provided is substantial, accessible, and integrated with academic courses and programs.

According to the literature, a strong counseling component is characteristic of successful developmental education programs (McCabe, 2000; Maxwell, 1997b; McCusker, 1999; Kozeracki, 2002; Boylan, Bonham, White, & George 2000). Key to this success is a program that integrates counseling with teaching and has a highly structured, easily accessible and proactive format. Maxwell (1997a) notes,

> In programs for under-prepared disadvantaged students, it is essential that counseling be an integral part of the academic program and that counselors provide both formal and informal assistance to students and staff. Counseling arrangements which consist of counselors who sit in their offices and wait for clients to schedule do not work with at-risk students who need more intrusive intervention. (p. 12)

She goes on to suggest that these students need comprehensive services including advising and mentoring as well as academic skill development and help to "undo the lingering effects of negative attitudes, emotions, and fears they experienced in their earlier schooling" (Maxwell 1997b, p. 2). In this respect, counselors who are effective in serving developmental students shift from a role of remote advising to adopt a more preventative, proactive function.

Offering counseling and advising services in connection with the developmental education program of colleges has been correlated to improved first-term GPA and success in developmental courses (Boylan, Bliss, & Bonham, 1997). In general, students in programs with a counseling and advising component are more likely to have higher pass rates than students from programs where a specific counseling-advising connection is lacking. This relationship was also highlighted by McCabe and Day (1998), who suggest that broad support services should include assessment, placement, orientation, tutoring, advising, counseling, peer support, early alert programs, study skills training, and support groups.

Various theoretical models regarding student engagement and its relationship to college persistence postulate that attachment to the institution develops when the student has a relationship with a significant member of the college community. This hypothesis has been tested in a variety of higher education settings and is well supported. The frequency and quality of these interactions have definite effects on student retention. Further, in summarizing available research on student persistence in college, Wycoff (1999) found that inadequate advising was the primary negative characteristic linked with student attrition. Another study that examined institutional characteristics associated with desired outcomes for low-income students in four-year universities concluded that a "high-impact" college typically provided services such as intentional academic planning via intrusive advising, freshman orientation courses, and special programs for advising and academic support of at-risk students (Muraskin & Lee, 2004).

The counseling function is also tied with intensive student monitoring and advising in effective developmental programs. Preregistration counseling, including that provided via mandatory orientation, helps students understand the need and value of pursuing suggested remediation routes. In a study of credential-seeking students at 58 national community colleges who entered as freshman in 2002, 86% of students who were placed in and completed developmental courses in their first term persisted to the second term, whereas only 57% of those who were placed but elected not to enroll in developmental courses persisted to the second term (Lumina Foundation, 2006). In situations lacking mandatory course placement after initial assessment, counseling and advisement play an especially vital role in referring students to appropriate courses to promote their persistence and success.

Structured advising (including mandatory, early meetings with advisers in a central location in proximity to classes) is supported by a recent study comparing students at colleges that reportedly had structured programs with those that lacked such structure (Person, Rosenbaum, & Deil-Amen, 2006). Students in the unstructured environment more often reported having mistakenly taken courses that did not apply to their degree requirements or were mistaken in their belief that remedial courses awarded degree-applicable credit. Students in the structured programs demonstrated a statistically significant positive difference with regard to the degree of confidence they felt about making correct course choices.

Two general types of advising are often mentioned in the literature. Prescriptive advising is characterized by an authoritative relationship in which the student is a passive receiver of advice and information delivered by the counselor. The student assumes no responsibility for decision making and instead relies almost exclusively on the counselor to plan and direct his activities. In contrast, developmental counseling emphasizes shared responsibility between the adviser and the student for clarifying the student's goals and making informed choices. The counselor, usually trained in developmental theory, supports the student in taking initiative to plan for his or her personal and academic growth, taking into account ongoing changes to the student's needs over time.

Although it might appear that the developmental advising approach is always superior to the prescriptive approach, both methods have merit in particular situations. Students do, in fact, value direct explanations of graduation and program requirements, registration procedures, and so on, and rely heavily on the expertise of counselors and other advisers to direct them in these matters. Furthermore, developmental advising is time intensive and requires the services of highly trained providers—a significant obstacle in circumstances where counseling caseloads are already too demanding. A hybrid approach has been successfully employed as appropriate for particular situations.

"Intrusive" advising models have been suggested as particularly appropriate for at-risk students. This action-oriented model assumes that students will not always take the initiative in seeking out help to resolve their academic concerns, and is connected with prescribed counselor contacts to intervene in a developing academic crisis. Intrusive advising for at-risk students has been positively associated with improvements in retention rates and credit hours completed (Bray, 1985; Nichols, 1986); increased GPA (Schultz, 1989; Spears, 1990); use of study skills, time management strategies, and increased attendance (Spears, 1990), and graduation rates and time to graduation among targeted groups (Glennen & Baxley, 1985).

Developmental students often lack the ability to assess their academic standing in a course in order to make necessary adjustments in a timely manner. McCabe (2003) notes that developmental students are unlikely to recognize how dire their academic situation may actually be; they "may have the false belief that they can pass . . . despite the mathematical impossibility of resurrecting a 50 percent average to a passing 70 percent" (p. 98). Given this concern, a variety of interventions have been implemented by colleges to provide timely academic assistance.

A popular approach to proactive academic intervention is the so-called "early alert," in which academic and student services personnel collaborate to identify students who need help and refer them for assistance. Bourdon and Carducci (2002) summarized a wide variety of recent literature sources on 27 areas of community college practice. This summary of published sources reported that, compared to students not involved in early alert programs, students in these programs were more likely to

- Successfully complete a course in which they were experiencing academic difficulty

- Maintain higher rates of continuous enrollment to the end of the academic year

- Have higher persistence rates for two or more consecutive semesters

- Exhibit higher persistence rates up to four years later (including transfer students)

However, several studies indicate that the "alert" alone may be insufficient to positively affect student achievement. In one college's initial implementation of an early alert letter referring students to services, an evaluation of student behavior after the letters were received indicated that the notices may have promoted an increase in the drop rate. The percentage of survey respondents who dropped their courses increased from 19.2 to 33.8% after receiving an early alert letter. A larger number of students stated that they "studied more" as a result of the early alert notice and more students also met with their instructors; however, beyond those initial student efforts, smaller proportions of students reported having used tutorial services and labs (Cartnal & Hagen, 1999).

Results such as these suggest that simply alerting students to their academic vulnerability may not be enough. "Much of the literature suggests that frequent and regular feedback on academic performance should be encouraged.... Multiple progress reports throughout the semester are necessary to have a positive impact on performance" (Eimers, 2000, p. 12). Moreover, effective referral mechanisms to provide the designated support services and to monitor how students are using the services in response to academic alerts are needed to evaluate the effectiveness of such measures. Finally, closing the loop with feedback to the instructor or adviser that initiated the alert or referral is essential in maintaining a strong, integrated connection between classroom instruction and support service providers.

Reports from the Community College of Denver (CCD) indicate that the college's student services practices have effectively promoted retention (Roueche, Ely, & Roueche, 2001). Denver's counseling and academic support services are organized in a comprehensive unit called the Academic Support Center (ASC) which employs a "case management" model, following up on individual students and directing them to services. Data indicates that the class withdrawal rate was 7.8% for students receiving ASC support, whereas the overall campus rate was 12.4% (Bailey, Alfonso, Calcagno, Jenkins, Keigl, & Leinbach, 2004).

Colleges also use a variety of nontraditional advisers to supplement the kinds of assistance available to underprepared students. The use of student peer advisers or peer mentors has been associated with higher grades, reenrollment, and higher graduation rates among participants, compared with those not having access to these supports (Bourdon & Carducci, 2002). In another approach, Broward Community College in Florida has adopted a suite of assistance options, including assignment of a Student Life Skills instructor as a "success coach" to each student who places into entry level remedial courses based on all three subject assessment tests (reading, writing, and mathematics). Coaches meet weekly in one-on-one sessions with assigned students to provide advising, academic tutoring, career counseling, and information about campus support services. Over the course of three semesters, coached students demonstrated higher retention and completion rates, and additional correlations demonstrated that the frequency of faculty interactions was positively associated with these desired outcomes (Husain, 2008).

Counseling in and of itself is not sufficient to significantly affect student success. The integration of academic and support services is repeatedly cited as a key for improving outcomes. According to research (Boylan & Saxon, 2002), effective counseling for remedial students must reflect the following characteristics:

- Integrated into the overall structure of the remedial program
- Based on the goals and objectives of the program
- Undertaken early in the semester
- Based on sound principles of student development theory
- Carried out by counselors specifically trained to work with developmental students

Maxwell (1997b) further suggests that true integration of counselors into the developmental program means including them in program planning, regular meetings with instructional staff, and program evaluation activities. In support of the instructional function, counselors who work closely with faculty know and can communicate the content-area goals and expectations to students and help them navigate the developmental sequence appropriately. They also serve to support faculty by helping them understand and deal with student motivational and behavioral problems.

2.3. Financial aid is disseminated to support developmental students. Mechanisms exist to ensure that developmental students are aware of such opportunities, and that they receive assistance to apply for and acquire financial aid.

Community colleges have long been labeled "democratizing" institutions because they provide high-quality education at an affordable price; however, even an affordable system is beyond the reach of some students if the financial aid process is too complicated, or if students are unaware of its benefits. According to Haycock (2006), college going among students from low-income families grew from 20% to over 50% in the years between 1992 and 2003, but even with increases in financial aid packages, the aid failed to meet the costs. Pell Grants are most often the first option for financial aid, whereas federal loan programs provide additional options. According to Haycock, "in 1975, the maximum Pell Grant covered approximately 84 percent of the cost of attending college or university. Today, it covers only 36 percent, effectively blocking access for thousands of aspiring college students from 'low-income families'" (p. 4).

In an Opening Doors study of financial aid approaches, Choitz and Widom (2003) assert that financial aid grants have a greater impact on student retention and certificate completion if the grants are more generous and offer incentives for enrollment in more units. Further, they maintain that some structural academic barriers may inhibit college success. For instance, many remedial courses are not eligible to demonstrate the "satisfactory progress" requirements for the Pell Grant (17). Finally, Choitz and Widom note that students may be intimidated by the financial aid process or unaware of the entire process. "At many colleges, financial aid staff have little time to meet with students individually, and written materials on how to apply for grants and loans tend not to be user friendly" (p. 12).

In a study by MDRC and the Louisiana Opening Doors program, researchers Brock and Richburg-Hays (2006) document the impact of financial incentives on student performance among low-income students. They found that students at Delgado Community College and Louisiana Technical College-West Jefferson participating in the study were more likely to demonstrate an explicit commitment to their academic goals and performance. Participating students were offered $1,000 performance-based scholarships for two semesters. The program also provided students with enhanced counseling services. The study found that participating students enrolled in approximately 8.9% more units than the control group students. Additionally, students passed "nearly half a course more" (p. 23) than their counterparts in the study. Among those attempting a course, almost 65% passed the course with a C or better. They also tended to withdraw less frequently.

Another recent study further confirms the positive outcomes associated with providing financial aid packaged as scholarship incentives (Glenn, 2007). In a large, randomized study of students at a Canadian university, 650 first-year students were divided into three experimental groups. One group was offered a suite of tutoring and support services, a second group was offered large merit scholarships in their sophomore year if they met certain grade-point averages, and a third group was offered both tutoring and scholarship incentives. At the end of the freshman year, the persistence and GPAs of these groups were compared with those of a matched control group that was offered neither services nor financial incentives. Results showed that those offered tutoring alone were no more likely to persist than the control group, but those offered scholarship incentives were statistically more likely to return for their sophomore year, and those offered both tutoring and aid did better still. A significant increase in GPA was also noted for those offered both tutoring and scholarship incentives. Moreover, these students used the proffered academic support services much more than the control group or the group that was not offered financial assistance. The authors of the study also noted that the positive outcomes were concentrated almost exclusively among female students.

A variety of rigorous analyses of the impact of financial aid on student persistence show that students who receive financial aid are likely to make more consistent progress in college. Receiving a Pell Grant was shown to decrease the probability of withdrawal among students during their first two years of college (Bettinger, 2004). Also, students who entered Adult Basic Education (ABE) or ESL courses without a high school diploma were far more likely to complete at least forty-five college credits if they received financial aid when they enrolled in credit-bearing courses (66% versus 16% for ESL; 42% versus 13% for ABE) (Prince & Jenkins, 2005).

Though more investigation is necessary to determine the long-term effects, these studies indicate a strong correlation between financial aid and student performance. In addition to providing more direct aid in the form of scholarships or grants to students, colleges can also contribute to student success by enhancing student opportunities to acquire available aid. Effective practices would include creating strong mechanisms for communication with developmental students, increasing student awareness of financial aid opportunities, and providing accessible assistance with aid application processes.

2.4. Regular program evaluations are conducted, results are disseminated widely, and data are used to improve practice.

Various studies provide evidence that comprehensive and systematic program evaluation is a hallmark of successful developmental education programs. In a nationwide benchmarking study of best practices in developmental education, all the programs that were eventually identified as exemplary reportedly engaged in ongoing and systemic evaluation activities (Boylan et al., 2000). Additionally, program evaluation was shown to be positively correlated with both student retention and success in developmental courses at both two-year and four-year schools (Boylan, Bliss, & Bonham, 1997). Among the various programmatic elements examined for their relationships to desired student outcomes, systematic program evaluation was among those demonstrating the strongest relationship to student success.

The recommendation for a strong evaluation component in successful developmental programs is called for by a number of authors (McCabe & Day, 1998; Neuberger, 1999; Perin, 2005; Grubb, 2001; Roueche & Roueche, 1999). Boylan et al. (2000) defines a systemic evaluation as one that is done at regular intervals, is part of an overall plan, includes both formative and summative activities, uses a variety of measures, and is shared with a variety of audiences. McCabe and Day (1998) recommend an evaluation system focused on outcomes as well as on continuous improvement. Roueche and Roueche (1977) concur that "the most successful developmental education programs are generally those that use a number of indices on which to evaluate their efforts" (p. 107).

Although most colleges engage in at least some evaluation activities related to their developmental programs, these are often fragmented and episodic. A systematic evaluation of developmental education activities should collect data at three levels:

Primary level: Includes descriptive data such as number of courses, hours of tutoring, students served

Secondary level: Includes short-term outcomes such as course completion, grades in courses, and semester-to-semester retention

Tertiary level: Includes data on long-term outcomes such as grade point averages, retention, and graduation rates

In terms of summative evaluation, Boylan, Bonham, White and George (2000) describe an "industry standard" for criteria to be used in evaluation of developmental education programs. The New York College Learning Skills Association (Neuberger, 1999) recommends that developmental programs should be measured by using more than one of the following:

- Course completion rates and grade distributions for developmental courses

- Course completion rates and grade distributions in related/subsequent courses

- Retention and persistence rates

- Graduation rates (at the very least, tracking students for three years for an Associate's degree)

- Rates of developmental students who maintain good academic standing; rates of those who experience probationary status

- Achievement rates as revealed by pre- and posttest gain, course and semester GPA, and cumulative GPA

- Rates of students who meet standards on competency-based assessments

- Rate of student goal attainment rather than graduation rates. Students should be asked to define their goals after their first semester, and be asked if those goals were achieved during an exit interview.

- Transfer rates (or transfer intentioned, as shown by transcript requests)

- Graduate school, military, other continuing education

- Employment rates and length of employment, including employment in degree field or related field

- Labor statistics: percentage not on welfare, percentage above poverty line, etc. (p. 10)

Weissman et al. (1997) also emphasize the need for a well-designed evaluation component for developmental education programs, noting that program evaluation not only answers public concerns for accountability, but also determines whether institutional policies and practices are succeeding and which, if any, need to be changed. These authors strongly advise that evaluation of developmental course effectiveness is not enough, and stress the need to examine all policies that the college has established to govern the developmental education program, including placement, the timing of remediation, and enrollment in college-level courses.

Although an emphasis on program outcomes is essential in any comprehensive evaluation of developmental programs, the collection of qualitative data is vital for formative evaluation and continuous program improvement. Boylan (2002) strongly recommends the development of a comprehensive assessment plan for the developmental education program, created by program stakeholders and including a well-developed plan for dissemination of program results. In addition, student learning outcomes at the course and program level should be developed and assessed, and the data collected used to inform program improvement.

Based on our review of effective practices for developmental education as documented in the research literature, the authors of this book developed an assessment tool that can be used by colleges wishing to examine various aspects of their developmental education programs (see Chapter Six). This tool aligns with the research-based effective practices that we identify in Chapters One through Five of this book and provides a framework for a college's self-evaluation in identifying strengths and opportunities for improvement relative to delivery of its developmental education program. Although this comprehensive assessment tool was not intended as a vehicle for use in cyclic review of developmental education programs, its use can inform the development of institution-specific criteria that might be assessed in an ongoing fashion in the context of regular program review. The action plan component of the tool particularly provides a focus for assessing targeted efforts strategically chosen to strengthen effectiveness.

Conclusions

By examining the ways in which assessment, placement, counseling, advising, financial aid, and program review are applied to the developmental education program, colleges empower the various stakeholders in these areas to create more optimal conditions to facilitate student success. The use of institutional data, combined with the research-based effective practices noted in this section, can provide the stimulus for thoughtful dialogue and continued inquiry to determine the desired actions to advance a particular institution's developmental education program. In the spirit of ongoing improvement, college leaders should validate the importance of these discussions, with a focus on the institutional goals relating to developmental education. Supporting ongoing, broad-based discussion with stakeholders in instruction, student services, and institutional research will not only lead to improved programmatic outcomes, but will also contribute to a culture of engaged professional learning and development.

Chapter 3

Instructional Practices

MEANINGFUL INSTRUCTION IS simultaneously art and science—mixed with a little inspiration and luck. In the United States, over 500,000 college teachers educate approximately 15 million students every year—all of them, at one point or another, wondering how they will effectively address the integrity of the material while also reaching the students who seem most underprepared (Fink, 2003). The issue of student readiness is an ever-present specter, haunting the territory beyond the English, math, reading, and ESL borders. If the issues of developmental learners were that easy to confine, perhaps the task of educating so many would be simpler. However, in current conditions, most college faculty, especially those in the community college, will find it necessary to incorporate some new strategies in order to maximize student learning and achievement. This chapter is an attempt to provide a comprehensive guide to the theories and strategies that most significantly impact the performance of underprepared students.

Effective instructional practices are the key to achieving desired student outcomes for developmental programs. Research has linked the following instructional practices with success for developmental learners:

3.1. Sound principles of learning theory are applied in the design and delivery of courses in the developmental program.

3.2. Brain-based research informs instructional design.

3.3. Curricula and practices that have proven to be effective within specific disciplines are employed.

3.4. Developmental education faculty employ a variety of instructional methods to accommodate student diversity.

3.5. Programs align entry and exit skills among levels and link course content to college-level performance requirements.

3.6. Developmental education faculty routinely share instructional strategies.

3.1. Sound principles of learning theory are applied in the design and delivery of courses in the developmental program.

Cognitive Models

Fundamentally, educational theorists agree that learning means a change in the learner; those changes may be as subtle as the modification of the learner's perspective or as dramatic as a shift in behavior. Most theorists also agree that learning is a process, not just a product. For years, learning theory was dominated by behaviorists who contend that the product of learning is shaped by the environment of the learner. The measure of a learner, as the name suggests, is evaluated on the basis of the behavioral changes of the student. Developmental education, despite the growth of other compelling theoretical frameworks, is still often dominated by behaviorist perspectives that support practice, rote learning, and reinforcement. Although these strategies can certainly support learning, other theoretical models have also made a significant contribution to the evolution of developmental education.

More recently, behaviorist frameworks have benefited from the inclusion of cognitive models based on the teachers' and learners' abilities to connect new learning with prior knowledge or understanding, evolving into metacognition models that emphasize the students' participation in the creation of meaning and comprehension. Metacognition refers to the students' awareness of their own learning and thinking processes. "Metacognition was the first way of theorizing to promote the idea that the learner had to be driving the process of learning" (Svinicki, 1999, p. 13). This shift gave rise to the concept of "learner-centeredness . . . which mirrors a larger social shifting to promote personal responsibility" (Svinicki, p. 13). Since then, theorists and practitioners have developed pedagogies harnessing the learners' active participation in the learning process. This quantitative perspective assumes that students "learn cumulatively, interpreting and incorporating new material with what they already know, their understanding progressively changing as they learn" (Biggs, 1994).

Constructivists promote the view that knowledge is created in relation to the web of knowledge students already have. The world is interpreted from a network of previous understanding, and "knowledge is 'constructed' by each learner in terms of his or her perceptions of the world and the learner's mental models" (O'Banion, 1997, p. 83). This theory lends support for contextual learning and a "learn by doing" approach, reinforcing the need for active learning strategies. O'Banion claims that the "old view of learning is mechanical; it is the factory model in which learners move through the line at the same rate imprinted with knowledge the school deems important. The new learning views learning as organic and natural; learning is unique for each person, and it is related to personal meaning and real life" (p. 89).

Mezirow (2000) describes this in terms of "meaning systems" which act as filters for information as students attempt to make connections to new information. Transformation Theory also includes the necessity of the learners to "become critically aware of [their] own tacit assumptions and expectations and those of others and [assess] their relevance for making an interpretation" (p. 4). Inherently, this idea emphasizes the importance of the learners' experiences and maturity, which is especially important for adult learners.

A social cognitive framework integrates both behaviorist and constructivist theories, supporting the notion that students learn by observing others, which is sometimes termed "observational" or "social" learning (Merriam, Caffarella, & Baumgartner, 2006). This theory emphasizes the thesis that learning is a naturally social act, and that by "observing others, people acquire knowledge, rules, skills, strategies, beliefs, and attitudes" (p. 288). Theorists like Bandura (1989) and Pascarella and Terenzini (1991) focus on the capacity for interaction with other learners to inspire imitation, motivation, empathy, and self-esteem. Willams and Sternberg (1988) studied small groups and concluded that the work produced in a collaborative setting was of higher quality than the work produced by individuals. Further, the study revealed that "both cognitive and social-cognitive skills are related to the effectiveness of a group" (Silverman & Casazza, 2000, p. 155).

Motivation Theories

For adult learners, motivation is an especially critical issue. Most theories centered on adult learners incorporate some aspect of motivational control. Attribution theory, for instance, explores the learner's motivation levels in relationship to the benefits or outcomes. When the learner feels in control of the learning process, it is more likely that he or she will be motivated to engage or try (Svinicki, 2004).

Andragogical perspectives are based on the fundamental beliefs that "(1) the individual learner is the primary focus, (2) the goal of learning is to promote personal growth and realization of the individual's potential, (3) autonomy and self-direction are important components of adult learning, and (4) the individual has the power to persevere against social, political, cultural, and historical forces" (Merriam quoted in Casazza & Silverman, 1996, p. 119). In this model, "rather than being the source of all knowledge, the instructor is a guide to students as they create their own knowledge" (Grubb, 1999, p. 32).

There are three characteristics of self-regulated learning. First, learners attempt to assert control over their learning, their behavior, and their environment. Second, learners are working toward a goal, which provides a standard by which success can be measured. Third, the individual student must be in control of his or her actions and decisions. Self-directed learning is a particularly appropriate approach for adult learners because these models "argue against the notion of intelligence as a characteristic that varies among students and is unchangeable after a certain point in life" (Pintrich, 1995, p. 8). Frequent feedback using assessment instruments can help students develop awareness about their own motivation and learning. This kind of self-monitoring can be either covert or overt; however, in order for students to benefit from self-monitoring, "students must be able to discern and interpret subtle changes in their functioning" (Pintrich, 1995, p. 18).

Motivation is also a key component of self-directed learning. Students may set different types of goals for themselves: mastery goals, performance goals, or both. In any case, adult learners may need initial assistance in setting goals that are realistic in order to experience success. "The more students can take responsibility for their own learning, the more likely they are to attribute success to their own efforts" (Trawick & Corno, 1995, p. 53). "Students will perform better if they know what goals they are seeking and if those goals are personally important to them" (Kleinbeck, Quast, & Schwarz, 1989, p. 54). The assertion of any goal implies the importance of personal control. McCombs argues that teachers must assume some of the responsibility for helping students to develop metacognitive awareness. She argues that once students establish a perception of self-direction, they will more ably use self-management skills and learning strategies (Casazza & Silverman, 1996).

Problem Solving and Critical Thinking

Students in general *and developmental students in particular* are rarely taught critical-thinking skills in high school or in their early college courses. As a result, "a lack of well-developed critical thinking skills is often a causative factor in the failure of developmental students" (Boylan, 2002, p. 95). Boylan cites long-term studies at LaGuardia Community College indicating that critical-thinking instruction improves course completion rates, grades, intellectual maturity, and satisfaction. Often remediation involves abstract and repetitive practice, which lacks application or connection to the students' goals. Grubb asserts that "the idea that remediation has to precede content learning creates a teaching problem" (1999, p. 184).

Many colleges and universities offer specific courses in critical thinking; however, the research generally suggests "that this is not the most effective way to teach critical thinking to developmental students" (Boylan, 2002, p. 96). The ineffectiveness could perhaps be explained by the impracticality of isolating thinking skills. Kurt Fischer's skill theory attempts to provide a descriptive range of cognitive development, ranging from functional to optimal; in between these is the developmental range. Students demonstrate varying levels of skills depending on the circumstances or environment. "Under conditions of low support, students function less skillfully and function at their functional level, which is adequate for their everyday [needs]" (King & VanHecke, 2006, p. 13).

In order to improve developmental levels of skill and help students achieve optimal levels of ability, the students must be consistently challenged and supported. According to King and VanHecke (2006), "skill theory suggests that students use cognitive frameworks to solve problems and that, concomitantly, problems inspire new learning" (p. 16). Unless students are challenged to think critically, even while they develop fundamental skills, they cannot begin to create the necessary cognitive framework to address their collegiate studies. Further, Chaffee (1992) argues that the integration of critical-thinking skills throughout the curriculum is even more beneficial than stand-alone courses, especially for the weakest students. Boylan (2002) asserts that "an emphasis on critical thinking at the early stages of developmental students' academic careers may enable them to gain more from their early remedial courses, and, therefore, reduce the amount of time spent in remediation" (p. 95).

Critical thinking, then, becomes part of a larger framework of "academic literacy," linking reading, writing, and thinking. As cited in *Academic Literacy: A Statement of Competencies Expected of Students Entering California's Public Colleges and Universities* (ICAS, 2002), "analytical thinking must be taught, and students must be encouraged to apply those analytical abilities to their own endeavors" (p. 15).

3.2. Brain-based research informs instructional design.

Historically, relatively little was known about the inner machinations of the brain. In the last few decades, brain research has exploded, with possibly its greatest ascent coming in the 1990s. In fact, the 1990s were declared "officially" as the "Decade of the Brain" by a United States House of Representatives Joint Resolution in 1989, signed into law by President George H. W. Bush (House Resolution #174, July 1989).

By most accounts, translation of the findings of the key brain research fields of cognitive science and neuroscience into practical education applications has been slow. The reasons for this are myriad; Jensen (2005) suggests that much of the answer is grounded in the differences between brain research and traditional educational research. Brain research tends to utilize paradigms of basic research and clinical research, whereas educational research tends toward more applied or action research.

However, as Zull indicates, educators know intuitively that when people learn they also change. Or, in other words, "learning makes a difference" (2004, p. 68). And the capacity to affect transformation in students and lives is part of the lure of education as a vocation. This premise about change, though, informs some of the contemporary discussions regarding brain-based learning theory, challenging the notion that the brain is static or fixed.

Even so, researchers are often hesitant to proclaim bold conclusions, couching their findings (correctly) as limited by the research design, the controlled nature of the study, and a number of other factors. Educators, however, are often looking for "answers" that they can immediately apply to the classroom. This structural tension has certainly contributed to the adoption curve of potentially relevant cognitive and neuroscience research findings. Wolfe (2001) also notes that educators are wary of fads and the newest "breakthrough," which may also contribute to the lack of early adoption.

In *The Art of Changing the Brain*, Zull (2004) examines the causal factors to creating learning, or changing the brain. He cites "practice" as the first change agent, explaining that when learners practice something, the "neurons that control and drive that action fire repeatedly. If a neuron fires frequently, it grows and extends itself out to other neurons. . . . These signaling connections are . . . synapses. . . . These networks are the physical equivalent of knowledge" (p. 69).

Like practice, Zull (2004) cites emotion as an equally significant change agent for learning. He explains that the chemistry associated with emotions have a powerful impact on the learning experience for students. According to Zull, "Emotion and thought are physically entangled" (p. 70). Damasio (1994) asserted that "somatic markers" match bodily experiences with cognitive experiences. In addition, he suggests that the learning environment also has an impact on the learning by creating "background feelings" that also affect the mood of the learning. This hypothesis implies that the better learning feels, or the more positively learners associate good feelings with the learning process, the more likely they are to be motivated and engaged.

These two principles imply that instruction must contain both practice and emotion in order to promote the change educators recognize as learning. Zull (2004) explores the following possibilities:

Don't Explain: Instructors often blame themselves when explanation alone seems to fail. However, brain-based research implies that because explanation may create minimal opportunity for either practice or emotion, it can only be marginally effective as the sole instructional approach.

Build on Errors: Instructors often see their role as "eradicators of error." However, mistakes may also provide fertile opportunity for new knowledge by taking erroneous thinking and contrasting it or building on it with new information.

Engage the Whole Brain: Instructors should provide experiences and assignments that engage all aspects of the cerebral cortex: "sensory cortex (getting information), integrative cortex (making meaning of information), integrative cortex near the front (creating new ideas from these meanings), and motor cortex (acting on those ideas)" (p. 71).

Researchers are just beginning to explore the impact that stress has on learning. Some initial studies conclude that the effectiveness of learning is compromised when the learner is stressed or fearful. According to Goswami (2008), "One important function of the emotional brain is assessing the value of the information being received. When the amygdala is strongly activated, it interrupts action and thought and triggers rapid bodily responses critical for survival" (p. 44).

The National Research Council's Commission on Behavioral and Social Sciences and Education 2000 volume *How People Learn* (Bransford & Brown, 2000) has been hailed as another critical step in formulating an all-encompassing connection between previously unattainable primary research in neuroscience, social psychology, cognitive psychology, developmental biology and psychology, and more practical application in the field of education. This volume traces the development of the science of learning and summarizes a wide range of research into how learning occurs and the effects of teaching and teachers on learning, formulating specific key findings and principles. Much of this volume is focused on how children learn, but the authors specifically suggest that the implications are analogous for adults. This would seem to be especially true in the domain of developmental education in the college environment.

The volume elevates three findings that are supported by a wide range of research as key findings. The first finding indicates that students come to the classroom with preconceptions about how the world works. If their initial understanding is not engaged, they may fail to grasp the new concepts and information that are taught, or they may learn them for the purpose of a test but revert to their preconceptions outside the classroom. In addition, to develop competence in an area of inquiry, students must: (a) have a deep foundation of factual knowledge; (b) understand facts and ideas in the context of a conceptual framework; and (c) organize knowledge in ways that facilitate retrieval and applications. Finally, a "metacognitive" approach to instruction can help students learn to take control of their own learning by defining learning goals and monitoring their progress in achieving them.

In addition, these findings also challenge the "myths" often associated with brain-based learning. Among these include the ideas associated with "left-brain" and "right-brain" learning, the capacity for learning at "critical periods" of the brain's development, and the notion that effective learning interventions need to be timed with brain development (Sternberg, 2008).

3.3. Curricula and practices that have proven to be effective within specific disciplines are employed.

Just as ongoing research informs the development of theory and practice for effective teaching and learning in general, similar work continues to advance recommendations for discipline-specific curriculum and pedagogical approaches that work for developmental learners. Although a comprehensive review of these elements across the various disciplines is beyond the scope of this literature review, a few selected approaches that frequently appear in the literature are discussed in this section.

Reading and Writing Curricula Integration

Literacy skills, at their most basic, encompass the ability to read and write. The literature generally supports the use of one of these skills to strengthen the development of the other. Theorists assert that directive reading instruction ends at approximately the third grade. Forget, Lyle, Spear, and Reinhart-Clark (2003) assert that "if a student has not mastered reading comprehension skills by the fourth grade, chances are that she/he will struggle with learning in grades four through twelve" (p. 3). In general, students who struggle with reading struggle with writing because they are unable to respond analytically to a text. The literature strongly supports an "embedded curriculum" model, where students are immersed in a learning environment which strongly promotes simultaneous reading and writing development, using reading to help students write and using writing to help students read. This approach is also referred to as the Strategic Reading and Writing (SRW) model (Laine, 1997). Ultimately, the goal is not just to develop reading and writing as discrete skills, but also to cultivate students' analytical thinking and reasoning abilities, which improves their ability to learn. Reading and writing skills are "conceptually and functionally but often taught separately" (Perin, 2003, p. 36).

This embedded curriculum might be accomplished in the following ways:

- Corequisite English and reading courses
- Learning communities with an English or reading component
- An emphasis on reading and writing across the curriculum
- Integrated reading and writing courses

Zhang (2000) asserts that mainstream faculty at the secondary level must share the burden of literacy problems with English and reading faculty and suggests "shared staff development activities where developmental and mainstream educators learn about better ways to help students learn" (p. 16).

The literature also strongly supports a reading and writing connection for students to develop their metacognitive abilities. Adults who are poor readers and writers reveal a lack of metacognitive ability about their own skills. Researchers (Rinehart & Platt, 1984; Tei & Stewart, 1985) suggest the following teaching techniques to assist students in developing awareness about their own reading and writing processes:

- Monitoring exercises
- Summarizing activities
- Self-questioning activities
- Reading logs

Most of these strategies involve post-reading activities. However, Elbow (2004) asserts that writing is an effective prereading tool, citing the tradition to treat reading as the primary activity: "when writing is assigned, it traditionally serves reading" (p. 10). However, because writing is considered a more active process, it also serves as a way to maintain student engagement. He suggests a variety of writing activities to help the students prepare for reading by summarizing what they already know about a topic, preparing questions for themselves to answer as they read, or experimenting with a particular writing form. In this way, writers develop a purpose for reading, and these strategies help students develop awareness about their own reading and writing processes.

Beyond the reading and writing classrooms, Perin (2008) asserts that there is "minimal connection" between reading and writing instruction within the content disciplines. She argues that contextualizing reading and writing instruction into a single content area may improve motivation and improve transferability of skills. In a study of approximately 300 students, researchers concluded that teaching "general" reading and writing skills had little impact on preparation for specific disciplines. Perin's study also revealed that students tended to overestimate their abilities on general writing tasks.

Reading and Writing Centers

Researchers also stress the importance of creating supportive writing and reading environments through labs or centers. Writing and reading centers can promote literacy skills by providing opportunities to practice skills in a safe and supportive environment, promoting community and social learning models, emphasizing process development, and supporting instruction (Rossini, 2002). Gale (2001) asserts that institutions without formal Writing Across the Curriculum (WAC) programs can reap many of the same benefits through activities based in a writing center. Similarly, reading centers can support reading instruction across the curriculum and reinforce holistic metacognitive strategies in an individualized environment (Nist & Hynd, 1985; Dorlac, 1994; Baker, 1989). Maitland (2000) also stresses the role of the reading center in helping students to become more active learners and readers.

Reading Pedagogy

In addition to literature supporting the strong connection between reading and writing skill development, other approaches specific to the teaching of reading appear in the literature. Unfortunately, although much is published, relatively few practices have documented effectiveness in the form of statistically significant results demonstrated through substantial controlled trials comparing the recommended techniques. In an extensive review of over 4,000 relevant papers published between 1980 and 2002, Torgerson et al. (2004) found only 36 controlled trials with rigorous controls and data reporting. Of these, 34 had a literacy focus, including the application of various strategies to develop basic reading skills and reading comprehension. Among these few studies, five reported a positive effect for a particular intervention, one reported a negative effect, and 10 reported no difference. Eighteen others were inconclusive.

Reciprocal teaching is one method which has strong evidence in support of its effectiveness in developing reading comprehension. Initially described by Palinscar and Brown (1984), this method is described as

> *[a] procedure . . . where the teacher and student took turns leading a dialogue concerning sections of a text. Initially, the teacher modeled the key activities of summarizing (self-review), questioning (making up a question on the main idea), clarifying and predicting. The teacher thereby modeled activities; the students were encouraged to participate at whatever level they could. The teacher could then provide guidance and feedback at the appropriate level for each student. (p. 124)*

Essentially, the principle of reciprocal teaching asserts that by observing modeling of effective comprehension strategies, those with poor comprehension can gradually strengthen their own abilities. Such dialogue and modeling can be mediated by either teachers or tutors. In their work applying this strategy to middle school students, Palinscar and Brown (1985) reported greater than 70% of students achieved a criterion-based level of performance on an assessment analyzing reading passages, whereas none of the control group receiving traditional individual instruction achieved the minimum criterion. A much more rigorous study by Rich and Shepard (as cited in Torgerson et al., 2004) confirmed significant positive gains in reading comprehension using the reciprocal teaching method.

Reading Apprenticeship

Reading Apprenticeship (RA) is another approach to reading instruction that has been demonstrated to have a significant impact on secondary students' reading abilities and scores on standardized tests (WestEd, 2004b; Grosso de Leon, 2002). Equally important, a rigorous but accessible staff development protocol has been developed around the principles and practices of Reading Apprenticeship that provides both reading and content faculty effective strategies for developing reading skills in more mature students. The Strategic Learning Initiative at the WestEd research and development agency has developed intensive faculty training workshops that have been demonstrated to produce classroom practices that provide secondary learners effective tools for reading improvement (WestEd, 2004a; Schoenbach, Greenleaf, Cziko, & Hurwitz, 2000).

Recently, a number of California community colleges (for example, Los Medanos College and City College of San Francisco) have participated in these WestEd RA training programs and are finding these methodologies to be a useful tool in reading and composition *and* disciplined-based classrooms.

In 2007, WestEd initiated the Community College Leadership Institute in Reading Apprenticeship, a *training-of-trainers* experience designed to prepare community college teams to lead professional development in Reading Apprenticeship.

Reading Apprenticeship calls on the teacher to weave four dimensions—social, personal, cognitive, and knowledge building—into classroom instruction using metacognitive conversations with students. The social dimension draws on peer interaction as well as larger sociopolitical and cultural issues and is focused on creating a "safe environment" for students to share their difficulties with texts and recognize diverse perspectives. The personal dimension "draws on strategic skills used by students in out-of-school settings," their self-awareness as readers, and their "goals for reading improvement." The cognitive dimension develops students' resources with specific comprehension and problem-solving strategies using classroom modeling of inquiry processes. Knowledge-building involves the understanding that the reader brings to the text including traditional skills such as word construction, vocabulary, text structure, and so on, as well as the reader's personal and social interaction with the text.

The RA method emphasizes metacognitive processes that the teacher models and the student uses to gain confidence and strategies for self-reliance in reading activities (Greenleaf, Schoenbach, Cziko, & Mueller, 2001). In addition, RA helps students develop an awareness that "reading is just like writing: a process of cognitive (and social) construction in which everyone builds up meanings from cues in the texts" (Elbow, 2004, p. 13), providing a strong basis for the integration of instruction in reading and writing. Jordan and Schoenbach (2003) add that if college administrators decide to focus on literacy, instructional leaders need to expect that attention to reading and literacy will be embedded in subject area instruction.

In summarizing a large number of studies and meta-analyses including both quantitative data and expert opinion, Torgerson et al. (2004) derived the following factors shown to correlate with better progress in reading:

- *Phonemic awareness and/or word analysis instruction may lead to increased achievement in other aspects of reading for adult beginning readers.*

- *Word analysis may be taught using approaches that include direct instruction in word analysis along with instruction in other aspects of reading.*

- *Fluency (greater speed in reading aloud) may be taught to adult basic education students and fluency practice may lead to increases in reading achievement.*

> • *Explicit instruction in reading comprehension strategies may lead to increased reading comprehension achievement. (p. 15)*

Effective Practices in Mathematics

As the call for critical literacy has fueled interest in reading and writing across academic disciplines, so has a movement for "quantitative literacy" influenced the ways in which the developmental mathematics curriculum is structured and delivered. The American Mathematical Association of Two-Year Colleges (AMATYC, 2006) recommends the following approaches to mathematics instruction:

- *Teaching with technology*: modeling the use of appropriate technology in teaching mathematics

- *Active and interactive learning*: fostering interactive learning through student writing, reading, speaking, and collaborative activities so that students can learn to work effectively in groups and communicate about mathematics both orally and in writing

- *Making connections*: actively involving students in meaningful mathematical problems that build upon their experiences, focus on broad mathematical themes, and build connections with branches of mathematics and between mathematics and other disciplines

- *Using multiple strategies*: interactive lecturing, presentations, guided discovery, teaching through questioning, and collaborative learning

- *Experiencing mathematics*: learning activities including projects and apprenticeships that promote independent thinking and require sustained effort

Further reports from this organization recognize the importance of student engagement in learning activities, and recommend the use of group work, case studies, and projects. In general, the movement to a more "learner-centered" environment constitutes the most substantial reform of mathematics education over the past few decades.

Another issue with implications for success in mathematics is the recency of prior preparatory course completion. In a study of five community colleges in Virginia, Waycaster (2001a) reinforces the need for students in foundation-level courses to enroll immediately after succeeding in the previous level math course, citing an almost 15% difference in performance when contrasting student groups. In addition, the study cites significant differences in student success when students completed the recommended preparation, reinforcing both prerequisite enforcement and careful curriculum sequencing.

Among the practices currently informing the direction of developmental mathematics education in community colleges, the following initiatives are noteworthy.

Addressing Environmental Factors

In their review of literature concerning environmental factors relating to student achievement in mathematics, Higbee and Thomas (1999) identified a number of affective considerations that had an impact on performance. These included students' attitudes, self-concept, and confidence in mathematics, as well as math anxiety, test anxiety, low motivation, and misplaced sense of locus of control. These same researchers also examined cognitive factors such as preferred learning style and critical-thinking skills. Based on this body of research, educators are beginning to explore various techniques to address the barriers and mismatches identified, including increased use of collaborative learning and verbalization of the problem-solving process.

Sheila Tobias, author of *Overcoming Math Anxiety* (1995), concurs that the predominant causes of math anxiety derive from environmental factors created by teachers, leading to destructive student self-beliefs. These obstacles include timed tests, overemphasis on "one right method and one right answer," humiliation at the blackboard, classroom atmospheres of competition, and the absence of discussion in typical math classrooms (Armington, 2003). Her suggestions for relieving math anxiety and reenvisioning math instruction to respond to the more prevalent verbal learning style of many developmental math students continue to influence the way developmental mathematics instruction is delivered in today's classroom.

Small-Group Instruction

In a study of preparatory algebra students at a large urban university, DePree (1998) demonstrated that those taking course sections taught in a small-group instructional format had higher confidence in their mathematical ability and were more likely to complete the course than those in comparison courses with traditional instructor-led teaching. This was particularly true of students from traditionally underrepresented groups (Hispanic, Native American, and female students). Among those completing the courses, there was no significant difference in overall course grades.

Problem-Based Learning (PBL)

Based on a constructivist approach, this instructional strategy emphasizes the learning and application of mathematical concepts in connection with student exploration of a complex problem, usually deriving from a "real-world" situation. Problems are posed in such a way that students need to gain new knowledge in order to solve the problem, and most problems have multiple correct solutions. Problem-based learning involves students gathering information, identifying possible solutions, evaluating the various alternatives, choosing a solution, interpreting results, and defending conclusions. Because complex problems are often solved collaboratively, this method also promotes teamwork, shared responsibility, and skill development for peer-to-peer mathematical communication. Proponents feel that PBL leads to deeper understanding of mathematical concepts and avoids the learning by imitation that may occur in traditional algorithmic approaches. Studies have shown that students who learn through a problem-based approach exhibit higher achievement on both standardized tests and on project tests dealing with realistic situations than do students taught in traditional content-based learning environments (Boaler, 1998).

Contextual Learning

Cognitive science teaches that students retain information longer and can apply it more effectively if it is learned in context. With respect to developmental mathematics, an approach gaining favor is the teaching of mathematics "across the curriculum": the notion that applied mathematics delivered in conjunction with business, technical, or other professional preparatory coursework enhances student motivation and acquisition of mathematical skills. This may also take the form of curricular enhancements in traditional developmental math courses, in which standard math concepts are enhanced with problems, examples, or applications from other fields. A stronger emphasis on reading-math integration (for example, analyzing word problems, building mathematical vocabulary, and teaching reading skills as they relate to learning from a math textbook) has also been suggested as a means to leverage interdisciplinary skills and help students see connections between vital components of a developmental curriculum (Haehl, 2003).

Use of Manipulatives

In a study of middle school students, Moyer and Jones (2004) conclude that the use of manipulatives to illustrate mathematical concepts may promote more autonomous thinking, curiosity, and understanding among math students. The study asserts that "communicating the value of representations and the importance of being able to move flexibly among different representational systems, including manipulatives, visual images, and abstract symbols, helps students develop a deeper understanding of mathematics"

(p. 30). The study suggests that the practice diversifies instructional delivery and may provide students with additional points of access when contrasted with traditional lecture models.

Use of Technology

A great deal of the literature in recent years has addressed the use of technology in developmental math instruction. This includes technology primarily used by teachers (for example, presentation technology), students (for example, calculators), or both (for example, computer-assisted instruction, or CAI). A seven-year study in five Virginia colleges examined developmental math classes of ten instructors whose primary instruction was either lecture with lab or individualized computer-aided instruction to determine how student outcomes from these courses compared to those of traditional lecture courses. Results from this study indicated that student pass rate was independent of the manner of instruction used (Waycaster, 2001b).

An extensive review of recent studies examining computer-assisted instruction found mixed results at a variety of colleges, each implementing slightly different forms of computer-assisted instruction (U.S. Department of Education, 2005). These included self-paced or lab-based instruction with products such as Academic Systems (Internet-delivered curriculum combining lecture, practice, and self-administered tests), ALEKS (a nonlinear, nontraditional Internet-based course), or PLATO (a popular computer-based program for K–adult learners). Instructor-created distance learning courses were also examined, as were courses using computer algebra systems (CAS programs that manipulate mathematical expressions in both symbolic and numeric forms). The authors of this extensive review find studies crediting CAI and CAS with higher, lower, or no difference in pass rate, no difference or higher rates of persistence to higher level math, and no difference in final grades compared to developmental math sections taught in traditional instructor-led formats. They ultimately conclude, however, that offering a variety of instructional formats may allow students more options for choosing a modality that best suits their particular learning styles. They also reiterate the views of Boylan and AMATYC that, for technology to be effective, it should be used as a supplement to, rather than a replacement for, regular classroom instruction. (U.S. Department of Education, 2005)

Further examples and recommendations for effective practices in mathematics can be found in *Effective Practices for Developmental Mathematics* (Armington, 2003).

Effective Practices in English as a Second Language (ESL)

Any discussion of effective practices for ESL must first recognize the inherent diversity of student background and literacy level that exists in this heterogeneous population of learners. The exceptional amount of diversity in this group makes meeting their educational needs especially challenging. ESL students are among a group of second language or "L2" learners: those who are acquiring English language proficiency secondary to having learned to speak, understand, and perhaps read and write in a different language. Within this group, individuals have acquired varying levels of proficiency in their native languages, ranging from those who are functionally illiterate to those who have attained a sophisticated, expert facility with spoken and written forms, and who have earned advanced degrees in their home countries. Among those who lack formal education and who have not learned to read and write in their first language, the challenge of ESL instruction takes on the additional complexity of teaching basic literacy skills while also assisting in English language acquisition.

In addition to the direct acquisition of English language skills, ESL students also face complexities arising from the impact of cultural adaptation. Effective instruction must take into account the cultural norms and learning styles that have influenced previous learning behaviors among these students. This consideration is likely to be highly variable within an ESL population, owing not only to a diversity of nationalities, but also to the amount of time individuals have spent in the United States. A typical ESL population in a community college contains a mixture of recent immigrants, long-term immigrants who have decided to pursue a career objective for which they need language skills, international students, and "generation 1.5" learners who may have been largely raised in the United States, but who are acquiring English as an academic medium and speak another language in the home.

Effective practices for ESL instruction among adult learners were the focus of a recent major national study, "What Works" (Condelli & Wrigley, 2004). Funded by the U.S. Department of Education, this is the first large-scale, empirical study designed to determine which instructional practices, student-related, and teacher-related variables actually correlate with measurable improvements in reading, writing, and speaking skills for adult ESL learners. Conducted over a three-year period and involving 495 students and 530 separate classroom observations, this study identified statistically significant correlations between various instructional practices and student gains on standardized assessments in basic reading skills, reading comprehension, and oral communication. Although the study also attempted to correlate practices with growth in writing, the authors were ultimately unable to make this assessment, perhaps due to the relatively short study time frame or the inability of the assessment instrument to adequately measure small gains in the development of this complex ability (Condelli, 2004).

Prior to conducting the "What Works" study, its authors identified eleven practices suggested by the literature as having a potential impact on adult ESL student achievement in reading, writing, and speaking. Following observations from the study which coded the prevalence and application of these practices in the classroom, the authors performed a factor analysis, which identified three main approaches that best represented the underlying practices actually used by teachers in the study. The study emphasized the need to vary practice and interaction, supporting multiple learning modalities. It also supported open communication, including open-ended questioning. Finally, the study supported the exploration of learning outside of the classroom, including field trips, speakers, and authentic materials.

Findings from the "What Works" study support statistically significant relationships between certain instructional or structural variables and student skill development over time (Condelli & Wrigley, 2004). Major findings from this study include:

1. Use of "connection to the outside" strategy significantly promoted student growth in the development of basic reading skills. This strategy was effective in raising the level of students' mastery in basic reading skills.

2. Use of a student's native language had a positive effect on linear growth in reading comprehension. The more the teachers used students' native languages to give directions or to clarify concepts, the faster students' reading comprehension grew. This is distinct from instruction in the native language, but instead represents an approach that ensures understanding of tasks to be performed and that students can communicate difficulties or questions in their native languages. Use of students' native language was also correlated with positive gains in oral communication abilities.

3. Gains in oral English skills were positively correlated with rate of student attendance, longer scheduled length of class in terms of hours per week, the use of students' native languages for instructional support, and the use of the varied practice or interaction strategy.

Additional sources cite support for the use of native languages in ESL instruction for adult literacy. A report authored through Teachers of English to Speakers of Other Languages (TESOL, 2000) recommends this strategy, stating that "the use of non-English languages facilitates the learning of English and develops proficiency in those languages"(p. 8).

Research indicates that literacy proficiency in the primary language facilitates literacy acquisition in English. Researchers also recommend the use of bilingual and native language texts as instructional materials when possible and appropriate and suggest that effective practices build on learners' existing knowledge, recognizing and developing the use of different learning styles and multiple intelligences. Instruction in grammar and discrete English language skills is also advised in the context of meaningful language use.

The use of explicit versus implicit instruction in basic literacy skills for ESL learners has not been thoroughly examined for adult learners. Evidence from studies of children in ESL classrooms supports the use of explicit instruction for reading skill development (AERA, 2004). At the present time, a large-scale study is under way to measure the effectiveness of explicit instruction for reading development in adult ESL students (Cronen, Silver-Pacuilla, & Condelli, 2004).

ESL practitioners also acknowledge the importance of learner motivation and interactions in second-language acquisition. ESL students may be motivated by "integrative" motivation (the desire to learn a language in order to identify with the community that speaks the language), or by "instrumental" motivation (the desire to learn the language in order to meet individual needs and goals for transacting the business of daily life). It has been suggested that ESL teachers can enhance student motivation by providing short-term goals, helping students to reflect on their progress and achievements, providing self-assessments or progress-tracking devices, and creating classroom environments that encourage group cohesion and a sense of community (Moss & Ross-Feldman, 2003). The use of assigned projects to stimulate group work and language both in class and out of class is also recommended. Research suggests that learners produce longer sentences and negotiate meaning more often in pair and group work than in teacher-led instruction.

The approaches suggested in the "What Works" study have been connected with positive outcomes for adult ESL students needing significant literacy development. However, many ESL students in the college setting have already acquired basic literacy in their native languages but need additional instruction to acquire sufficient English language proficiency to pursue college-level coursework. Achieving proficiency in this so-called academic English may involve additional instructional strategies and take longer to acquire. For these students, a "participatory approach" has been recommended (Berlin, 2005). This approach sees the ESL classroom as a microcosm of society, in which development of English language fluency is socially co-constructed along with an understanding of other concepts including democracy, multiculturalism, and social justice. Berlin suggests the use of "problem posing" as a critical pedagogy to engage students through stages of naming, reflection, and action relating to the problem. Interactive dialogue among students and between the teacher and students in examining the problem creates a vehicle for developing more advanced language skills and building confidence in oral communication.

3.4. Developmental education faculty employ a variety of instructional methods to accommodate student diversity.

Teaching and pedagogy have most recently been transformed by the concepts of "learner-centeredness" rather than "teacher-centeredness" as well as the inclusion of active learning strategies rather than passive learning strategies. These concepts have given rise to shifts in institutional paradigms from the "college-ready student" to the "student-ready college," or to what Terry O'Banion calls "The Learning College." Overall, these shifts have fundamentally changed the roles of teachers and learners, and contemporary pedagogies are likely to emphasize student engagement, individualization, learning styles, collaboration, critical thinking, and classroom assessment. These practices are echoed in Chickering and Gamson's "Seven Principles for Good Practice in Undergraduate Education" (1991):

1. Good practice encourages student-faculty contact.

2. Good practice encourages cooperation among students.

3. Good practice encourages active learning.

4. Good practice gives prompt feedback.

5. Good practice emphasizes time on task.

6. Good practice communicates high expectations.

7. Good practice respects diverse talents and ways of learning.

Of these principles, Cross asserts that "what the principles really tell us is how to get and keep students actively engaged in learning" (2005, p. 8). Similarly, she offers a list of guidelines for effective teaching and learning, which include the following instructional or classroom factors as keys to success: communicate high expectations; encourage active learning; provide consistent assessment and prompt feedback.

Active Learning

An emphasis on active learning methodologies correlates with unique strategies that are effective for adult learners. Boylan (2002) describes this correlation as follows:

> *Whatever they are called, active learning methods are characterized by the fact that they are designed to elicit students' active participation in the learning process. Such involvement is critical for adult students because, as Grubb points out, these students have already been exposed to the typical lecture, discussion, drill and practice approaches used in high school courses and college remediation and they have not worked. (p. 102)*

In a classroom emphasizing active learning the instructor departs from the front of the classroom and the "sage on the stage" model and becomes a facilitator within the classroom. As Cross (2005) points out, other terms that are often explored to replace "teacher" are, for instance, "coach," "observer," "trainer," "arranger," "manager," or "colearner" (p. 6).

"There is a convergence in the literature advising flexibility coupled with sufficient structure to assure productive learning toward articulated goals" (Cross, 2005, p. 6). Cross argues that "the role of the instructor in active learning includes these responsibilities: orienting students to the goals and purposes of active learning, making decisions about the size and operation of learning groups, assigning and structuring learning tasks, assuring active participation of all students, and monitoring and assessing learning" (pp. 6–7).

The most important role of the instructor is the design of the instructional experience in order to provide structure and goals, even if he or she relinquishes control. Weinstein and Meyer (1991) conclude that "there is a great deal of intuitive appeal to the cognitive approach to teaching. . . . Applying the approach is more difficult, however, because [instructors] must give up the illusion of control. That change shakes the foundation of content as the primary focus of our teaching" (p. 36).

Partly, this means departing from a traditional model focused on effective teaching performance and moving instead to one which emphasizes the goal of teaching expressed as student learning. Weinstein and Meyer view this change as optimistic as the result is more likely to be "more productive learners who will function effectively and independently in the uncertainties of the future" (p. 36).

Cross (2005) summarizes this paradigm change by analogizing teaching to farming:

A successful farmer is judged by the quality and quantity of his crops— not by whether or not he wears bib overalls or rises with the sun. A farmer's attention is concentrated on understanding the nature of the things he is trying to grow. He knows that some plants require fours hours of sun a day; others do well in shade. Some plants are drought resistant; others require irrigation. Some plants require one kind of fertilizer; others something else. The point is that the farmer's actions are determined by the needs and nature of his crop. . . . Teaching today is more like home gardening than scientific agriculture. Care, attention, and experience will certainly result in better crops than neglect, and some home gardeners get wonderful results. (p. 10)

The students' role is also changed in this pedagogical paradigm from passive listener to engaged participant. MacGregor (1990) defines some of these changes as follows:

- From listener, observer, and note taker to active problem solver, contributor, and discussant

- From low or moderate expectations of preparation for class to high expectations

- From private presence in the classroom with few or no risks to public one with many risks

- From attendance dictated by personal choice to attendance dictated by community experience

- From competition with peers to collaborative work with them

- From responsibilities and self-definition associated with learning independently to those associated with learning interdependently

- From seeing teachers and texts as the sole sources of authority and knowledge to seeing peers, self, and the thinking of the community as additional and important sources of authority and knowledge (p. 25)

Lectures, then, from a cognitive-motivational standpoint, may not be the most effective method of instruction, especially for developmental learners. In order for a lecture to be an effective method of instruction, it must promote enthusiasm about the subject and provide students with an avenue of response so that their interaction is intrinsic to the activity rather than additive.

Engagement

The validity of active learning strategies is closely related to the valuation of "engagement" among community college students. The results of the Lumina Foundation's study "Connecting the Dots: Multi-Faceted Analysis of the Relationships between Student Engagement Results from the National Survey of Student Engagement (NSSE), and the Institutional Practices and Conditions That Foster Student Success" indicate that meaningfully including students in the creation of their own learning has particularly significant results on traditionally underrepresented groups. The study (Kuh et al., 2006b) points to the following findings about engagement:

- *Student engagement in educationally purposeful activities is positively related to academic outcomes as represented by first-year and senior student grades and to persistence between the first and second year of college.*

- *Engagement has a compensatory effect on first-year grades and persistence to the second year of college at the same institution. (p. 68)*

The study includes an exhaustive list of collaborative and active learning opportunities (for example, asked questions in class, made a presentation, sought tutoring, discussed issues outside of class, sought instructor assistance, discussed career plans with an adviser, worked with other students on a project) (Kuh et al., 2006b, p. 81). Tinto (1997) quotes a typical student from a recent study who expresses his understanding of why engagement enhances learning:

> *You know the more I talk to other people about class stuff, the homework, the tests, the more I'm actually learning. . . . I learn more about the subject because my brain is getting more, because I am getting more involved with other students in the class. . . . I'm getting more involved with the class even after class. (p. 4)*

The most recent report from the Community College Survey of Student Engagement (2008) emphasizes the point that rigorous education and high expectations also require high levels of support. The report states that "data consistently show that students are more engaged in the classroom than anywhere else" (p. 2). As just one illustration, approximately 20% of the students surveyed indicate that they work with classmates outside of class on projects or assignments, and 46% indicate that they often or very often work with other students collaboratively. However, the study also reveals that 53% of faculty respondents allow less than 10% for collaborative or small-group activities. These results demonstrate the need for colleges to engage faculty and students in the benefits of active learning strategies and to construct opportunities to make these activities more possible.

Collaborative Learning

Collaborative learning is based on social cognitive theories suggesting that students' learning can be facilitated and enhanced by connectivity to peers. "Collaborative learning is based on the idea that learning is a naturally social act in which participants talk among themselves" (Gerlach, 1994, p. 8). This model assumes that students create learning within this social context, rather than within the solitary confines of their own studying. This approach is also distinct from "cooperative learning," which many theorists deem more appropriate for children; collaborative learning is more closely aligned with the needs of adult learners and adult education.

Of course, in order for this approach to be successful, students and instructors need to understand each others' roles; furthermore, students need to learn collaborative skills. Bosworth (1994) asserts that teachers should train students to learn what skills will be necessary, ask students to demonstrate those skills, model those skills in their instruction, provide feedback about students' collaborative skills, and give students an opportunity to reflect on the collaborative experience. Students require this training because "in the traditional classroom setting, where individuals compete for grades and academic standing, cooperation and collaboration are usually not rewarded" (p. 24). Barkley, Cross, and Major (2005) assert that collaborative learning contains the following features: intentional design, co-laboring, and meaningful learning.

Obviously, then, in order for collaborative learning to be effective, the academic and campus climate must support these activities. This climate must emphasize the importance of learning, which involves risk taking, collaborative work, academic integrity, and mutual support. According to Hallinan (2003), when "students are provided with rich educational opportunities and experiences, they are most likely to attain high achievement" (p. 99). Learning, then, must be an institutional priority. Tinto asserts that colleges and universities should "stop tinkering at the margins of institutional life . . . move beyond the provision of add-on services and establish those conditions with universities [and colleges] that promote the retention of all, not just some, students" (pp. 1–2).

Barkley, Cross, and Major (2005) reference studies indicating that collaborative learning models are particularly effective for diverse populations. The evidence strongly confirms that nontraditional students greatly benefit from the opportunity to participate in group learning settings: "Women, members of under-represented racial and ethnic groups, adult and re-entry students, commuters, and international students have been identified as students for whom peer and group learning seem especially valued and valuable" (p. 21). However, they also assert that "taken as a whole, the research appears to substantiate the claim that both underprepared and well-prepared students benefit from group learning, but perhaps for different reasons" (p. 21).

This technique is widely applied across the disciplines. Mathematics instruction has been enhanced by providing students with the opportunity to work problems and discuss them with peers. Hartman (1993) describes the use of a collaborative learning process by which "Thinker and Listener" pairs work on problems together. "Students take turns serving as thinkers (problem-solvers) who externalize their thought processes by thinking aloud, while analytical listeners track and guide the problem solving process as needed" (p. 272). However, Hartman cautions that to be successful, any collaborative technique will require careful student training and consistent feedback from the instructor.

Collaboration is also a key feature in Writing Across the Curriculum (WAC) models. Rather than treating writing as a discrete skill, WAC programs attempt to use writing as a thinking tool, making literacy a core value in every discipline. The use of collaborative writing projects, writing groups, blogs, and discussion boards all contribute to the students' ability to participate in the discipline discourse, as well as improve their overall literacy. Many WAC programs also support the collaboration of writing experts with other discipline faculty. Stout and Magnotto (1991) surveyed 1,200 community and junior colleges to collect data about WAC programs across the country. They conclude that the investment in WAC programs yields the following benefits: "increased faculty interaction among the disciplines," "more writing outside of English courses," and "increased faculty interaction within the disciplines" (p. 11).

Within composition studies programs, collaborative writing is often lauded for its benefits; however, it also poses a number of potential problems. Elbow (1999) asserts that collaborative writing is often "difficult and unpleasant"; it is often "bland" because the writers must agree on their thinking; and it often "silences weaker, minority, or marginal voices" (p. 1). He notes that carefully designed assignments, student training, and fair assessment techniques can ameliorate these issues.

Contextual Learning

Constructivist theories hold that learners incorporate new information by relating it to what is already known. In this way, meaning is attached to the new information as it is placed in the context of previous knowledge. Instruction can capitalize on this principle of brain learning by directly seeking to provide relevance and application of new information through presenting it in relation to real-world aspects of the students' lives. Contextual teaching and learning (CTL) "helps teachers relate subject matter content to real world situations and motivates students to make connections between knowledge and its applications to their lives as family members, citizens, and workers" (Ohio State University, 1999, p. 1). In addition to facilitating constructed meaning from new knowledge, this method also enhances student motivation and helps to translate often abstract concepts into concrete examples.

Contextual teaching and learning differs from traditional, conceptual instruction in several ways. In general, CTL is characterized by:

1. *Centralization of pragmatic life/work issues*

2. *Integration of academics with real-life experiences*

3. *Personalization of instruction*

4. *Visualization of abstract ideas*

5. *Demonstration of utility (Bond, 2004)*

Contextual learning methods have also been termed "cognitive apprenticeships," a reference to the acquisition of academic knowledge or skills in a manner similar to that which has historically been employed among craftsmen in technical occupations (Bond, 2004). Much as in a traditional apprenticeship, CTL makes the knowledge to be mastered visible and presents it in a way that makes immediate sense to the learner. Instructional methods shift from lecture-dominated formats to those in which instructors provide modeling, scaffolding, and coaching as the novice learner trains to do the "task" in which he or she will apply the information gained.

Most often, CTL has been used to connect learning in academic subject areas with vocational training. Researchers have concluded that teaching academic applications in the career context is an effective way to engage hard-to-reach students and to motivate them in the areas of math, written and oral communication, critical-thinking skills, and problem solving (Paris & Huske, 1998). Others have noted the affective benefits of increased learner confidence, development of enthusiasm and interest toward students' long-term goals, and the education that is required to achieve them (Weinbaum & Rogers, 1995; Baker, Hope, & Karandjeff, 2009). In reviewing studies on "work-based" learning in high schools, Medrich, Calderon, and Hoachlander (2002) found that this method led to increased student attendance, decreased dropout rates, and increased student engagement with school. Specifically, these studies noted that work-based learning significantly improved a student's grade point average and attendance and was correlated with students' enrolling in higher level math and science courses more frequently than their peers.

In Washington, a statewide initiative has recently demonstrated the significant potential of contextual learning for improving student outcomes in basic skills and workforce training. At 10 two-year colleges, the Integrated Basic Education and Skills Training Program (I-BEST) paired ESL adult basic skills instructors in classrooms with professional-technical instructors to simultaneously deliver intensive instruction aimed at developing English language or literacy skills in the context of workforce education. Project results indicated that I-BEST students earned five times more college credits on average and were fifteen times more likely to complete workforce training than a control group of ESL students over the same amount of time (Washington State Board for Community and Technical Colleges, 2005). The success of the program was profound enough to prompt a change in the system's full-time equivalent (FTE) calculations for funding reimbursement to accommodate the unique instructional mode involving two instructors present simultaneously in the classroom, along with enhanced support services.

Learning Communities

Learning communities can occur within a course or exist as paired courses. Either way, the goal of learning communities is that "students encounter learning as a shared experience rather than isolated experience" (Tinto, 1997, p. 602). Extensive data indicate that these shared experiences contribute to the overall success and retention of developmental and transfer students. Further, Tinto claims that learning communities "emphasizing collaborative learning have a positive impact on student attitudes toward learning" (p. 602). His research also suggests that learning communities and collaborative learning activities have a positive effect on the academic performance and persistence of developmental students.

Tinto (1997) argues that "though it is apparent that the college classroom is, for many if not most students, the only place where involvement may arise, it remains the case that most college classrooms are less than involving" (p. 602). For the most part, students take courses in detached and isolated units. However, a number of colleges are exploring the potential for paired courses or formal learning communities. In paired courses, a cohort of students enroll in the same two courses, and usually one course is designed to complement the other. The Puente Project and MESA in California are based on this model, as is an MDRC project at Kingsborough Community College. The instructors of these courses work together to promote shared curriculum and to support each other's learning goals.

In a study of Seattle Central Community College students, Tinto (1997) concluded that a learning community of paired courses resulted in supportive peer groups, shared learning, and greater voice in the construction of knowledge (p. 608). Students enrolled in learning communities at the college persisted at a rate that was 25% higher than those in the traditional curriculum, and reported an increased sense of personal responsibility for their own learning and that of their community members (Tinto, 2000a). The learning communities resulted in the development of learning networks that extended beyond the boundaries of the classroom and assisted students in their ability to manage assignments and feel more secure in an unfamiliar academic environment. In addition, Tinto asserts that a "multidisciplinary approach also provided a model of learning that encouraged students to express the diversity of their experiences and world views" (p. 610). This means, of course, that the instructors modeled methods of expressing both comparisons and contrasts in course materials and personal viewpoints.

Boylan (2002), however, indicates that learning communities are labor intensive and not necessarily effective for all students, despite the research documenting their success. Therefore, learning communities must have a strong training and staff development component. Furthermore, the "overall effect of learning communities is strengthened by weaving advising, counseling, tutoring, and other support services into the learning community" (pp. 70–71). This last salient point is perhaps overlooked in terms of the contribution of these features toward the documented successes of learning communities.

Indeed, as suggested by effective practices previously identified in this review, the inclusion of these support service components and their concomitant focus on increased engagement and motivation may account in large part for the success of the learning community structure.

Much of the available research on learning communities has been conducted at four-year, residential colleges and universities. More studies are needed to examine the impact of these models at commuter and two-year colleges. One promising study by MDRC (Bloom & Sommo, 2005) at Kingsborough Community College in New York indicates that learning communities have the capacity to accelerate basic skills improvement and, therefore, improve students' chances of completing their undergraduate goals. Despite the promise of substantial gains associated with the implementation of learning communities, they are not without their limitations. Colleges should be thoughtful and deliberate in selecting a learning community approach to meet the needs of specific cohorts of developmental students.

3.5. Programs align entry and exit skills among levels and link course content to college-level performance requirements.

If basic skills courses are to assist underprepared students in achieving college success, the issue of sequential course alignment with college-level requirements is fundamental to effective developmental programs. Grubb (2001) notes that along the pathway from initial student placement to successful completion of degree or transfer requirements, there are many critical points at which the system may break down. Assessment instruments not carefully aligned with course content may result in either over- or underinclusion of students in the remedial pathway. Likewise, improper alignment between sequential course exit and entry-level skills may lead students to repeat previously mastered material or may result in gaps in acquired knowledge and skills needed for success. Grubb recommends that colleges examine the entire trajectory of the developmental curriculum, from initial placement through all levels of remedial coursework to the collegiate-level content course, to ensure consistency and appropriateness of coursework prescribed for developmental learners.

Research confirms that remedial courses are most effective when regular efforts are made to ensure consistency between exit standards for remediation and the entry standards for content courses (Boylan, Bonham, Claxton, & Bliss, 1992). At institutions where such consistency was present, students passing remedial courses had a higher likelihood of also passing their college-level courses. Higher retention rates have also been linked to entry and exit skill alignment in sequential developmental courses (Boylan & Saxon, 1998). In their studies of successful developmental programs, both Boylan (2002) and Roueche and Roueche (1999) found that ensuring linkage between basic skills and college-level courses was a key component, leading them to advocate strongly for colleges to embrace this function.

3.6. Developmental faculty routinely share instructional strategies.

Although the literature reveals a great deal regarding the defining characteristics of developmental students, little research has been conducted regarding the preparedness of faculty to teach this diverse group of learners. As Kisker and Outcalt (2005) observe, developmental educators are more likely to be involved in "community college-specific organizations and attend association meetings more often than [do] non-developmental faculty" (p. 7). This trend is an important aspect of the success of developmental educators, who provide both formal and informal professional development for one another. The study also revealed that developmental faculty are more likely to rely on colleagues for advice or input.

Effective teaching practices should be shared among faculty to increase the benefits to a larger population of students. Though many faculty do this with their colleagues informally, highly effective developmental programs are characterized by formal, embedded mechanisms to facilitate such exchanges. In a national benchmarking study of best practice institutions for developmental education, 89% indicated that they had some sort of mechanisms in place to promote creation and exchange of instructional strategies among faculty at the discipline level and across the program (Boylan, 2002). Additionally, many also noted that they made deliberate efforts to support collaboration between faculty and student service personnel.

Boylan (2002) suggests that sharing mechanisms must be routine rather than occasional, and that these must be structured into the activities of the developmental program. Mechanisms that facilitate sharing might include:

- Set-aside time at faculty meetings to talk about teaching/learning issues and pedagogical approaches

- Share syllabi or other course materials

- Form instructional teams to develop or adapt materials

- Encourage mentoring relationships among faculty

- Provide opportunities for faculty returning from conferences to "share out" regarding their learning and/or materials obtained

- Frequent collegewide forums devoted to dialogue and discussion of instructional practices

McCusker (1999) also notes a recommendation for cross-level sharing and collaboration between faculty in developmental and content-area courses. Because they represent a significant proportion of developmental instructors, adjunct faculty must also be strongly encouraged to routinely communicate and share strategies with others in the program.

Chapter 4
Student Support Services and Strategies

FOR MANY STUDENTS, especially those in community colleges, the transition into higher education is especially challenging—not just because they lack the academic tools to thrive, but because they lack the emotional or psychological maturity or the cultural capital to comfortably immerse themselves into both the expectations and norms of this new world. As Levitz, Noel, and Richter (1999) observe, incoming students "enter with some anxiety or apprehension about beginning a new educational venture. Some of these students also bring complex educational and personal issues that dictate the need for even more comprehensive and individualized support services than many institutions are set up to provide"(p. 37). As previously discussed, the most successful developmental education programs provide an integrated approach to education, connecting academics with student services. These services and approaches are instrumental for a college to shift from a deficit culture to an achievement culture. This chapter provides an overview of just some of the most promising practices in student support services and student success strategies.

4.1. The developmental education program addresses holistic development of all aspects of the student. Attention is paid to the social and emotional development of the students as well as to their cognitive growth.

4.2. Culturally Responsive Teaching theory and practices are applied to all aspects of the developmental instructional programs and services.

4.3. Faculty and advisers carefully structure learning environments and closely monitor student performance.

4.4. Colleges assist students in developing social connections to others.

4.5. Programs provide comprehensive academic support mechanisms, including the use learning assistance centers, tutoring, and student development courses.

4.1. The developmental education program addresses holistic development of all aspects of the student. Attention is paid to the social and emotional development of the students as well as to their cognitive growth.

Although the terms "developmental" and "remedial" are often used interchangeably, a key philosophical difference between the two relates to how students are perceived. "Remedial" approaches derive from a deficit model, assuming that students who have not acquired skills and abilities from previous instruction need additional or modified instruction to correct the deficiency. The preferred "developmental" approach recognizes that all students have strengths and weaknesses, and that learners not only progressively acquire content-specific knowledge, but also attain the skills and attitudes necessary to facilitate higher-order thinking and learning. This view is connected with so-called whole student approaches that consider metacognitive, affective, and social aspects of student development in addition to cognitive growth.

According to the literature, best practice developmental programs are those that address the holistic development of the student. In an early study of colleges reporting good retention rates for developmental programs, Roueche and Snow (1977) found that course objectives and methods employed at these institutions integrated the use of cognitive, affective, and psychomotor skills. McCabe and Day (1998) cite a study of 10 colleges having model developmental programs, and note a common finding that "each recognizes that the programs must deal with all aspects of student development—personal, as well as academic" (p. 24).

A more recent study of exemplary developmental programs again identified that these colleges shared common beliefs that were both holistic and developmental, addressing students as "total beings with both affective and cognitive characteristics shaping their attitudes and behaviors" (Boylan, 2002, p. 62). Maxwell (1997b) notes that studies of developmental students consistently show that programs where faculty members are concerned with students' emotions and attitudes about their work are more successful than those where the faculty concentrates only on teaching the subject. She states firmly that "without exception, the one variable that separated the successful developmental program from those with moderate success . . . was that instructors spent as much time on self-concept development as on teaching basic skills" (p. 19).

Based on these studies, the literature contains various recommendations that developmental programs pay close attention to the social, emotional, and personal development of learners. McCabe and Day (1998) recommend that model developmental programs should integrate learning and personal development strategies and services. Hennessy (1990) suggests that colleges should consider personality variables, particularly self-esteem and self-confidence, as well as academic achievement and persistence. In her commentary on developmental education, Higbee (1995) asserts that developmental educators should address not only student competence, but also the development of identity and purpose, interdependence, mature interpersonal relationships, and integrity. Finally, in defining an underlying philosophy of practice for developmental education, Casazza (1996) advocates a talent development approach that aims to maximize learner potential, advising that the process "takes place in a meaningful context and is sensitive to the cognitive, emotional and social needs of the learner" (p. 8).

Underprepared students have diverse needs, many of which extend beyond the need to learn fundamental skills. To succeed, "at-risk" students often require child care, financial aid, and transportation, as well as an array of personal services. This issue is further exacerbated by the fact that most community college students are commuters, contributing to an overall sense of disconnection and isolation. Intentional efforts by colleges to overcome this isolation and to encourage students to identify with the college are important vehicles for enhancing students' intrinsic motivations to persist and succeed.

Research has consistently shown that students who actively engage with faculty, staff, and other students at their colleges are much more likely to succeed in attaining their educational goals (Tinto, 1993; Astin, 1985; CCSSE, 2006; Kuh et al., 2006b). Essentially, when students identify strongly with their college, they perform better. Tinto's integration model (1993) suggests that students coming into a college undergo phases in which they separate to some degree from groups of their former association (such as family or high school peers), transition to interacting with members of a "new" group (college personnel and students), and ultimately incorporate the values and behaviors that lead to acceptance into the new group. He further suggests that students who leave college may be those who have been unsuccessful in adopting the values and behaviors that allow them to integrate into college life. Such integration has both academic and social aspects. Though research documenting the linkage between academic integration and persistence is modest, the support for social integration as a predictor of persistence is considerable (Braxton, Sullivan, & Johnson, 1997).

An exhaustive review of literature to determine "what matters to student success" recently affirmed the powerful relationship between institutional affinity and positive student outcomes (Kuh et al., 2006a). A key finding of this study stated, "Students who find something or someone worthwhile to connect with in the postsecondary environment are more likely to engage in educationally purposeful activities during college, persist, and achieve their educational objectives" (p. 3).

Among the approaches associated with high student engagement are student-faculty contact, cooperation among students, active learning, prompt feedback, time on task, high expectations, and respect for diverse talents and ways of learning (Chickering & Gamson, 1991). Many initiatives that have proven effective with developmental learners (such as learning communities and freshman experience programs) owe much of their success to the associated affective and motivational attributes that build connections and develop a shared sense of responsibility among students in these programs. Colleges seeking to increase achievement of developmental learners might first consider expanding mechanisms to build affinity and social integration as platforms for intensifying student commitment and motivation.

An example of a comprehensive program that engages students with a variety of college services is the first-year experience program at Bronx Community College, with its focus on personal and academic counseling. Students in the program were those who, based on their assessment results, were required to take at least three remedial courses in English composition, reading, or mathematics. These students were required to meet with counselors at least three times, while also enrolling in an orientation and career development course meeting once a week. The course included the Noel-Levitz Retention Management System, the Myers-Briggs Type Indicator, and the California Occupational Preference Survey. The tests emphasized students' assets, and the counselors emphasized self-esteem development. In addition, students were encouraged to seek tutoring and additional academic support. The program resulted in a 29% increase in retention and an overall increase in GPA and course completion for program participants (Baron, 1997).

Student success courses (also called student orientation, study skills, first-year experience courses) are a common practice in the network of support services that colleges offer to support student performance, especially the performance of underprepared learners. And though these courses have the capacity to reach a wide number of students with a diverse set of issues, they are highly valued but not widely studied. In a recent study, Dr. Windham and other researchers at the Florida Department of Education compared the performance of students who had completed a "student life skills" course with those who did not, and they concluded that course completers were more likely to earn a credential, transfer to university, or persist at the college after five years (Zeidenberg, Jenkins, & Calcagno, 2007). Although researchers caution that the study indicates a correlative relationship between the course and success rather than a causal one, the data strongly suggest the efficacy of the practice.

Muraskin (1997) cites the importance of addressing student motivation in successful student services programs, which use reward and reinforcement in order to promote and enhance the students' motivation to engage in academic careers. She cites the following commonalities of five highly effective programs:

- A project-designed freshman experience for most or all participants
- An emphasis on academic support for developmental and popular freshman courses
- Extensive student service contacts
- Targeted participant recruitment and participation incentives
- Dedicated staff and directors with strong institutional attachments
- An important role on campus

Muraskin further states that "we do not know that these commonalities of approach and practice are the reasons these projects are successful, but we know that these features are important elements of successful projects" (p. 14).

Another motivational factor is the influence of teachers' expectations and the students' learning styles or preferences on achievement and success. The research on learning styles is vast and wide, even contradictory. However, researchers agree that students' preferences and personalities have a profound impact on their learning. Therefore, an environment that takes these differences into consideration has a better opportunity to maximize learning.

According to Svinicki, "prior knowledge impacts what learners pay attention to, how they perceive and interpret what they are experiencing, and how they store new information based on what they already know" (2004, p. 185). This prior knowledge is not limited to what students bring to the particular discipline, but also includes their cultural orientation and personal view of themselves and the world.

Personality differences may cause learners to prefer a specific set of learning modalities. Indicators like the Myers-Briggs point to varying factors that influence a learner's tendency to gravitate toward particular experiences.

Kolb's learning style indicator is yet another tool commonly used to make similar determinations. All of these tools assist the instructor in designing learning experiences that will lead to deeper understanding and easier comprehension for the students.

Anderson (1988) asserts that culture plays an important role in the worldview of the learner, and therefore on the development of learning. For instance, "a culture that values cooperation and places more emphasis upon the good of the group rather than the individual may produce students who have a natural preference for learning environments that allow for cooperation rather than competition" (Sanchez, 2000, p. 37). These preferences set a framework for the learner's perspective and inform behavior and expectations. It may also have an impact on the way that students process and prioritize information (Jonassen & Grabowski, 1993).

4.2. Culturally Responsive Teaching theory and practices are applied to all aspects of the developmental instructional programs and services.

Culturally Responsive Teaching (CRT) theory and practice articulates basic principles and pedagogical strategies designed to enhance learning among all students, regardless of the students' ethnic, socioeconomic, and educational backgrounds. Although this theory and practice builds on earlier efforts to diversify the content of curriculum (for example, readings from different cultures), Culturally Responsive Teaching focuses more directly on the pedagogy for developing students' skills, competencies, and knowledge.

Most of the research in this area has concentrated on the elementary and secondary levels. There are isolated examples of community colleges implementing CRT strategies (for example, Baltimore County Community College and work at Native American tribal colleges); however, there is very little published research on the impact of these strategies in the community college environment. Nonetheless, given the emerging substantial research that verifies the effectiveness of these practice in the precollege learning environments (Gay, 2000; Banks, Magee, & Cherry, 2001; Banks, 2004), we cannot ignore the importance of these practices to the precollegiate developmental education programs designed for those students when they move on to the community college from K–12 or other educational environments.

A number of the core practices of Culturally Responsive Teaching overlap with other effective practices described in this review. However, it is important to view these practices in the context of the needs of students from diverse backgrounds. First, communication of high expectations is fundamental. "Trying to teach from . . . [a] deficit mindset sounds more like a basis for 'correcting or curing' than educating," warns Gay (p. 24). Rather than "blaming the victim" by focusing on negative socioeconomic factors, CRT calls for positive perspectives on parents, families, and the diverse experiences students bring to their learning environments (Banks, McGee, & Cherry, 2001; Banks, 2004).

The communication of high expectations and positive perspectives relies on *cultural sensitivity* and *culturally mediated instruction. Cultural sensitivity* depends upon the "teacher's . . . knowledge of the cultures represented in their classrooms and [their ability to] translate this knowledge into instructional practice." This cultural knowledge goes beyond the stereotypical "artifacts of the culture, such as food and art" to a thorough understanding of how communication and learning take place within each culture (Knowledgeloom, 2006, p. 10). *Culturally mediated instruction* involves the following:

1. Culturally mediated cognition, that is, a pedagogy that reflects "the ways of knowing, understanding, and representing information within a given culture" (Knowledgeloom, 2006, p. 12)

2. An understanding and application of the various cultural perspectives on the relationships of students to students and of students to faculty (McCarty, Lynch, Wallace, & Benally, 1991)

3. The inclusion of knowledge that is valued and relevant in the student's personal experiences

4. A curriculum that "capitalizes on students' cultural backgrounds" by fully infusing materials, examples, and strategies drawn from the students' various cultural backgrounds (Abdal-Haqq, 1994, pp. 2–4)

Culturally Responsive Teaching embraces the active learning methodologies described in other sections of this literature review. Within those active strategies, the teacher becomes a facilitator responsible for organizing instruction so that diverse voices can be incorporated into the learning process, as well as a cultural mediator who engages students in dialogue about cultural identity, while also helping students address critical differences in cultural systems. Finally, the instructor must "orchestrate" social contexts to create compatible frameworks for ethnically diverse groups (Gay, 2000).

CRT methodologies also emphasize giving the student "control [of] some portion of the lesson" to ensure that the student's cultural and family learning experiences and the language used to communicate those experiences inform the classroom learning environment (Knowledgeloom, 2006, p. 15). Small-group and cooperative learning strategies provide students the opportunity to develop academic competencies using "underlying values of human connectedness and collaborative problem solving [that] are high priorities in cultures of most groups of color in the United States" and that play "a central role in these groups' learning styles, especially communicative, procedural, motivational, and relational dimensions" (Gay, 2000, p. 158).

4.3. Faculty and advisers carefully structure learning experiences and closely monitor student performance.

Early researchers noted the effects of structured learning environments in developmental education programs. In her book *Accent on Learning*, Cross (1976) noted that developmental learners tended to lack the organizational schema necessary to comprehend many academic concepts, and advised that highly structured learning experiences helped students by modeling appropriate methods of organizing information. In their study of colleges with good retention rates in developmental programs, Roueche, Baker, and Roueche (1985) determined that the offering of highly structured courses was a characteristic feature. More recent reviews of developmental literature have reinforced this element as an effective practice for instructional improvement (Perin, 2005). Snow (1977) further showed that structured learning environments provided the most benefit to the weakest students, a position also validated by subsequent studies (Kulik & Kulik, 1991; Boylan, Bonham, Claxton, & Bliss, 1992).

The benefits of structure have also been noted at the program level, where the use of a well-planned, step-by-step sequence of offerings with proactive academic support has been advised (Roueche & Snow, 1977; McCusker, 1999; Maxwell, 1997b; Roueche & Roueche, 1999).

According to Cross (2001), "one of the basic principles of learning is that learners need feedback." The concept of "curriculum bits" or units was first articulated in Bloom's concept of mastery learning:

Bloom saw dividing the material to be learned into units and checking on students' learning with a test at the end of each unit as useful instructional techniques. He believed, however, that the tests used by most teachers did little more than show for whom the initial instruction was or was not appropriate. . . . With this in mind, Bloom outlined a specific instructional strategy to make use of . . . feedback and corrective measures, labeling it "mastery learning." (Gusky, 1994, pp. 9–10)

Mastery learning, therefore, emphasizes individualized instruction and frequent classroom assessment. Boylan (2002) asserts that techniques using this framework are particularly effective for developmental learners because they provide "regular reinforcement of concepts through testing. An emphasis on mastery requires students to develop the prerequisite knowledge for success in a given course and to demonstrate this knowledge through testing" (p. 88). Mastery learning also provides "regular reinforcement" as well as a high degree of structure (Boylan & Saxon, 2002). Although this approach is not as popular as it was 30 years ago, the evidence still supports its efficacy. However, "frequent testing does not necessarily imply the exclusive use of paper and pencil or computerized testing. Any activity that requires students to demonstrate their skills according to a standard can represent frequent testing" (Boylan, 2002, p. 79). Consequently, the feedback from these assessments gives students an opportunity to practice and study more effectively.

According to Craven (1987), the disciplines that are most compatible with mastery learning share the following traits: "[t]hey require a minimum of prior knowledge, they are learned sequentially, they emphasize convergent thinking, and they are closed" (p. 82). Generally, this description applies to science and some mathematics instruction. Craven asserts that the process of mastery learning—informing the students of what they need to learn, providing opportunity for practice, providing feedback about what students can do to correct errors, and assessing achievement—is relatively easy to employ. Studies show that achievement can be expected to rise with this more individualized model.

This concept of mastery learning has been further explored and popularized through the "classroom assessment techniques" described and validated by Angelo and Cross. The purpose of classroom assessment is for the teacher to obtain continuous information about the quality and depth of student learning, and for students to obtain continuous information about the development of their skills so that they can reflect, monitor, and correct. Some of the most popular techniques include the "minute paper," which is easy to administer and provides immediate feedback about student learning. *Classroom Assessment Techniques* by Angelo and Cross (1993) outlines approximately 50 techniques that are adaptable for a wide variety of disciplines and that help engage students in the evaluation of their own learning while also informing their instructors as to the progress of their skills and comprehension. This, in turn, provides an opportunity for instructors to conduct their own classroom research about the progress of their classes. The institutionalization of the student learning outcomes cycle provides similar opportunities.

In addition to classroom feedback, the literature strongly supports evaluating student progress through student services, either through a counselor or "case manager." Roueche, Ely, and Roueche (2001) describe a case management approach at the Community College of Denver, where case managers work as "advocates, problem solvers, and friends" for their student charges (p. 94). Case managers meet routinely with students to map approaches for the students' course of study and to designate appropriate services as they progress.

Monitoring student performance is an important element in most developmental programs, but the best programs make monitoring a shared responsibility for faculty and advising staff (Boylan, 2002). Current theories maintain that affective factors such as attitude, motivation, and self-efficacy contribute toward academic achievement as much as a student's cognitive ability. Though faculty are in the best position to monitor cognitive progress, advisers may have additional insight regarding affective factors. This collaborative monitoring model provides for the development of comprehensive interventions.

Commonly, such monitoring is manifested as an "early warning system" in which faculty may refer students needing help to an academic adviser who meets with the student to recommend solutions or services. After referring the student to the appropriate services, the adviser follows up to ensure that the student actually takes advantage of the recommended services and reports the outcomes back to the faculty (who may make further assessments or adaptations to instruction). Advisers who are able to work with the same students throughout their developmental programs are better able to build relationships with students, understand their goals, and promote student engagement with the institution.

Kulik, Kulik, and Schwalb (1983) found that college interventions for high-risk students were more successful when they began as early as possible in students' academic careers. Similar findings were reported by McCabe and Day (1998) who noted that "early intervention appears to be a key to the success of monitoring activities in developmental education" (p. 59).

4.4. Colleges assist students in developing social connections to others.

Many colleges have also successfully used peer mentors for monitoring. Peer mentors must be carefully selected and very well trained in areas including interviewing skills, academic policies, and advising ethics. This strategy has proved to be particularly effective for students who may feel culturally disenfranchised or isolated. Peer mentors have also been effective at introducing students to the norms and expectations of a professional environment, providing valuable insight into vocational or professional fields that students may be insecure about exploring.

Beatty-Guenter (1994) identifies "connecting students with one another and with the institution" and "supporting students in dealing with life's problems or responsibilities" as two critical retention strategies (Stromei, 2000, p. 57). Mentoring accomplishes both of these goals by providing the students with a personal guide who can ameliorate some of the stresses of isolation while also coaching students through threatening personal and academic scenarios.

In 1991, James conducted a study evaluating the retention of two groups of black students—one group participated in mentoring while the other did not. Mentors consisted of both part-time and full-time faculty at the college. The study concluded that of the students who were mentored, 66% completed all of their credit courses. In the nonparticipant group, 55% completed their coursework. In addition, among mentored students, 80% returned to the college to reenroll, whereas only 73% of the nonparticipating students persisted (Stromei, 2000).

In addition to faculty mentors, peer mentors have also shown to be promising and inspirational guides. Indiana University created an initiative called "Access to Success" as part of a Lumina Foundation project (Miller & Spence, 2007). The goal of the program is to connect underserved students with peer mentors who can help them navigate the complex and disorienting world facing incoming freshman. The director of the program states, "Students have a lot of barriers to overcome. . . . There are a lot of things that they don't know. They are apprehensive and many times don't know what to expect. Having peer mentors helps them make the transition from life experience to becoming a student" (2007, p. 16). Participants in the summer "Access to Success" project had a 93% retention rate in 2004 and an 86% retention rate in 2005, rates well above those of their nonparticipant cohorts.

According to Wilcox, Winn, and Fyvie-Gauld, "social integration" is a key factor in retention and persistence (2005). Their study concluded that the creation of social support was a meaningful predictor of student success and ultimately assisted students with their ability to learn while helping students with "material factors" related to success (for example, finances, unfamiliar surroundings, and so on). The sense of belonging supported by a social network helped students "find a sense of place" and feel part of the campus community (2005, p. 712).

Other examples of mentoring programs—Partners for Success in Illinois, Puente Project in California, and AMIGOS in New Mexico—support similar results, suggesting that mentoring is a strategy that supports the academic achievement of participating students, while addressing some of the affective issues that many incoming students face. Additionally, First Year Experience programs provide similarly powerful learning networks, easing students' transition by providing a safe community in which to learn the norms and strategies that will help them thrive in higher education.

4.5. Programs provide comprehensive academic support mechanisms, including the use of learning assistance centers, tutoring, and student development courses.

The most common form of academic support or learning assistance occurs at the community college in the form of a lab or center featuring a variety of services. Because most developmental students simultaneously enroll in transfer or occupational courses, learning assistance programs are particularly important for the students' ability to successfully move through their courses of study. Noel, Levitz, and Kaufman (1982) assert that remediation services alone were unable to ensure student success. In a comprehensive program, they write,

> [s]tudents must learn to motivate themselves, to understand their learning strengths and weaknesses, to negotiate the academic and social system, to adapt effective and efficient methods of processing information, and to alter previously established attitudes about their own potential and their sense of self-worth. (p. 7)

Despite the proliferated availability of tutoring services on most college campuses, many are underutilized by the students who most need the service. The reasons are sometimes difficult to pinpoint, but some theorists and researchers indicate that many students who need help will make a conscious effort to avoid help. According to Karabenick, "help seeking behavior is generally subject to the same influences of other learning strategies" (2004, p. 569). The research indicates that students who "adopt performance goals" are much more likely to demonstrate help-seeking behavior. Conversely, students whose instructors put a strong emphasis on student performance when they are uncertain about their own goals are less likely to exhibit help-seeking behaviors, attitudes, or intentions. Other research indicates that students with higher self-esteem were more likely to seek tutoring assistance, and students with lower esteem used tutoring in "marginal" ways (Clegg, Bradley, & Smith, 2006, p. 112) These findings are important because they explain why students who should be most likely to seek support do not—the failure to seek help is directly associated with the students' desire to avoid the perception of being a failure. This suggests that the more these support services are destigmatized, the more likely they can reach the students who need them most.

Tutoring is often effective because it reinforces social learning models and theories. When students collaborate during the learning process, they see themselves as part of a network, which can help students more readily accept their roles as creators of meaning rather than as receivers of meaning (Ryder, 1994). This approach is not only effective for underprepared students, but for all students.

These services may be housed under the guise of other names as well (for example, academic support centers, reading centers, study skills centers, success centers, educational development centers, or resource centers). The literature generally supports the efficacy of tutoring; however, many educators recommend that in order to be effective, these services must include a number of key characteristics.

One elemental consideration involves the metaphors associated with any form of academic support, often underscored by the name of the service. McQueeney (2001) and Carino (1995) contend that many academic support services suffer under the nomenclature of medical terms such as "labs" or "clinics." Such connotations underscore the stigma implying that students who need help are damaged or injured and seeking "treatment," further stigmatizing the status of students with basic skills issues. Arendale (1997a) further argues for the need for a paradigm shift away from the "medical model."

Similarly, when these services are created for the sole support of basic skills students or dedicated solely to the goal of remediation, they also suffer a kind of marginalization in the community college environment. The effect, unfortunately, dissuades students from usage rather than encouraging it because the service is seen as a designation for failure or inadequacy. To that end, Burns (1994) argues that learning assistance centers should be accessed by all students, faculty, staff, and administrators, emphasizing interrelationships.

Burns goes so far as to assert that learning assistance programs solely devoted to underprepared students actually decrease effectiveness. In this way, the notion of seeking help can be destigmatized through the development of a philosophy that all learners require support. For instance, the University of California provides a network of learning support services founded on the notion that their job, as Adolfo Bermeo, former associate vice-provost for student diversity at UCLA, put it, is to "work with students not on surviving, but on excelling" (Burdman, 2001, p. 36). According to Johanna Dvorak (2001), "although tutoring can carry the stigma of remediation, today we recognize that most college students need some academic support" (p. 39). In addition, academic support centers are often necessary to balance the traditional lecture models, within which most developmental students do not thrive.

Other structural aspects of the center operation also can impact overall effectiveness. Dvorak (2001) recommends that learning center administrators consider the following elements of the operation:

- The development of a mission statement that is aligned with the college

- The availability of individual as well as group learning, where students may learn more in a social construction

- The availability of either walk-in tutoring, appointment-based tutoring, or both

- A varied staff that includes peer tutors, but may also include graduate students

- The development of regular program assessment measures that are both quantitative and qualitative in order to demonstrate the benefits of tutoring or support services

Many researchers comment on the overall lack of quantitative analysis on the benefits of tutoring services, probably because the notion of academic support as a universal good is so widely accepted. However, the difference that tutoring makes on student achievement is only one aspect of how a student may be affected by such services. For instance, a research study on the learning centers at the University of Minnesota indicates that part of the reason that tutoring is valuable is because it can help to "eliminate barriers to learning" (Duranczyk, Goff, & Opitz, 2006). In a student survey regarding experiences in the Math Center, researchers verified that center usage improved confidence gains as well as grades. Goolsby, Dwinell, Higbee, and Bretscher (1994) found that confidence was one of the most significant variables when predicting student success in a developmental mathematics program. However, both of these studies rely heavily on self-reported data, and further research is probably needed in order to correlate these affective changes with grades or achievement.

Further, location plays a key role in the overall effectiveness of the services. The location promotes either access through "visibility" or marginalization through "invisibility." Haviland, Fye, and Colby (2001) argue that isolation can prevent instructors from engaging in the learning processes of an academic support center by relegating them to the fringe of the institution. Therefore, they promote geographic centrality as the best location for an academic support center.

Tutoring is generally considered the most common function of a learning center. Tutors should be well trained, and the tutoring services should be subject to program evaluation. Although some research (Irwin, 1980) indicates that tutoring may have little impact on student achievement, it does seem to have a more significant effect on college persistence (Koeler, 1987; Vincent, 1983). However, tutor training significantly contributes to the overall effectiveness of peer tutors (Gier & Hancock, 2006; Maxwell, 1995; Gourgey, 1994; Condravy, 1995; Damashek, 1999). Specifically, Boylan, Bliss, and Bonham assert that tutors participating in a systematic training component are more likely to promote higher pass rates and higher grade point averages. Generally, the tutor training model sponsored by the College Reading and Learning Association (CRLA) is most widely supported (Gier & Hancock, 2006). Generally, tutor training helps to emphasize the students' need to learn rather than focusing on improvement of specific assignments. Additionally, training helps alert peer tutors to their own metacognitive strategies so that they can more effectively assist students in their own engagement and learning. Ashwin's study (2003) on peer support asserts that peer support has the potential to change the way students study by improving their metacognitive skills, therefore improving the quality of their learning.

Beyond the training issues, learning centers should also provide a structural framework that reinforces the values of learning and features strong instructional design. Though many learning centers embrace the individualization possible in this environment, the center is often used as a practice format. However, "workbook pages or ditto sheets used without teacher intervention are simply a type of test and can lead to the reinforcement of mistakes and total frustration" (Smith & Simmons, 1978, p. 403). In addition, write Smith and Simmons, "students should be made aware of the purposes for their learning activities" (p. 403) so that they understand the connections of the activity to their own educational need and context.

In addition to the instructional design features of center assignments, the overall effectiveness of the learning center is often tied to the strength of its connection to the classroom instruction. At Hartnell College in California, initial research into tutoring services indicates that in order to establish significant benefits, the center must be the nexus of connection to other services and programs on campus and must work closely with faculty to develop support services like workshops (Kane & Henderson, 2006).

Researchers generally agree that tutoring is only one possible component to an academic support center. Effective assistance requires that the services are focused on the students' specific learning needs as well as on their metacognitive development. In order to meet the students' needs, an academic support center can serve many functions by providing the following:

- Appropriate academic resources such as computer access and academic resources

- Diverse and active learning experiences such as workshops, study groups, self-paced instruction via video or software, and experiential learning

- Flexible hours

- Referrals to other services (medical, psychological, financial)

Many researchers agree that such a diverse set of goals requires full-time faculty leadership and full institutional support.

Generally, learning centers diversify student support through the use of technology and software support. However, some caution that the software itself cannot provide positive results (Stoik, 2001). Software and technological support must be used within the context of the larger departmental and institutional curriculum. Caverly (1994) recommends a careful evaluation process and lists the following applications as some of the most common uses of technology in a learning environment: diagnostics, practice, tutorials, and simulations. Caverly agrees that software can facilitate learning by providing opportunities to practice skills, but from a holistic perspective students must also have access to direct instruction, modeling, and guidance; this suggests that it is not the technology that makes a difference in student success but the opportunity to enhance learning using technology accompanied with human interaction.

Another approach to academic support is the offering on Student Life Skills (SLS) courses. Recently, the Florida Department of Education (2006) published a study indicating that student life skills courses have an affect on community college student success. These courses are designed to teach students fundamentals such as time management, study skills, and test-taking strategies. Using data from the Florida Community College System over a five-year period, researchers concluded that students who enrolled in these courses were 17% more likely to succeed academically and 16%

more likely to be retained at the institution. Results were also disaggregated by their college readiness, and both college-ready and basic skills students were similarly affected. In addition, the course had the greatest impact on African American students. In every ethnic group, success improved approximately 1.5 times more as compared with nonparticipating students.

A recent MDRC study (Scrivener, Sommo, & Collado, 2009) concluded that a student development course coupled with other forms of academic support also shows some promising results for students on probation or dismissal. The study suggests that connecting more than one intervention can be effective for even the most discouraged student population. The students in the study were on academic probation at Chaffey College in California, and in order to maintain their enrollment, they were required to participate in a personal development course. Participants were randomly assigned, and thus the study has a high degree of reliability. At the end of the term, students who participated in the student success course did not demonstrate a statistically significant level of achievement compared to the control group. However, when the student success course was enhanced with required participation in carefully structured Success Center activities, their achievement rates exponentially improved. Program students were twice as likely to progress to good academic standing, more likely to increase their GPA to 2.0 or higher, and complete more credits.

Another common form of academic support is Supplemental Instruction (SI), which was created by Deanna Martin at the University of Missouri-Kansas City in 1973 and has since become a common practice at many colleges and universities. Whereas many other intervention programs target at-risk students, SI targets historically difficult courses (classes with a 30% failure or withdrawal rate) or "gatekeeper" courses. According to Ogden, Thompson, Russell, and Simons (2003), "student performance cannot be addressed effectively by serving only those students who demonstrate predisposed learning weakness" (p.13). Historically, students participating in effective SI programs earn higher final course grades, succeed at a higher rate, and tend to persist at higher rates.

Bowles and Jones (2003) attempted to further validate the results of SI by controlling for the selection bias, which suggests that a higher course grade may result from SI because "better students choose to attend" (p. 241). From their model, Bowles and Jones concluded that "inherently less able students are more likely to attend SI" (p. 242). Therefore, some of the current studies correlating student success and participation in SI may be undervaluing its overall effect.

Hensen and Shelley (2003) confirm this research in their SI study of entry-level biology, chemistry, mathematics, and physics students. Their study found that "SI participants have lower pre-entry characteristics than non-SI participants, contradicting the belief of many that participants' higher mean final course grades can be attributed to higher-achieving students participating in the program" (p. 258). They concluded that "students of all levels are utilizing the program and being impacted by that participation" (p. 258).

SI focuses on both content issues as well as learning process habits, contributing to the students' overall learning improvement while decreasing their sense of isolation, which is commonly viewed as a cause of attrition among first-year college students. Maxwell (1995) asserts that "college social relations are so invariably isolating" (p. 3) that they have an impact on overall student success.

The SI user's role is to take an active part in providing the material for the session, whereas the SI leaders are responsible for structuring the session (Ashwin, 2003). The SI leaders are trained to incorporate a number of collaborative and review techniques to help the student learn the course material within a safe and familiar context. Arendale (1997b) stresses the importance of continuous program evaluation and training in order to promote success. Casazza and Silverman (1995) stress the importance of training, especially as it relates to supporting adult learners; because the learning focus for adults is on empowerment, "details of assignments may be negotiated rather than prescribed, with the learner taking an active role in the decision making and the [tutor] functioning with less authority" (p. 119). This allows the "tutor to mediate the session while letting the adult learner determine the direction of assistance" (p. 119).

SI integrates what to learn with how to learn. Video-based Supplemental Instruction is the newest variation of this model for students who need a more intensive experience of learning how to apply study strategies immediately with difficult course work (Martin & Blanc, 1994).

Martin and Blanc, however, point to a number of challenges for the delivery of Supplemental Instruction, which include the students' inabilities to do the following:

- Hear and understand professor's language

- Read and understand course texts

- Sit through lectures and take meaningful notes

- Write well enough to express ideas in an essay

These limitations inhibit the overall effectiveness of the session and the SI leaders' ability to assist in learning. Even with these potential challenges, "supplemental instruction or SI is probably the single most well documented intervention available for improving the academic performance of underprepared students" (Boylan, 2002, p. 75).

These strategies attempt to address the wide range of challenges that underprepared students often face. During the journey toward academic competency, students often require the guidance, support, and mentoring of the entire college community in order to address the numerous obstacles that threaten to undermine their ultimate goals of program completion, graduation, or transfer. Anticipating these obstacles and planning accordingly can make a significant difference in the students' ability to advance toward the achievement of their goals.

Chapter 5

Professional Learning and Development

THE IDENTIFICATION OF effective practices—such as those described in other chapters—will have no impact on student outcomes if those practices are not adopted by faculty and support professionals and applied across the educational experiences that students have in courses and support services. Though specific training in pedagogy and student development are widely accepted prerequisites to employment in the P–12 systems, the research literature finds—and the perspective from the field agrees—that postsecondary faculty rarely encounter the rudimentary aspects of instructional design and delivery as part of their graduate training. (Grubb, 1999; Brawer, 1990; Eble, 1985; Gaff, 1975; Svinicki, 1990). This is particularly problematic for community college professionals because so many students enter with insufficient academic success skills and weak backgrounds in reading, writing, and mathematical reasoning. Whether the instructional activity focuses on basic skills, general education, traditional academic disciplines, or vocational training, the teacher or academic support professional is confronted with students whose success is dependent on the implementation of effective practices that were not a part of the professional's academic preparation.

Therefore, the importance of comprehensive training and professional development opportunities for faculty and staff cannot be overestimated. Programs with strong professional development components have been shown to yield better student retention rates and better student performance in developmental courses than those without such an emphasis (Boylan, Bonham, Claxton, & Bliss, 1992). Boylan goes so far as to state that "no matter what component of developmental education was being studied, an emphasis on training and professional development improved its outcomes" (Boylan, 2002, p. 46). However, community colleges rarely devote significant resources—human or financial—to professional development. Coordinated and ongoing professional learning is the exception rather than the rule.

So, what is the "case for professional development"? To effectively assess the extent to which professional development can and should be used to improve student outcomes, three questions must be addressed:

1. What do we know about the impact of professional development?

2. What are the evidence-based principles that should guide effective professional development?

3. What types of professional development produce the greatest impact on student learning and success?

This chapter reviews the literature and evidence supporting the answers to these central questions.

What Do We Know About the Impact of Professional Development?

Evaluating the value and impact of faculty development programs and activities is a vexing problem for community college researchers, administrators, and faculty involved in professional development activities. "There is abundant information concerning the structure and organization of professional development," concludes Sydow (2000) in her analysis of the long-term fiscal and human resources investment necessary for effective staff development, "but no data to measure program effectiveness" (p. 383). Actually, there are significant data on participants' perceptions about various types of staff development activities. It is common practice to conduct surveys that assess the number of participants, their satisfaction with the activity, and their perceptions of the relevance of the development activity (Murray, 2002; Grant & Keim, 2002). However, the connection between faculty development and student learning is much more elusive.

Using research terms, the problem is the "dependent variable"; that is, what are we using as the measure of success? Maxwell and Kazlauskas (1992) define three measures: (1) the assessment of the activity itself (re: participation and satisfaction); (2) changes in teaching behavior; and (3) improvements in student learning. Beno, Smith, DeVol, & Stetson (2003) add organizational development and the return on investment as additional measures. However, even measuring changes in teaching behavior poses significant challenges in the culture of community colleges. Classroom observations are generally restricted to faculty evaluation procedures and generally must adhere to contractual and other policy restrictions, unless the observations are part of the staff development activity itself (Grubb, 1999). The connection of a specific staff development activity to an evidence-based assessment of improvements in student learning is even more difficult to accomplish.

As the other chapters in this book demonstrate, significant data exist that validate the effectiveness of specific institutional practices, program components, and pedagogies. However, research in community colleges that clearly connects a particular professional development activity or practice to specific improvements in student outcomes is rare. There may be a simple, commonsense reason for this: professional development is not designed to directly produce changes in students. Instructional practices and institutional programs produce changes in student outcomes. Therefore, it may be more useful to address the extent to which professional development produces changes in instructional practices and institutional programs, that is, in research terminology, to treat professional development as an "intervening variable" or a "cofactor" that is an essential element in producing improvements in student outcomes. Professional development *enables* effective practices which, in turn, can produce positive student outcomes.

The California Postsecondary Education Commission, an oversight agency charged with providing the legislative and the executive branches of government with advice and information about major policy and planning issues, undertook a study of the effectiveness of professional development in 1998. Not surprisingly, the Commission's report could not directly tie professional development activities with specific improvements in student performance but concluded that "even if it is impossible to prove certain faculty activities result in particular student learning, the development of clear purposes or objectives [for professional development] . . . can help ensure that individual and institutional resources are directed towards the highest priority needs and are effective in meeting those needs" (1998, p. 22).

Unfortunately, much of the research on the *types* of professional development that are most common in community colleges—one-time workshops and conference attendance—suggests that these activities lack "clear purposes and objectives" and are not necessarily "directed towards the highest priority needs." Murray (2001), in one of several studies on the content of professional development activities in community colleges, concludes that "faculty development at most community colleges is . . . a randomly grouped collection of activities lacking intentional coordination with the mission of the college or the needs of the faculty members" (p. 497).

At community colleges, professional development has tended to focus on individual activities, such as attendance at professional conferences and sabbaticals, or institutional activities such as campuswide events or workshops on a broad spectrum of topics from pedagogical issues to career planning and personal development. Murray (2001) notes, "During the 1970s and 1980s, many colleges formalized professional development in three areas: professional development, personal development, and organizational development" (p. 90). In this trilogy, professional development represented work-related knowledge and skills, personal development covered career management, and organizational development included curriculum and program development. Although any of these professional learning opportunities *may* stimulate improvements in instruction and support services, they do not reflect "intentional coordination with the mission of the college." Instead, educators most frequently find themselves facing a smorgasbord of academic and nonacademic topics.

Although the research literature on community colleges shows only very limited evidence of a direct relationship between coordinated professional development and improved student outcomes, the literature does provide substantial evidence regarding the principles that should be applied to professional development in postsecondary education. Equally important, there is an emerging body of evidence regarding the impact of staff development that uses these principles in P–12 education that can inform the application of those practices to community colleges. The subject matter and the expectations of students in community colleges are different from P–12, but the two segments do share a number of similarities: both segments are primarily teaching institutions; address students who are academically and culturally diverse; have limited resources for professional development; and face increasing demands from internal and external stakeholders for improving student outcomes.

Judith Warren Little, in a study prepared for the National Education Association, describes the qualities of a "learning-centered school" based on an extensive review of literature on effective professional development in P–12 environments. Little argues for a focus on the environment established in the school "where the work of teaching and learning resides . . . where the problems of practice take on a particular face, where pressures for achievement are most directly felt, and where investments in professional learning pay off or not" (2006, p. 3). She describes four major goals for teacher learning that illustrate the ways that professional development is an essential part of a broader educational reform, rather than an intervention on its own:

1. Making headway on the school's central goals, priorities, or problems.

2. Building the knowledge, skill, and disposition to teach to high standards.

3. Cultivating strong professional community conducive to learning and improvement.

4. Sustaining teachers' commitment to teaching. (p. 2)

Summarizing the research of Borko (2005); Cohen and Hill (2001); Desimone, Porter, Garet, Yoon, and Birman (2002); Garet, Porter, Desimone,

Briman, and Yoon (2001); Grossman, Schoenfeld, and Lee (2005); and Wilson and Berne (1999), Little concludes that professional development is more effective where it is content focused, active, collective, coherent, and sustained (pp. 7–8).

Defining the larger social setting of the school as the vehicle for professional learning breaks down the isolation of teaching and builds shared responsibility for student learning. "A school that systematically supports professional learning and promotes effective forms of professional community," concludes Little, "is more likely to be effective with students." (p. 22) The research that Little synthesizes—including Grodsky and Gamoran (2003), Louis and Kruse (1995), and McLaughlin and Talbert (2001)—demonstrates that "schools that exhibit high levels of success with students, sometimes against considerable odds, tend to supply consistent portraits of work environments conducive to teacher learning" (p. 22).

Inverson, Meirs, and Beavis (2006) report similar findings in a major study of successful professional development in Australian initiatives. They found that a sense of "professional community" among teachers had a significant impact on the acquisition of knowledge and the implementation of that knowledge into practice. "The level of *school support* influenced the extent of *active learning, follow-up, and feedback,* and was related to the level of professional community activity" (p. 15). In addition, they conclude that "programs with an emphasis on subject matter that is being taught, how it is learned and how to teach it, tend to facilitate more active school based professional learning processes" (p. 14). And finally, "the relative success of programs also depended on the extent to which programs were extended in time, and planned so that they included activities that strengthened interaction and collaboration in the school—the level of professional community activities" (p. 17).

The most recent and perhaps the most significant evidence supporting a strong link between professional development and student achievement comes from a worldwide study of "best performing school systems" by McKinsey and Company (2007). Using data from the Programme for International Student Assessment (PISA), McKinsey compared the performance of 15-year-old students on the PISA assessments and found wide differences in student achievement among countries. Surprisingly, these differences were not associated with unusually high funding investments in education. The study found five countries that had achieved a high level of student performance at a reasonable cost (Canada, Finland, Singapore, Japan, and Korea) using quantitative data supplemented by qualitative information. The study also benchmarked school systems in the United

States with a trajectory that showed strong improvement including systems in Atlanta, Boston, Chicago, and New York.

McKinsey (2007) concludes that while these systems have widely divergent characteristics, they share a number crucial principles and practices:

- *They have high standards for selecting teachers.*

- *They invest in the professional development of their teachers to become effective instructors—the only way to improve outcomes is to improve instruction.*

- *They systematically ensure that every child is able to benefit from excellent instruction—the only way for the system to reach the highest performance is to raise the standard of every student. (p. 13)*

The study of successful school districts, McKinsey continues, underscores that "the quality of an education system cannot exceed the quality of its teachers" (2007, p. 16). Even with increased qualifications for entry into teaching and standards of teacher preparation, strong districts invest in the ongoing professional learning and development of their teachers. Singapore, for example, provides teachers with a hundred hours of professional development per year (p. 27). A Boston policymaker noted that 5% of the district's budget went to professional development, and 80% of those funds went to teachers. "The only way to improve outcomes," he concluded, "is to improve instruction."

All top school systems organized different methods to support professional development. Expert teachers and designated instructional leaders went into classrooms to model, coach, and give feedback to teachers. In school systems in Japan and Finland, in particular, schools created ways for teachers to work together and learn from each other. "These systems create a culture in their schools in which collaborative planning, reflection on instruction, and peer coaching are the norm and constant features of school life" (McKinsey, 2007, p. 28). McKinsey's study consistently illustrates that the commitment of an educational institution to support an individual's professional learning contributes to the overall institutional effort to increase student learning.

Principles of Effective Practice in Professional Development

As noted above, the review of the literature on professional development in postsecondary education does not generally provide a direct connection between a particular professional development activity and improvements in specific student outcomes. Rather, the effects are mediated through the culture and environment. Effective professional development *enables* effective practice which *produces* improved student outcomes. However, as noted above, *the importance of comprehensive training and development opportunities for faculty and staff who work with developmental students cannot be overestimated*. Multiple studies have demonstrated that specific training is one of the leading variables contributing to the success of a variety of components of developmental education, including tutoring, advising, and instruction. Though the relationship of professional development and student outcomes may be indirect, the research literature does clearly establish a set of guiding principles for professional growth that consistently produce improved practices in instruction and support services. These principles include:

5.1. Administrators support and encourage faculty development in basic skills, and the improvement of teaching and learning is connected to the institutional mission.

5.2. The faculty play a primary role in needs assessment, planning, and implementation of staff development programs and activities in support of basic skills programs.

5.3. Staff development programs are structured and appropriately supported to sustain them as ongoing efforts related to institutional goals for the improvement of teaching and learning.

5.4 Faculty development is clearly connected to intrinsic and extrinsic faculty reward structures.

5.5. Staff development opportunities are flexible, varied, and responsive to developmental needs of individual faculty, diverse student populations, and coordinated programs and services.

5.1. Administrators support and encourage faculty development in basic skills, and the improvement of teaching and learning is connected to the institutional mission.

The research and analytical literature consistently points to the relationship of high-level administrative support to the success of faculty development programs and services. (Brawer, 1990; Eble, 1985; Murray, 2002; Sydow, 2000). Administrative leadership must establish institutional goals related to the improvement of teaching, create a climate that fosters and encourages faculty development, and, most important, communicate to faculty the "belief that good teaching is valued by administrators" (Murray, 1999, p. 48).

Faculty development is most effective when it is directly tied to the institutional mission, and executive administration usually provides the leadership for the development and implementation of institutional mission processes (Murray, 2002; Richardson & Wolverton, 1994; Tierney, Ahern, & Kidwell, 1996). Although the literature also strongly advocates for the primacy of faculty involvement in the development and implementation of staff development initiatives, several national surveys (Murray, 2002; Grant & Keim, 2002), reports of successful programs, and numerous analytical commentaries (Eble, 1985; Nwagwu, 1998; Vineyard, 1994) clearly substantiate the important role that chief academic and chief executive officers play in successful developmental programs.

Ironically, although the support and leadership of chief academic officers is vitally important, the literature also points to the limitations of that leadership. Murray (1999) and others report that in the absence of a designated staff development coordinator, the chief academic officer is identified as having responsibility for leading staff development in the vast majority of community colleges—a task that clearly requires more time and focus than can be expected of a chief officer. Given the importance of faculty ownership of staff development, a careful balance needs to be established in which the administrative leadership sets the context for faculty development and then "remove[s] the stones from the path of faculty" (Travis, 1995, p. 85).

5.2. The faculty play a primary role in needs assessment, planning, and implementation of staff development programs and activities in support of basic skills programs.

In a paper on faculty development, The Academic Senate for the California Community Colleges states that "faculty development activities should be designed by faculty who know their needs, who can develop forums geared toward teaching excellence, and who can design sustained and collective efforts" (Academic Senate, 2000, p. 10). There is ample support for this assertion found over the 40-year history of contemporary literature on staff development theory and practice. Starting with the seminal works of Gaff (1975) and Berquist and Philips (1975), continuing in the faculty-based theories related to the scholarship of teaching and learning, classroom research, and reflective teaching practices (Hutchings & Shulman, 1999; Angelo & Cross, 1993; Brookfield, 2002), and culminating with recent research (Murray, 1999 and 2002; Grubb, 1999; Grant & Keim, 2002), it is absolutely clear that the key to successful faculty development programs is the direct involvement of faculty in every aspect of the planning, implementation, and evaluation of developmental activities.

Beyond the obvious truism that professional staff members are more likely to benefit from developmental activities that they feel they have created to meet their own needs, there are also several issues related to the professional identity of community college faculty that emerge from the literature as significant factors. First, there is an inherent conflict between the role of the faculty member as a professor in higher education and the needs of the highly diverse, heterogeneous student populations found in community colleges, particularly in basic skills courses and programs. The literature on community college faculty consistently points to the adjustment that community college faculty must make when they move from graduate programs in research-oriented universities into teaching institutions that serve students who have weak academic skills and preparation (Grubb, 1999; Murray, 2002; Brawer, 1990; Boylan, 2002). Although community college hiring practices attempt to emphasize teaching theory and practice, Grubb (1999) and others note that the amount of time and procedural limitations imposed on the hiring practices mean that hiring committees "do not gather valid information about teaching" even from teaching demonstrations which are usually "so short and artificial as to be laughable" (p. 289). Murray (2002) summarizes a common theme found throughout the literature: "if instructional improvement efforts are to succeed, faculty must first accept the unique mission of the community college" (p. 90). Even faculty who seek preparation for teaching in graduate programs directly related to basic skills instruction (such as university-level reading programs) find that their training programs are frequently not specific to adult learners and, once hired by a community college, they find that their status in the institution is sometimes viewed by some colleagues as lower than traditional discipline-based faculty (Kozeracki, 2005; Grubb, 1999).

A second significant factor might be described as the gap between the faculty's own educational experiences and their students' educational experiences and needs. There is overwhelming evidence that graduate programs in most colleges and universities provide graduate students with little or no training in the art of teaching (Grubb, 1999; Brawer, 1990; Eble, 1985; Gaff, 1975; Svinicki, 1990). This produces two common results. First, many faculty, without the benefit of specific staff development, teach as they were taught—placing an emphasis on lecture, large-group discussion, and what might be described as relatively passive student learning styles. "A second defining aspect of instructor's lives," notes Grubb "is isolation" (1999, p. 283). The literature on instructor isolation is rich with explanations related to the independence assured by academic freedom (Grubb, 1999), the teacher as expert or scholar, and even suggestions that faculty fear that their pedagogical weaknesses, either real or imagined, will be "found out" (Collay, Dunlap, Enloe, & Gagon, 1998). However, Grubb concludes that "the isolation of instructors is created by the lack of any activities that draw them together *around teaching*" (p. 285).

Finally, the works of Boyer (1990) and Hutchings, Shulman, and Huber and Sherwyn (Hutchings, 2000; Hutchings & Shulman, 1999; Huber & Sherwyn, 2002) address the real and perceived links between the organization of knowledge within a discipline and the methodologies commonly used to teach that discipline. This literature suggests that certain disciplinary structures are inherently connected to certain pedagogical frameworks. However, the literature also points to ways faculty can reconceptualize these frameworks to promote better learning among students who lack the academic background or bring other perspectives to the college learning environment (for example, diverse learning styles and multicultural life experiences of community college students).

Effective faculty development not only imparts specific skills that can improve the faculty member's effectiveness in promoting student learning, it also seeks to change the basic identity of the community college instructor, striking a balance between the higher education scholar and the adult education practitioner. There is much discussion in the literature regarding which faculty participate in staff development. A common theme is summarized by Angelo (1994): "those faculty who do participate [in staff development programs] are often the ones who seem to need them least" (p. 3). However, there is virtually no reliable research to support this assertion except surveys that ask faculty and administrators to share their *perceptions* of who benefits (Blackburn, Boberg, O'Connel, & Pellino, 1980; Maxwell & Kazlauskas, 1992). In fact, some recent research suggests that faculty participation in relevant staff development activities is significantly increasing among all types of faculty (Grant & Keim, 2002).

5.3. Staff development programs are structured and appropriately supported to sustain them as ongoing efforts related to institutional goals for the improvement of teaching and learning.

The most common criticism of staff development activities found in the literature is that these programs "appear to be a plethora of activities: it is difficult to detect the desired outcomes or identify how activities are linked to institutional goals" (Beno, Smith, DeVol, & Stetson, 2003, p. 4). Richardson and Wolverton (1994) found that "professional development opportunities in higher performing institutions were linked in systematic ways to institutional priorities" and that in lower-performing institutions "faculty had no sense of priorities" (p. 46). Clearly articulated goals linked to systematic sets of programs and activities are a key factor in successful staff development (Travis, 1995; Murray, 1999; Beno, Smith, DeVol, & Stetson, 2003; Grubb, 1999).

Workshops are the most common form of staff development offered by community colleges; yet they are also the most consistently rejected as ineffective by research, expert analysis, and even the faculty and administrators who participate in these activities (Murray, 1999, 2002; Maxwell & Kazlauskas, 1992; Brawer, 1990; Grubb, 1999). There is little evidence that "one-shot" workshops produce any change in pedagogical practice; and, even when workshops *do* affect faculty performance, the improvements are short-lived unless they are reinforced and developed with ongoing staff development activities (Clark, Corcoran, & Lewis, 1989; Lenze, 1996; Grubb, 1999). "A well formed faculty development plan recognizes that many diverse activities are needed over a long period of time," concludes Murray (1999). "It also recognizes that these activities must be united around a common institutional mission—the systematic, demonstrable, and highly regarded improvement of teaching" (p. 48).

Leadership is another central feature of a formalized staff development structure. As noted above, strong support from the chief academic and executive officers is important. However, the key to effective program development and implementation is the designation of specific staff with direct responsibility for staff development and adequate professional time to work on development activities. In national studies, Murray (1999) found that the chief instructional officer was identified as the leader of staff development in 68% of community colleges, and Grant and Keim (2002) found similar designations in 48% of two-year colleges. The amount of time that the designated leaders of staff development reported spending on development activities was generally very limited. In Murray's study, 83.3% of the institutions had staff development leaders who spent *less than* 50% of their time on development activities. Only 2.3% of the institutions had a faculty leader assigned full-time. While Grant and Keim argue that commitment to staff development is improving, Murray and others "found a glaring lack of commitment on the part of leadership for faculty development" (p. 58).

One of the most reliable and accessible methods for achieving well planned and executed staff development is the establishment of a teaching and learning center, responsible for overseeing a broad-range of staff development activities, providing individual faculty training and consultations, and promoting staff development at the institutional, program, and department levels (Cross, 2001; Singer, 2002; Travis, 1995). Cross notes that these centers are effective in "(1) maintaining high visibility, high credibility, campus-wide conversations focused on forward-looking learning and teaching and (2) providing quality support for all teachers, from beginning instructors to experienced, highly regarded faculty members" (p. 59).

Although teaching and learning centers have become a central feature of instructional development activities at many four-year institutions, their growth at two-year colleges has been significantly more limited. As indicated above, the lack of a clearly articulated organizational structure for staff development within the institution is one reason why these centers have not flourished at community colleges. However, the limitations and instability of funding is another major factor inhibiting the implementation of these centers and almost all other forms of staff development. The source of funding for staff development appears to have changed very little over the last thirty years. Centra (1975) and Grant and Keim (2002) report that over 70% of the funding for staff development came from general funds through state apportionments, with the balance from foundations and governmental grants. But the Academic Senate for California Community Colleges notes that the "lack of funding has constantly plagued professional development programs" and there has been no increase in state staff development funding "since early in the 1990s" (Academic Senate, 2000, p. 4). In addition, the Academic Senate finds that local senates frequently are not consulted on the allocation or expenditure of those funds. The lack of faculty control and limited institutional resources are significant in light of the findings of Eble and McKeachie's frequently cited study (1985) of faculty development in which they concluded, "a firm conclusion from this study is that faculty development programs need to be *shaped by the individual college or university* and be invested with *a sense of faculty ownership*" (p. 210, emphasis added).

5.4. Faculty development is clearly connected to intrinsic and extrinsic faculty reward structures.

As noted above, the most effective staff development evolves from faculty members' direct participation in setting the goals, developing the activities, and using the results of those activities to improve instruction. Bland and Schmitz (1990) note that "whether faculty activities are considered productive or not depends on whether they relate to the faculty member's personal and professional goals and to the institution's mission" (p. 45). Therefore, it is not surprising that the research suggests that faculty's most important rewards from participation in staff development are intrinsic rather than extrinsic rewards. As early as the 1970s, Gaff, Centra, and Berquist and Philips were contending that "faculty development activities . . . enable faculty members to find intrinsic satisfaction in their teaching" (Centra, 1978, p. 15). The Grant and Keim study (2002) found that "intrinsic incentives of professionalism and commitment are incentives for most faculty," although they did point to certain extrinsic factors such as salary advancement and release time as important for broad-based participation. Murray and others (Nwagwu, 1998; Harnish & Creamer, 1986; Ferren, 1996) assert that "recognition needs to include praise and support for experimentation *even when it fails* . . . faculty need to know . . . that taking risks is *not damaging to their careers*" (Murray, 1999, p. 95, emphasis added).

Support of colleagues is another intrinsic reward that is an important aspect of professional development. Many of the development activities described above involve colleague-to-colleague interchanges. The perception among faculty that pedagogy is inherently connected to disciplinary structures and values (Hutchings, 2000; Hutchings & Shulman, 1999; Huber & Sherwyn, 2002) means that pedagogical advice and praise for instructional innovation from colleagues in the same discipline carries particular value (Maxwell & Kazlauskas, 1992). Braxton (2006) and Brothern and Wambach (2004) describe the characteristics of a "culture of teaching" in which colleagues across disciplines broaden their sense of scholarship to include teaching and learning and thus develop an alternate "community of scholars" (Kozeracki, 2005, p. 45).

5.5. Staff development opportunities are flexible, varied, and responsive to developmental needs of individual faculty, diverse student populations, and coordinated programs and services.

The literature and research on faculty development contains a broad spectrum of theoretical frameworks and specific programmatic activities that can support the improvement of teaching and learning. These range from individualized peer mentoring to structured reflective teaching practices to broad-based efforts promoting the scholarship of teaching and learning across large groups of faculty. Though there is extensive literature on the specific processes and benefits for each type of development activity, the literature generally does not specify or provide adequate research for assessing the applicability of each framework to basic skills staff development. However, when viewed in the context of the other effective practices articulated in this review, each framework has the potential for effective development related to basic skills. This concise literature review can only briefly cite a few of the more prominent methodologies.

Types of Professional Development

Professional development is a means toward an end, not an end unto itself. The research literature demonstrates its indirect, but essential, contribution to student outcomes. There is significant evidence regarding the principles that should be applied to the development and implementation for professional learning activities. But, as noted earlier, "faculty development at most community colleges is . . . a randomly grouped collection of activities lacking intentional coordination with the mission of the college or the needs of the faculty members" (Murray, 2001, p. 497). Therefore, it is important to identify the types of professional development activities most likely to produce changes in the practices used by faculty that will lead to improved student outcomes based on principles of effective practice.

Peer Mentoring

One of the oldest and most varied forms of faculty development is peer mentoring. In its simplest form, it involves two faculty members working together to improve their teaching. Some peer mentoring involves a "master teacher" format in which an experienced faculty member is teamed with a less experienced instructor. In the "master teacher" format, the development is focused primarily on the less experienced instructor and is usually related to evaluation or tenure review procedures. Other forms of peer mentoring involve more of an equal exchange between faculty, sometimes combined with a particular developmental methodology such as "microteaching" in which faculty incorporate a specific teaching strategy into their classroom work and use video and peer feedback to assess the strategies' success. (Levinson-Rose & Menges, 1981). This peer-to-peer approach ensures that faculty play the primary role in professional development and provides for one of the most flexible and personally responsive forms of professional growth.

Instructional Consultation

Instructional consultation involves the use of an outside expert to work with individual instructors or groups of faculty on specific pedagogies.

Although the literature suggests (Brawer, 1990; Levinson-Rose & Menges, 1981) that the use of outside consultants for single-session workshops has a limited impact, if any, the use of experts within a specific discipline or across disciplines with clearly defined shared interests can be an effective resource (Maxwell & Kazlauskas, 1992; Murray, 2002). This type of content-based consultation supports the faculty member's identity as a teacher-scholar and promotes pedagogical solutions that address the structure of the discipline adapted to the learning styles and personal experiences of diverse community college student populations.

A number of these approaches—Scholarship of Teaching and Learning, Classroom Assessment Techniques, Reflective Teaching and Faculty Inquiry—take the practice of teaching and learning as the subject of critical examination. In this sense, they underscore the intellectual work of teaching.

The Scholarship of Teaching and Learning

Scholarship of Teaching and Learning (SoTL) began with the work of Ernest Boyer (1990) as an effort to reframe the organizational culture of four-year institutions to recognize that faculty accomplishments in such areas as teaching, learning theory, and practice have the same status and professional validity as accomplishments in the more traditional discipline-based research and theory. As refined by Shulman, Huber, and Hutchings (Hutchings, 2000; Hutchings & Shulman, 1999; Huber & Sherwyn, 2002), SoTL has become an effective model for promoting individual faculty members' efforts in using their classroom as a laboratory for self-improvement as well as receiving recognition for their accomplishments by contributing to the literature on effective teaching and learning practices (Paulson & Feldman, 2006). When incorporated into the evaluation of faculty or other institutional processes, SoTL provides a crucial link between the intrinsic rewards of teaching and extrinsic reward structures of the academic institution.

Classroom Assessment Techniques

Based on the work of Thomas Angelo and Patricia Cross (Angelo, 1991, 1994; Angelo & Cross, 1993), Classroom Assessment Techniques (CAT) provides faculty with specific techniques for conducting, evaluating, and responding to research in the classroom. The Classroom Assessment Techniques developed by Cross and Angelo have been widely used in both two- and four-year institutions (Cross & Steadman, 1996; Belcher & Glyer-Culver, 1998). CAT is a highly effective strategy for ongoing professional development that is not dependent upon the continuous availability of institutional resources or the involvement of anyone other than the classroom instructor. Each faculty member determines the goals of the assessment and is solely responsible for use of the information gathered.

Teaching portfolios are another technique used in conjunction with classroom-based research in which faculty develop documentation of their work that can be used for evaluation, promotion, or other professional development (Travis, 1995). Though CATs can be used by all community college faculty, these methodologies provide a particularly useful context for addressing basic skills issues within nonbasic skills, content-based classrooms. Individual discipline-based faculty can use these techniques for insight into students' learning processes and skills levels with limited or no support from staff development specialists.

Reflective Teaching

Reflective Teaching is a practice-oriented approach in which faculty engage in self-reflection on specific instructional issues, articulate their personal theories on the issues, and engage with peers in developing alternate approaches to those issues. Reflective teaching can be a highly structured process using facilitators and rigorous protocols or it can be informally implemented at the department or program level (Chung, 2005; Weimer, 1990; Hirshfield, 1984). Brookfield (2002) describes the reflective process as a "set of lenses" the instructor uses to understand his or her teaching. These include the *autobiographical lens* of the faculty member's experiences as a student, the *learner's eyes* using students' perceptions of the faculty member's teaching, the *colleagues' experience* in which faculty reframe and broaden their theory and practice through consultation with peers, and the *theoretical framework* in which individual faculty members compare their personal theories and practices with literature on research and theory. Regardless of the methodology used for reflective teaching, the process cultivates the "strong professional community conducive to learning and improvement" described by Little (2005), McKinsey (2007), and Inverson et al. (2005).

Faculty Inquiry Groups (FIG)

Faculty Inquiry Groups combine a number of the features of reflective teaching, SoTL, and CAT into a collaborative process for addressing curriculum reform and pedagogical effectiveness that can be adapted to many purposes. FIGs focus on a few essential elements of the inquiry cycle. First, an inquiry group of faculty is formed around a specific problem or objective, though the focus may be specific to a class, department, or discipline, or it may be interdisciplinary. The group formulates questions—subjects for inquiry—related to the problem or objective. Once the questions are formulated, the group gathers evidence including qualitative and quantitative data, which addresses the initial questions. Frequently this process is iterative, as evidence leads to additional questions and gathering more evidence. Depending on the nature of the problem or objective, the FIG may implement or develop curricular reform or pedagogical strategies that the evidence suggests might improve student outcomes. The innovation is then tested in the classroom or support service. And, in turn, data is gathered on the impact of the innovation and the members of the FIG group evaluate the evidence, determining the extent to which their original questions were answered and how much student performance improved. Depending on the results, the group may develop new questions and new strategies based on the evidence of student learning.

Effective FIGs require ongoing and sustained work by a group of faculty (and other staff, including counselors, administrators, and institutional researchers) working collaboratively over time. "As a form of practitioner research, FIGs depend first and foremost on evidence generated in the regular routines of teaching and learning: student performance on exams, projects, papers, etc." (Carnegie Foundation for the Advancement of Teaching, 2008, p. 29). The pattern of developing questions, gathering evidence, creating responses to the questions in the form of practice, and testing the practice against evidence of student learning creates a dynamic opportunity for faculty engagement with a direct impact on student outcomes.

Projects to revise and refocus curriculum and support services are a form of staff development that receives little attention in the higher education research literature. Frequently, these initiatives are not viewed as professional growth opportunities for faculty, even though their impact frequently extends well beyond the specific focus of a particular project or initiative. However, several studies of P–12 initiatives demonstrate that the collegial interchanges and clear focus on student outcomes related to curriculum reform efforts promote faculty understanding of how students learn content and can result in positive changes in pedagogy (Schmidt, Houang, & Cogan, 2004). This type of staff development may be more pervasive in community colleges than the current literature documents.

Great Teachers Seminars and Academic Alliances

Great Teachers Seminars (GTS) and Academic Alliances have comparatively long histories. GTS involves an extended set of highly structured, process-oriented workshops held over several days. The agenda for the workshops is developed as part of the process to address the specific needs of the participants (Travis, 1995; Gottshall, 1993). Academic Alliances are usually structured like a GTS but involve participants from different levels of education (P–12, community colleges, and four-year institutions) in a specific discipline (or closely related disciplines) within a geographic region. Although both of these types of professional development are well documented in journals and conference presentations, there is little evidence of their broad-based impact on student outcomes beyond specific studies related to individual projects.

Culturally Responsive Teaching

Culturally Responsive Teaching (CRT) is a significantly different way of approaching student behaviors, needs, and cultural values that addresses the cultural differences between instructors and students. Professional development in CRT focuses on the teacher's knowledge of, and sensitivity to, the students' cultural contexts and the use of culturally mediated instruction—translating the knowledge of students' cultural contexts into effective instructional practices. One of the tenets of CRT is that there is not one correct way to teach any particular student or group of students; rather, programs and instructors must use their experience and knowledge to be most effective in the context of particular students and particular classes. There is substantial literature on the theory and practice of CRT. However, research showing specific data with replicable results is very limited and almost exclusively addresses the success of this approach for elementary and middle school children.

Content-Based Professional Development

As noted earlier in this chapter, a number of effective practices that have been shown to have an impact on student outcomes at the P–12 level deserve consideration for community college practitioners. The success of subject-specific professional development in secondary education suggests that similar initiatives at the community college level may be key to improving student success. Although P–12 teachers must go through specific pedagogical preparation to gain certification for teaching in public education, community college instructors are not required to have any formal training in instructional theory and methodology. The primary "credential" for community college instructors is an advanced degree in the discipline. Graduate programs rarely address pedagogical issues related to teaching in their discipline, and community college faculty frequently rely on their own experiences as students to develop instructional strategies and teaching methodologies.

Several studies of mathematics and science education in secondary education demonstrate that professional development is most effective when it focuses specifically on discipline-based content. Evidence of these linkages comes from many sources. A 1998 analysis of evaluative studies of professional development programs in math and science found that programs focusing contextually on subject knowledge and on student learning of particular subject matter had a greater effect on student learning than those prescribing generic sets of teaching behaviors (Kennedy, 1998). A study by the National Education Goals Panel, a federal agency formerly charged with monitoring achievement of national educational goals, found that professional development activities geared to the science and math curriculum were a major factor in unusually high achievement rates of the eighth-grade students in Minnesota (Smreker, et al., 2001). Studies by Cohen and Hill (2001) and Kennedy (2002) found that the most successful professional development programs in mathematics focused on *how students learn specific mathematic ideas,* rather than emphasizing generic teaching strategies for mathematics.

The National Writing Project (NWP, see www.nwp.org) has been conducting local and regional research on the impact of the NWP professional development programs on student achievement in English classes in middle and high schools. The NWP model is rooted in the philosophy that teachers can create a *professional community* and be prepared to lead professional development for other teachers, address common issues of teaching and learning, and produce teaching strategies customized to specific learning environments. In fact, to work as an NWP teacher-consultant, teachers go through an intensive summer program that involves writing and creating classroom lessons and sharing them with colleagues. These teacher-consultants then work with local schools to determine and deliver the forms of professional development that the local schools and teachers need. Thus, professional development is directly connected to classroom content and assessment.

In nine independent studies, students whose teachers participated in NWP professional development were compared to students of nonparticipating instructors. Student writing was assessed for content, structure, sentence fluency, diction, and conventions as well as an overall holistic score. In all cases, the students in the NWP teachers' classes earned higher ratings than students in non-NWP classes. The studies took place in sites as diverse as St. Louis County, Missouri; Mississippi (statewide); Alabama; New York City (Lehman College working with six urban high schools); and Ventura and Kern Counties in California—in other words, the studies occurred across rural, urban, and suburban settings with over 3,000 students in 58 schools with widely varying economic, language, racial, and ethnic backgrounds. In all studies, student writing was assessed by independent outside readers, using a common evaluative framework. They evaluated student writing on seven dimensions: content, structure, stance, sentence fluency, diction, conventions, and a holistic score. On all measures in all studies, the NWP students outperformed their non-NWP counterparts, and in more than half of these comparisons, the differences were large enough to be statistically significant. Student writing showed particularly strong improvement in content, structure, and stance (NWP, 2008, pp. 2–3).

Conclusions

This overview of professional development leads to the conclusion that the field of community colleges has underestimated and underutilized professional development as a resource for strengthening instruction over-all, and basic skills instruction in particular. Despite the limitations of the research literature in higher education, research from the broader education field clearly illustrates the essential efficacy of professional development. However, for professional development to be effective as part of an overall effort to improve instruction in community colleges, the current practice would have to be changed. As the research illustrates, there are many ways to organize professional development. But what is also clear is that the most common approach to professional development is, in fact, one of the few ways clearly identified as ineffective. Instead of a series of workshops, a smorgasbord of options, or occasional attendance at a conference, both the institutions and the individuals would have to redefine the meaning of professional development. Professional development would have to become an ongoing sustained effort that is part of the professional work of the educator and the educational work of the institution.

All professions—architecture, medicine, law, and so forth—expect and require that professionals continue to learn and develop over the entire course of their careers. This dedication to ongoing professional learning should be an even more central commitment for educators. Moreover, educators have two professional domains with a specialized base of knowledge and skills: their chosen academic content area and the field of education. Well-designed professional development could become the vehicle for continuing growth in both domains and could provide the essential connection between disciplinary knowledge and engaging students in that knowledge.

The research on professional development still faces the challenge of understanding the relationship between professional development and student learning. This will not be a simple linear relationship. Professional development can be evaluated as a part of any overall initiative rather than as an initiative on its own. Professional development may prove to be the (sometimes missing) link between a model and its implementation. As an institutional commitment and an individual responsibility, professional development that is focused on teaching and learning can be a powerful way to implement, support, and enhance other institutional practices that have been shown to increase student success.

Part Two
Tools for Planning

PART ONE PROVIDED an integrated analysis of the effective practices that have been demonstrated to produce improvements in student outcomes in developmental courses, programs, and services. Part Two provides a methodology for colleges—and programs and services within colleges—to assess the extent to which they use those effective practices and to develop and implement plans to improve their courses, programs, and services based on practices described in Part One. Because cost and limited resources are the most frequently cited obstacles to implementing change, Part Two also provides a tool for estimating the "up-front" costs and the long-range fiscal benefits of implementing improvements in programs and services that promote student retention and goal attainment.

Making the case for institutional transformation is much easier than describing how to do it. Each institution is different, with its own organizational culture, history of past practice, internal and external constituencies, and goals for future development. Community college systems across the nation have significantly different funding mechanisms, governance structures, and relationships with other postsecondary and K–12 systems. What works in one system or individual college may be impossible to put into practice in another.

The *process* for implementing change also varies considerably among systems, colleges, and programs and services. Frequently, top-down efforts to stimulate change at the program or course level inspire practitioner resistance and superficial compliance (Lipsky, 1980), even when practitioners agree with the proposed changes (Evans, 2001). Bottom-up change is frequently stymied by budgetary limitations, institutional stasis, and a lack of understanding of the need for change. To foster effective change, leaders and practitioners must collaborate to develop a culture of institutional learning that facilitates ongoing improvement throughout the organization. Such institutional learning should be informed by data and the processes for assessing and implementing change must be inclusive.

Part Two provides the tools for implementing a change strategy. The self-assessment tool in Chapter Six is organized into three distinct stages: (1) compilation of quantitative baseline measures; (2) completion of a reflective, qualitative assessment of effective practices and related strategies; and (3) identification of priorities for change. Using the self-assessment tool, the college (or program) can develop a clear, detailed, and shared understanding of the current state of developmental education within the college or program. This understanding provides the foundation for an action plan that can be developed using the templates provided in the chapter. The action plan will create long-term goals and identify the specific steps necessary to achieve those goals. Using the tools provided in Chapter Six, a college or program can conduct a thorough evaluation of its approach to developmental education and develop a step-by-step plan for change and improvement.

Chapter Seven argues that the perceived cost of programs frequently is not accurately counterbalanced with a full understanding of associated revenue and benefits. This chapter offers an additional tool that assists with the analysis of the costs and revenue associated with making changes in developmental education programs. This tool allows colleges and programs to more realistically estimate the costs of a particular innovation and to project the long-range financial benefit that the college or program will receive from increased persistence and program completion. The tool can be used to project the costs and benefits of extending programs that have been demonstrated to be successful for a limited cohort of students to a much larger cohort. It can also be used to estimate the costs and benefits of using a combination of programs and services among a variety of student cohorts. While "extending a program to scale" is frequently cited as a limitation of successful "boutique programs," this cost-benefits tool also recognizes that not all programs should be brought to scale and that a combination of innovations in programs and services can produce significant financial and student-outcome benefits.

The combination of the self-assessment procedures and cost-revenue tools provides the college (or program) with a strong foundation for effectively using the practices articulated in Part One to develop and implement data-informed plans for programmatic improvement and "affordable change."

Note: The tools included in Part Two are also available electronically on the Web site at http://www.rpgroup.org/publications/Student SuccessBook.htm. Finally, please communicate your successes and challenges in using these tools by contacting us at info@rpgroup.org.

Chapter 6
The Self-Assessment Tool

The self-assessment tool comprises:

- A matrix of baseline measures that will provide the institution with an initial, quantitative overview of its developmental education programs

- Five broad sections that provide a framework for reflective assessment—these sections mirror the chapter structure of the literature review, incorporate the twenty-six effective practices, and draw from the literature review suggested strategies for accomplishing each effective practice

- A worksheet for developing a list of priorities from the changes, enhancements, or modifications identified by the institution through the reflective assessment

What Is the Purpose of the Self-Assessment?

The self-assessment tool is designed to allow colleges and programs to reflect on how their current practices fit with and reflect the findings from the literature regarding effective practices for basic skills students. The reflection encourages institutions to examine the scope and efficacy of current practices. Based upon this internal review, an institution may determine which augmentations, changes, or new initiatives might be beneficial and plan for how they can occur. In addition, the self-assessment can serve as a baseline measure, allowing an institution to identify its practices and priorities as of a particular point in time.

How Is the Self-Assessment Related to the Literature Review?

The self-assessment is directly related to the literature review in Part 1. The self-assessment tool consists of five broad sections—organizational and administrative practices, program components, instructional practices, student support services and strategies, and professional learning and development—that mirror the structure of the literature review. *We strongly suggest that participants in the self-assessment process read the literature review prior to beginning the self-assessment.* In addition, we suggest that the literature review is frequently consulted during the self-assessment process. Each item in the self-assessment is drawn directly from the literature review, and the literature review describes each item in more detail than is feasible within the self-assessment tool.

Who Should Participate in the Self-Assessment?

The reflection and planning processes should incorporate a variety of college constituents who will need to meet to discuss the various effective practices included in the tool. A group of 12 pilot colleges in California used the self-assessment tool in spring 2007; the colleges expressed strong agreement regarding the benefit of the cross-college conversations opened up by using the tool. The conversations created shared understandings and new working relationships. Open exploration of how various areas of the college can contribute to and improve success rates of developmental students is essential, and these meetings are a crucial venue for an inclusive discovery process. Responses to the assessment tool should flow directly from these meetings.

Consider including these leaders in the self-assessment process, listed in no particular order. In addition, you may wish to ask key department chairs (English, ESL, mathematics, counseling, learning assistance) to recommend two to four faculty members for participation.

- Developmental educational operation-level administrator
- Faculty or peer mentoring program(s) director(s)
- Financial aid officer
- Institutional researcher
- Learning assistance, tutoring center director, or tutoring staff
- Matriculation, counseling or advising dean(s) or staff
- Student services dean(s) or staff
- Students who recently matriculated and assessed into developmental education
- Faculty member(s) serving on the College Curriculum Committee
- Lead faculty members in developmental education programs, including reading, writing, mathematics, ESL, college success or study skills, and counseling

- Lead faculty members who teach college-level courses in English and mathematics

- Other college-level faculty who do not teach English or mathematics

- Others as appropriate (for example, academic senate representatives, provost, college president, chief financial officer, public information officer)

What Are the Stages of the Self-Assessment?

The self-assessment tool is organized into three distinct stages: compilation of baseline measures, completion of a reflective assessment of effective practices and related strategies, and identification of priorities for change. Each stage is outlined in detail later in this chapter. Certainly every institution utilizing self-assessment can and should adapt this process in ways that make it productive and manageable for the particular institutional needs and local environment.

How Can We Make the Self-Assessment Process Productive and Manageable?

The self-assessment process can be a lengthy and involved one. In particular, the reflective stage can be prolonged or truncated. We suggest determining a time line in advance and providing visible leadership and support for the efforts. The 12 pilot colleges who engaged in the process spent, on average, 16 hours of concentrated meeting time over the course of four months in the reflective stage. In our experience, leveraging the resources of existing planning committees or other preexisting structures is likely to ease the work in the reflective stage. Alternately, a "retreat" approach can be helpful. Consideration should be given as to whether there are other projects under way that might compete for time and other resources, or which might provide an opportunity for synergy. Although an institution might determine a priori that it wishes to focus more of its scrutiny in a particular section (for example, program components), keep in mind that each of the broad sections has implications for the other sections. Even if one or more sections are emphasized, we encourage institutions to spend some amount of meaningful time assessing effective practices in the de-emphasized areas.

The tools included in Part Two are also available in an Excel file that can be downloaded from the Research & Planning Group for the California Community College's Web site at www.rpgroup.org/publications/StudentSuccessBook.htm.

Stage One: Baseline Measures—Creating a Foundation for Discussion

Measures (Baseline, Additional Recommended, Locally Determined)

Prior to or during the inception of its self-assessment, each institution should collect and report on as much data as it can reasonably assemble for developmental education. We realize that most institutions will not be able to assemble all the desired measures. It is important to develop as clear a quantitative picture as possible in order to help ground and direct the reflective stage. To accomplish this, you may wish to identify key measures that are most important given your local context.

Sample data matrixes and suggested definitions are provided on the following pages.

Baseline measures are intended to provide a broad overview of developmental education at each college. Additional recommended measures are also listed. Though the recommended measures might be more difficult to identify, it is anticipated that these additional measures will promote more meaningful internal discussion. An individual institution may also identify other local data which it believes will promote fruitful discussion.

When considering local measures, colleges may wish to refer to Effective Practice 2.4: "Regular program evaluations are conducted, results are disseminated widely, and data are used to improve practice." In addition to any "new" measures that the college wishes to employ based on the literature review, colleges should also include any locally completed research that assists in better understanding of developmental education students or courses. These items should be referenced or attached along with the baseline measures so that institutional representatives completing the self-assessment can refer to and use the information as appropriate. Also, though not suggested specifically in the literature review, an understanding of local grading variability may help colleges in correctly interpreting student success data.

Levels of Measurement (Data for All Development Education, Discipline-Specific Data, Course-Specific Data, by Demographic Groups)

At a minimum, we suggest that colleges report aggregate data on all developmental education students, course offerings, and staffing. However, an exploration of data at the discipline level (math, English, and others) would augment the data's usefulness. The matrix on the following page allows for the inclusion of this optional level of measurement. Though strongly encouraged, the breadth and depth of exploration is left to the discretion of each institution.

Institutions might consider an even more refined course-level reporting for some selected measures. For example, "Student Success Rate in Developmental Education Courses" is likely to vary between disciplines, but it will also vary by course level. A course that is four levels below college-level, for example, is likely to have a success rate different from a course that is one level below college-level. Although this level of detail is not required for the self-assessment process, the more informed the college is about how it is currently serving students, the more meaningful the self-assessment process will be. This data can also serve in the future when an institution reflects on the progress it has made toward helping students in developmental education achieve their goals.

In addition to looking at the data overall, by discipline, and by course, it will be important to review data by various demographics. It is often the case that student experiences vary considerably on the basis of ethnicity, gender, age, and full-time or part-time enrollment status. Other pertinent demographics, such as socioeconomic status, may be unavailable. Consider selecting key measures to elaborate on and run these by each salient demographic. A matrix for ethnicity is provided as one example.

Baseline Measure Operational Definitions

The following definitions use MIS (Management Information System) data elements which all California community colleges report. These operational definitions are included here as a guideline. The MIS Data Element Dictionary is publicly available through the state's Web site, located at www.cccco.edu. You may find that using the site map helps in locating the relevant MIS documents.

- Percentage of New Students Assessed into Developmental Education Courses:

  - *New Student:* MIS Data Element SB15 = "1" (New Student).

  - *Assessed into Developmental Education:* Using the institution's assessment instruments, students enrolled during a fall term who were recommended to enroll in developmental education courses, MIS Data Element CB08 code of "P" (Precollegiate Basic Skill) or "B" (Basic Skill), divided by the total number of new students receiving assessment, multiplied by 100.

TABLE 6.1

Data for Developmental Education by Discipline (*Adapt as Necessary*)

Baseline Measures for Developmental Education (DEV) *Indicate Timeframe (i.e., Selected Term, Semester, or Quarter):___*	All Developmental Education	Levels of Measurement					
		Discipline-Specific, Developmental Education (DEV) Data					
		Math (DEV)	English (DEV)	Reading (DEV)	Writing (DEV)	ESL (DEV)	Study Skills (DEV)
Percentage of new students assessed into developmental education courses[1]							
Number of developmental education sections offered							
Percentage of section offerings that are in developmental education							
Unduplicated number of students enrolled in developmental education							
Student success rate in developmental education courses							
Student retention rate in developmental education courses							
Student course repetition rate in developmental education courses*							
Persistence rate of developmental education students*							
Percentage of developmental ed. sections taught by full-time faculty							

Levels of Measurement

Baseline Measures for Developmental Education (DEV) *Indicate Timeframe (i.e., Selected Term, Semester, or Quarter):* ___	All Develop-mental Education	Discipline-Specific, Developmental Education (DEV) Data				
		Math (DEV)	English (DEV)	Reading (DEV)	Writing (DEV)	ESL (DEV)	Study Skills (DEV)
Percentage of developmental education students who subsequently enroll in transfer-level courses**							
Success rate of developmental education students in transfer-level courses							
Percentage of students who successfully completed a developmental course and earned a degree or certificate**							
Percentage of students who successfully completed a developmental education course and subsequently transferred**							
Locally Determined Measures							
Your measures here							

1. It is also useful to investigate what percentage of new students are referred to placement testing and how many subsequently enroll within some specified time period (within their first year, for example) in developmental education courses.

*within some specified, extended timeframe, e.g., one year

**within some specified, extended timeframe, e.g., two years, three years, four years

TABLE 6.2

Data for Developmental Education by Ethnicity *(Adapt as Necessary)*

Baseline Measures for Developmental Education (DEV) *Indicate Timeframe (i.e., Selected Term, Semester, or Quarter):* ___	All Develop- mental Education	Levels of Measurement					
		Ethnicity-Specific, Developmental Education (DEV) Data					
		African American	American Indian	Asian American/ Pacific Islander	Hispanic/ Latino	White	Other
Percentage of new students assessed into developmental education courses							
Unduplicated number of students enrolled in developmental education							
Student success rate in developmental education courses							
Student retention rate in developmental education courses							
Student success rate in developmental education courses*							
Persistence rate of developmental education students*							
Additional Recommended Measures							
Percentage of developmental education students who subsequently enroll in transfer-level courses**							

Baseline Measures for Developmental Education (DEV) *Indicate Timeframe (i.e., Selected Term, Semester, or Quarter):* _____	Levels of Measurement						
		Ethnicity-Specific, Developmental Education (DEV) Data					
	All Developmental Education	**African American**	**American Indian**	**Asian American/ Pacific Islander**	**Hispanic/ Latino**	**White**	**Other**
Success rate of developmental education students in transfer-level courses							
Percentage of students who successfully completed a developmental course and earned a degree or certificate**							
Percentage of students who successfully completed a developmental education course and subsequently transferred**							
Locally Determined Measures							
Your measures here							

*within some specified, extended timeframe, e.g., one year

**within some specified, extended timeframe, e.g., two years, three years, four years

- *Unduplicated Number of Students Enrolled in Developmental Education:* Number of students enrolled in at least one development education course, counted only once if enrolled in multiple developmental education courses. A student is defined as follows:

  - *Student:* (MIS Data Element STD7 = A *and* MIS Data Element SX04 = A, B, C, D, F, CR, NC, I, FW, or W) *or* (MIS Data Element STD7 = B, C, or F).

- *Number of Developmental Education Sections Offered:* Number of sections with an MIS Data Element CB08 code of "P" (Precollegiate Basic Skill) or "B" (Basic Skill).

- *Percentage of Section Offerings That Are Developmental Education:* Number of sections coded as "B" or "P," divided by the total number of section offerings (MIS Data Element CB08 = "P," "B," or "N"), multiplied by 100.

- *Student Success Rate:* MIS Data Element SX04; number of A, B, C, and CR grades divided by the number of all grades, multiplied by 100. To calculate all grades, include A, B, C, D, F, CR, NC, I, FW, and W grades; exclude IP, RD, UD, UG, MW, and XX grades.

- *Student Retention Rate:* MIS Data Element SX04; number of A, B, C, D, F, CR, NC, I, and FW grades divided by the number of all grades, multiplied by 100. See "Student Success Rate" definition for details on how to calculate all grades.

- *Student Course Repetition Rate:* Number of students who earned a nonsuccessful grade (MIS Data Element SX04 = D, F, FW, NC, I, or W) in developmental education courses who subsequently re-enrolled in the same developmental education course (MIS Data Element CB08), multiplied by 100.

- *Persistence Rate of Developmental Education Students:* Number of developmental education students in a particular term who were counted as a student in a specified, following term, divided by total number of developmental education students in the initial term, multiplied by 100.

- *Percentage of Developmental Education Sections Taught by Full-Time Faculty:* Number of developmental education sections taught by full-time faculty (regular staff not on overload assignment as identified by MIS Data Element XE01 = 3), divided by total number of developmental education sections, multiplied by 100.

Additional Recommended Measure Operational Definitions

The following recommended measures require institutions to consistently define relevant student cohorts (such as new students in a fall semester who enroll in one or more developmental education courses). Though it is anticipated that colleges might identify different cohort characteristics based upon intervening variables unique to their institutions, significant thought and discussion should occur that will result in the establishment of consistent cohort definitions over time (for example, the same methodology should be employed to identify 2002, 2003, and 2004 cohorts, leading to an "apples-to-apples" comparison of identified cohort groups).

- *Percentage of Developmental Education Students Who Subsequently Enrolled in Transfer-Level Courses:*
  - "A": Identify a consistent cohort of students who successfully completed a developmental education course (such as by term or annual period; use baseline operational definitions to identify developmental education courses and successful completion).
  - "B": Among group "A" students, identify how many of these students subsequently enrolled in a transfer-level course. A transfer-level course is defined as MIS Data Element CB05 code of "A" (transferable to both a UC and CSU) or "B" (transferable to a CSU only). Define consistent track-out period for students identified in "A" (such as three years, five years, or six years).
  - Divide "B" by "A": multiply by 100.
  - *Example:* 345 students successfully completed a developmental education course in the Fall 2001 semester. Within a three-year period (for example, by end of Spring 2004), 225 had enrolled in a transfer-level course. 225/345 100 = 65.2%. Repeat for similar cohorts (for example, Fall 2002 and Fall 2003, tracked through Spring 2005 and Spring 2006, respectively).
- *Success Rate of Developmental Education Students in Transfer-Level Courses:* Among students identified in group "B," use baseline operational definitions to identify the success rate of the population in transfer-level courses.
- *Percentage of Students Who Successfully Completed a Developmental Education Course and Subsequently Earned a Degree and Certificate:* Among students identified in group "A," identify the number who

earned a degree or certificate within a consistently defined period (for example, three years, five years, or six years). Divide the number who earned a degree or certificate by all students in original cohort; multiply by 100.

- *Percentage of Students Who Successfully Completed a Developmental Education Course and Subsequently Transferred:* Among students identified in group "A," identify the number who subsequently transferred to another postsecondary educational institution. Submit original cohort to National Student Clearinghouse (NSC) after a consistently defined period of time (for example, three years, five years, or six years). Divide the number who transferred by all students in original cohort; multiply by 100.

Stage Two: Reflective Assessment—Strategy and Effective Practice Analysis

Stage One provides an important quantitative understanding of what is occurring at the institution and, as such, creates some basis for discussion. However, the heart of the qualitative self-assessment occurs in Stage Two, in which each of the five broad sections of the literature review are addressed separately through a strategy analysis, followed by an effective practice analysis. Strategies relate directly to a particular effective practice; all are drawn directly from the literature review.

Strategy Analysis

The college is asked to review each identified strategy associated with an effective practice. This process is meant to guide but not restrict the self-assessment analysis. Therefore, as appropriate, colleges are encouraged to also indicate any significant additional strategies not listed in the self-assessment tool but which the college employs *and strongly feels contribute to its ability to implement the effective practice.* To the extent possible, these additions should be presented with some evidence as to their efficacy. *It is not expected that every institution will engage in every strategy.*

To provide flexibility, we have left open the questions(s) to be investigated vis-à-vis the strategies. We suggest that this area be used as a means to identify which strategies are currently in use at your institution and where. If you take this recommended approach, the investigation directive would be "Where Strategies Occur." If the approach is used, the college might be asked to enumerate all the levels at which the strategy occurs (institution-wide, specific programs, or specific departments). In this way, the college can identify at a glance which strategies it currently employs and where these strategies are embedded within the organization.

Example: Each effective practice is associated with a matrix like the following. The institution is asked to complete the "Where Strategies Occur" section of the matrix.

(The following example is based on Effective Practice 1.4: A comprehensive system of support services exists, and is characterized by a high degree of integration among academic and student support services.)

	Strategies Related to Effective Practice	Where Strategies Occur (Or Insert Alternate Investigation Question(s))
1.4.4.	Peers and /or faculty provide mentoring to developmental students	• Mathematics (all developmental math courses encourage use of peer mentoring services) • English (peer mentoring encouraged for developmental writing) • Currently no other developmental education-specific mentoring

Effective Practice Analysis

Upon completing the initial analysis of strategies in which the college currently engages, the self-assessment proceeds to the effective practice level. Participants are asked to reflect in more detail on the effective practice as a whole by responding to the following prompts, which culminate in an analysis of priorities for change. These are the prompts we recommend, but each institution should consider whether these are the best prompts for its local context. These prompts can be supplanted by others, as desired.

1. Describe how this practice occurs or exists at your institution. Using the initial analysis of strategies as a basis, describe how the effective practice occurs at your college. Consider beginning your description with a statement which indicates one of the following:

   A. We have experience or strength in this area which we can build on and extend.

   B. This is an area which is emerging or shows promise.

   C. Results in this area have been mixed.

   D. This practice has not been addressed.

2. Identify what evidence exists to support the efficacy of this practice at your institution. Evidence is a measurable outcome that validates the effectiveness of the practice. Evidence might be found in the form of improved student persistence, for example. Indicate whether your college has such evidence for this practice. To the extent possible, include an indication not only that such evidence exists, but also where it is located and how it is shared or distributed within the college.

3. Identify barriers or limitations that exist to implementing or enhancing this practice. Barriers or limitations may be related to availability of resources, but they could also be more intangible, such as institutional culture. What barriers exist at the department level, or at other levels, such as interdepartmental, programmatic, institutional, regional, or statewide? Is the barrier related to lack of staffing, staff development, data, institutional commitment, money, or other capacity issues? What would be required to remove or substantially decrease the barrier?

4. Describe how this practice might be advanced or expanded upon in the future. List the actions (augmentations, changes, or new initiatives) that the institution believes will advance the efficacy or expand the delivery of the effective practice. Briefly indicate the specific problem(s) the action is expected to remedy: What will it fix and how will it work? What sorts of results are expected? What evidence can be used to verify results?

Reflective Assessment for Effective Practices and Strategies Related to Section 1: Organizational and Administrative Practices

Effective Practice 1.1: Developmental education is a clearly stated institutional priority.

	Strategies Related to Effective Practice	Where Strategies Occur (Or Alternate Investigation Question(s))
1.1.1	Clear references exist that developmental education is an institutional priority; references are public, prominent, and clear.	
1.1.2	Institutional leadership demonstrates a commitment to developmental education.	
1.1.3	Developmental educators are systemically included in broader college planning activities.	
1.1.4	Developmental education is adequately funded and staffed.	
1.1.5	Institutional commitment is reflected in the level of comprehensiveness and the extent to which developmental education is integrated into the institution.	

Suggested questions include:

1. Using the initial analysis of strategies as a basis, generally characterize the existence of this effective practice at your college.

2. What evidence exists to support the efficacy of this practice at your institution?

3. What barriers or limitations exist to implementing or enhancing this practice?

4. How might this practice be advanced or expanded upon in the future?

Effective Practice 1.2: A clearly articulated mission based on a shared, overarching philosophy drives the developmental education program. Clearly specified goals and objectives are established for developmental courses and programs.

	Strategies Related to Effective Practice	Where Strategies Occur (Or Alternate Investigation Question(s))
1.2.1	A detailed statement of the mission for developmental education is clearly articulated.	
1.2.2	Diverse institutional stakeholders are involved in developing the developmental education mission, philosophy, goals, and objectives.	
1.2.3	Developmental education mission, philosophy, goals, and objectives are reviewed and updated on a regular basis.	
1.2.4	Developmental education goals and objectives are clearly communicated across the institution.	

Suggested questions include:

1. Using the initial analysis of strategies as a basis, generally characterize the existence of this effective practice at your college.

2. What evidence exists to support the efficacy of this practice at your institution?

3. What barriers or limitations exist to implementing or enhancing this practice?

4. How might this practice be advanced or expanded upon in the future?

Effective Practice 1.3: The developmental education program is centralized or highly coordinated.

	Strategies Related to Effective Practice	Where Strategies Occur (Or Alternate Investigation Question(s))
1.3.1	A clear institutional decision exists regarding the structure of developmental education (centralized or decentralized, but highly coordinated).	
1.3.2	Based upon the institutional structure, a dedicated administrator or lead faculty is/are clearly identified and accorded responsibility for collegewide coordination of basic skills program(s).	
1.3.3	A designated budget allocation exists for developmental education.	
1.3.4	Formal mechanisms exist to facilitate communication/ coordination between faculty and staff in different developmental disciplines as well as with student services.	
1.3.5	Formal mechanisms exist to facilitate communication/ coordination between pre-collegiate and college-level faculty within disciplines.	

Suggested questions include:

1. Using the initial analysis of strategies as a basis, generally characterize the existence of this effective practice at your college.

2. What evidence exists to support the efficacy of this practice at your institution?

3. What barriers or limitations exist to implementing or enhancing this practice?

4. How might this practice be advanced or expanded upon in the future?

Effective Practice 1.4: A comprehensive system of support services exists and is characterized by a high degree of integration among academic and student support services.

	Strategies Related to Effective Practice	Where Strategies Occur (Or Alternate Investigation Question(s))
1.4.1	Course-related learning assistance (e.g., supplemental instruction, course-based tutoring) exists.	
1.4.2	Comprehensive learning systems (e.g., learning communities, course-embedded counseling, team teaching) exist and include developmental education students.	
1.4.3	A comprehensive learning assistance center provides support to developmental education students.	
1.4.4	Peers and/or faculty provide mentoring to developmental education students.	

Suggested questions include:

1. Using the initial analysis of strategies as a basis, generally characterize the existence of this effective practice at your college.

2. What evidence exists to support the efficacy of this practice at your institution?

3. What barriers or limitations exist to implementing or enhancing this practice?

4. How might this practice be advanced or expanded upon in the future?

Effective Practice 1.5: Institutional policies facilitate student completion of necessary developmental coursework as early as possible in the educational sequence.

	Strategies Related to Effective Practice	Where Strategies Occur (Or Alternate Investigation Question(s))
1.5.1	Students are required to receive early assessment and advisement for sound educational planning.	
1.5.2	Students are advised and encouraged to enroll only in college-level courses consistent with their basic skills preparation.	
1.5.3	Mechanisms/cultures exist to alleviate potential marginalization or stigma associated with isolation of basic skills students.	
1.5.4	Outcomes for basic skills students concurrently enrolled in college-level and basic skills courses are carefully monitored; data are used to adjust policies and/or recommendations to students.	

Suggested questions include:

1. Using the initial analysis of strategies as a basis, generally characterize the existence of this effective practice at your college.

2. What evidence exists to support the efficacy of this practice at your institution?

3. What barriers or limitations exist to implementing or enhancing this practice?

4. How might this practice be advanced or expanded upon in the future?

Effective Practice 1.6: Faculty who are both knowledgeable and enthusiastic about developmental education are recruited and hired to teach in the program.

	Strategies Related to Effective Practice	Where Strategies Occur (Or Alternate Investigation Question(s))
1.6.1	Recruitment and hiring processes for faculty/staff in basic skills programs emphasize expertise and/or experience in developmental education.	
1.6.2	Specific training in developmental education instructional strategies is provided to faculty teaching developmental education courses.	
1.6.3	Faculty choose to teach developmental education courses as opposed to being assigned to developmental education courses.	
1.6.4	A sufficient portion of developmental education course sections are taught by full-time faculty and the full-time to part-time ratio for basic skills is similar to the ratio for college-level classes and disciplines.	

Suggested questions include:

1. Using the initial analysis of strategies as a basis, generally characterize the existence of this effective practice at your college.

2. What evidence exists to support the efficacy of this practice at your institution?

3. What barriers or limitations exist to implementing or enhancing this practice?

4. How might this practice be advanced or expanded upon in the future?

The Self-Assessment Tool   **145**

Effective Practice 1.7: Institutions manage faculty and student expectations regarding developmental education.

	Strategies Related to Effective Practice	Where Strategies Occur (Or Alternate Investigation Question(s))
1.7.1	A clearly defined and widely shared definition of "successful developmental education" exists.	
1.7.2	Faculty new to the developmental program receive an orientation to convey to them the goals and expectations of the program.	
1.7.3	Faculty and other program personnel know/understand their individual roles and accept responsibility for the developmental program.	
1.7.4	Formal mechanisms exist to facilitate accurate communication of institutional values and expectations for developmental students.	
1.7.5	Colleges establish strong pre-enrollment advisement, including work with feeder high schools to convey expectations for appropriate pre-collegiate student preparation.	
1.7.6	Faculty/staff communicate clear expectations for student behaviors/performance in developmental courses and programs.	
1.7.7	Communication of expectations to students occurs early and often and is the shared responsibility of all developmental program providers.	

Suggested questions include:

1. Using the initial analysis of strategies as a basis, generally characterize the existence of this effective practice at your college.

2. What evidence exists to support the efficacy of this practice at your institution?

3. What barriers or limitations exist to implementing or enhancing this practice?

4. How might this practice be advanced or expanded upon in the future?

Reflective Assessment for Effective Practices and Strategies Related to Section 2: Program Components

Effective Practice 2.1: Orientation, assessment, and placement are mandatory for all new students.

	Strategies Related to Effective Practice	Where Strategies Occur (Or Alternate Investigation Question(s))
2.1.1	Mandatory orientation exists for all new students.	
2.1.2	Mandatory assessment exists for all new students.	
2.1.3	Mandatory placement exists for students assessed at developmental levels.	
2.1.4	Expanded pre-enrollment activities exist for students placed into developmental education courses.	
2.1.5	Diverse institutional stakeholders engage in routine review of the relationship between assessment instruments and student success in courses.	

Suggested questions include:

1. Using the initial analysis of strategies as a basis, generally characterize the existence of this effective practice at your college.

2. What evidence exists to support the efficacy of this practice at your institution?

3. What barriers or limitations exist to implementing or enhancing this practice?

4. How might this practice be advanced or expanded upon in the future?

Effective Practice 2.2: Counseling support provided is substantial, accessible, and integrated with academic courses and programs.

	Strategies Related to Effective Practice	Where Strategies Occur (Or Alternate Investigation Question(s))
2.2.1	A proactive counseling/advising structure that includes intensive monitoring and advising serves students placed into developmental education courses.	
2.2.2	Counseling and instruction are integrated into the developmental education program.	
2.2.3	Counseling staff are specifically trained to address the academic, social, and emotional needs of developmental education students.	
2.2.4	Counseling of developmental education students occurs early in the semester/quarter.	

Suggested questions include:

1. Using the initial analysis of strategies as a basis, generally characterize the existence of this effective practice at your college.

2. What evidence exists to support the efficacy of this practice at your institution?

3. What barriers or limitations exist to implementing or enhancing this practice?

4. How might this practice be advanced or expanded upon in the future?

Effective Practice 2.3: Financial aid is disseminated to support developmental students. Mechanisms exist to ensure that students are aware of such opportunities and are provided with assistance to apply for and acquire financial aid.

	Strategies Related to Effective Practice	Where Strategies Occur (Or Alternate Investigation Question(s))
2.3.1	Outreach and proactive mechanisms exist to educate developmental students about various opportunities to acquire financial aid.	
2.3.2	Developmental students receive timely assistance in identifying and applying for appropriate sources of financial aid.	
2.3.3	The institution actively solicits additional aid sources in support of developmental students (e.g., potential scholarship donors or textbook grants).	
2.3.4	The institution creates incentive programs that financially reward students who achieve/persist in developmental programs.	

Suggested questions include:

1. Using the initial analysis of strategies as a basis, generally characterize the existence of this effective practice at your college.

2. What evidence exists to support the efficacy of this practice at your institution?

3. What barriers or limitations exist to implementing or enhancing this practice?

4. How might this practice be advanced or expanded upon in the future?

Effective Practice 2.4: Regular program evaluations are conducted, results are disseminated widely, and data are used to improve practice.

	Strategies Related to Effective Practice	Where Strategies Occur (Or Alternate Investigation Question(s))
2.4.1	Developmental education course content and entry/exit skills are regularly reviewed and revised as needed.	
2.4.2	Formative program evaluation activities occur on a regular basis.	
2.4.3	Summative program evaluation activities occur on a regular basis.	
2.4.4	Multiple indices exist to evaluate the efficacy of developmental education courses and programs.	
2.4.5	Data obtained from course/program evaluation are disseminated and used for future planning and continuous improvement.	

Suggested questions include:

1. Using the initial analysis of strategies as a basis, generally characterize the existence of this effective practice at your college.

2. What evidence exists to support the efficacy of this practice at your institution?

3. What barriers or limitations exist to implementing or enhancing this practice?

4. How might this practice be advanced or expanded upon in the future?

Reflective Assessment for Effective Practices and Strategies Related to Section 3: Instructional Practices

Effective Practice 3.1: Sound principles of learning theory are applied in the design and delivery of courses in the developmental program.

	Strategies Related to Effective Practice	Where Strategies Occur (Or Alternate Investigation Question(s))
3.1.1	Developmental education focuses on self-directed learning, with students engaged in actively assessing and monitoring their own motivation and learning.	
3.1.2	Problem-solving and critical-thinking skills are integrated into developmental education curriculum.	
3.1.3	Developmental education curriculum recognizes and emphasizes the cognitive development of students (e.g., contextual learning, metacognitive skill development, and constructivism).	

Suggested questions include:

1. Using the initial analysis of strategies as a basis, generally characterize the existence of this effective practice at your college.

2. What evidence exists to support the efficacy of this practice at your institution?

3. What barriers or limitations exist to implementing or enhancing this practice?

4. How might this practice be advanced or expanded upon in the future?

Effective Practice 3.2: Brain-based research informs instructional design.

	Strategies Related to Effective Practice	Where Strategies Occur (Or Alternate Investigation Question(s))
3.2.1	Instructors use formative assessments to reveal students' errors, preconceptions, and preexisting understandings in order to facilitate genuine incorporation of new knowledge.	
3.2.2	Instructors can clearly articulate the desired competencies they want students to master.	
3.2.3	Courses are designed to provide a firm factual foundation as well as permit students to practice, allowing students to develop skills in the desired competencies.	
3.2.4	Instruction is designed to "engage the whole brain," providing experiences which include getting information, making meaning from it, creating new ideas, and acting on new ideas	

Suggested questions include:

1. Using the initial analysis of strategies as a basis, generally characterize the existence of this effective practice at your college.

2. What evidence exists to support the efficacy of this practice at your institution?

3. What barriers or limitations exist to implementing or enhancing this practice?

4. How might this practice be advanced or expanded upon in the future?

Effective Practice 3.3: Curricula and practices that have proven to be effective in specific disciplines are employed.

	Strategies Related to Effective Practice	Where Strategies Occur (Or Alternate Investigation Question(s))
3.3.1	Developmental courses/programs implement effective curricula and practices for English (e.g., reading/ writing integration, writing across the curriculum, and use of writing labs).	
3.3.2	Developmental courses/programs implement effective curricula and practices for mathematics (e.g., addressing environmental factors, problem-based learning, small-group instruction, contextual learning, appropriate use of technology, and learning labs).	
3.3.3	Developmental courses/programs implement effective curricula and practices for ESL.	
3.3.4	Developmental courses/programs implement effective curricula and practices for development of study skills.	

Suggested questions include:

1. Using the initial analysis of strategies as a basis, generally characterize the existence of this effective practice at your college.

2. What evidence exists to support the efficacy of this practice at your institution?

3. What barriers or limitations exist to implementing or enhancing this practice?

4. How might this practice be advanced or expanded upon in the future?

Effective Practice 3.4: Developmental education faculty employ a variety of instructional approaches to accommodate student diversity.

	Strategies Related to Effective Practice	Where Strategies Occur (Or Alternate Investigation Question(s))
3.4.1	Instructors in developmental education courses assess, employ, and incorporate a variety of active learning strategies (e.g., student engagement, collaborative learning, learning communities, supplemental instruction, and service learning).	
3.4.2	Developmental education promotes individualized student learning, focusing on learner-centeredness rather than teacher-centeredness.	
3.4.3	The academic and campus climate supports active learning strategies and connects developmental education students to the institution, faculty, staff, and other students.	

Suggested questions include:

1. Using the initial analysis of strategies as a basis, generally characterize the existence of this effective practice at your college.

2. What evidence exists to support the efficacy of this practice at your institution?

3. What barriers or limitations exist to implementing or enhancing this practice?

4. How might this practice be advanced or expanded upon in the future?

Effective Practice 3.5: Programs align entry and exit skills among levels and link course content to college-level performance requirements.

	Strategies Related to Effective Practice	Where Strategies Occur (Or Alternate Investigation Question(s))
3.5.1	Developmental education course entry/exit standards are regularly reviewed and revised as needed.	
3.5.2	The entire trajectory of developmental course sequences (including entry by placement instruments) is periodically reviewed and aligned to ensure appropriate student progression through sequential levels.	
3.5.3	A systemic approach exists within disciplines to align developmental education course content and pedagogy to degree-applicable and transfer-level course content.	

Suggested questions include:

1. Using the initial analysis of strategies as a basis, generally characterize the existence of this effective practice at your college.

2. What evidence exists to support the efficacy of this practice at your institution?

3. What barriers or limitations exist to implementing or enhancing this practice?

4. How might this practice be advanced or expanded upon in the future?

Effective Practice 3.6: Developmental education faculty routinely share instructional strategies.

	Strategies Related to Effective Practice	Where Strategies Occur (Or Alternate Investigation Question(s))
3.6.1	Formal processes exist that facilitate and promote the exchange of effective instructional strategies among faculty within disciplines.	
3.6.2	Formal processes exist that facilitate and promote the exchange of effective instructional strategies among faculty across disciplines.	
3.6.3	Formal processes exist that facilitate and promote the exchange of effective instructional strategies between faculty in general and developmental education programs.	

Suggested questions include:

1. Using the initial analysis of strategies as a basis, generally characterize the existence of this effective practice at your college.

2. What evidence exists to support the efficacy of this practice at your institution?

3. What barriers or limitations exist to implementing or enhancing this practice?

4. How might this practice be advanced or expanded upon in the future?

Reflective Assessment for Effective Practices and Strategies Related to Section 4: Student Support Services and Strategies

Effective Practice 4.1: The developmental education program addresses the holistic development of all aspects of the student. Attention is paid to the social and emotional development of students, as well as to their cognitive growth.

	Strategies Related to Effective Practice	Where Strategies Occur (Or Alternate Investigation Question(s))
4.1.1	In classroom teaching/learning, attention is paid to students' attitudes and emotions (e.g., self-concept and self-efficacy development) as well as to teaching basic subject skills.	
4.1.2	Student support services exist to address the external needs (e.g., child care, financial assistance, and transportation) of developmental education students.	
4.1.3	Timely interventions occur with students to address emotional, social, or nonacademic obstacles that arise, and to prevent student attrition resulting from such circumstances.	
4.1.4	Formal mechanisms in developmental courses and programs enhance student motivation and engagement to promote learning.	
4.1.5	College programs promote basic skills in students' social integration into and identification with the college environment.	

Suggested questions include:

1. Using the initial analysis of strategies as a basis, generally characterize the existence of this effective practice at your college.

2. What evidence exists to support the efficacy of this practice at your institution?

3. What barriers or limitations exist to implementing or enhancing this practice?

4. How might this practice be advanced or expanded upon in the future?

Effective Practice 4.2: Culturally Responsive Teaching theory and practices are applied to all aspects of the developmental instructional programs and services.

	Strategies Related to Effective Practice	Where Strategies Occur (Or Alternate Investigation Question(s))
4.2.1	Instructional content and pedagogy capitalize on perspectives and life experiences of students from diverse backgrounds.	
4.2.2	Developmental instruction communicates high expectations, engages students in critical dialogue regarding cultural conflicts, and establishes compatible sociocultural contexts for group learning.	
4.2.3	Developmental instruction reflects cultural sensitivity and culturally mediated instruction (e.g., the way communication and learning takes place in students' cultures).	

Suggested questions include:

1. Using the initial analysis of strategies as a basis, generally characterize the existence of this effective practice at your college.

2. What evidence exists to support the efficacy of this practice at your institution?

3. What barriers or limitations exist to implementing or enhancing this practice?

4. How might this practice be advanced or expanded upon in the future?

Effective Practice 4.3: Faculty and advisers carefully structure learning environments and closely monitor student performance.

	Strategies Related to Effective Practice	Where Strategies Occur (Or Alternate Investigation Question(s))
4.3.1	Mechanisms exist to frequently and consistently provide course performance feedback to students.	
4.3.2	Faculty and advising staff provide early intervention and support to students experiencing academic and/or personal difficulties.	

Suggested questions include:

1. Using the initial analysis of strategies as a basis, generally characterize the existence of this effective practice at your college.

2. What evidence exists to support the efficacy of this practice at your institution?

3. What barriers or limitations exist to implementing or enhancing this practice?

4. How might this practice be advanced or expanded upon in the future?

Effective Practice 4.4: Colleges assist students in developing connections to a community of learners.

	Strategies Related to Effective Practice	Where Strategies Occur (Or Alternate Investigation Question(s))
4.4.1	A structured peer or community mentoring program exists.	
4.4.2	Mentors are selected and trained appropriately.	
4.4.1	A variety of mechanisms promote social integration (e.g., First Year Experience programs).	

Suggested questions include:

1. Using the initial analysis of strategies as a basis, generally characterize the existence of this effective practice at your college.

2. What evidence exists to support the efficacy of this practice at your institution?

3. What barriers or limitations exist to implementing or enhancing this practice?

4. How might this practice be advanced or expanded upon in the future?

Effective Practice 4.5: Programs provide comprehensive academic support mechanisms, including the use of trained tutors.

	Strategies Related to Effective Practice	Where Strategies Occur (Or Alternate Investigation Question(s))
4.5.1	Learning support services emphasize an interrelationship between all levels of course offerings (developmental, degree-applicable, transferable, and others).	
4.5.2	Learning support services are visible and centrally located, minimizing marginalization and isolation.	
4.5.3	Various learning support services provide active learning experiences (e.g., Supplemental Instruction, workshops, and study groups).	
4.5.4	A formal referral system exists between academic and student support services.	
4.5.5	Tutoring is available and accessible in response to student needs/desires.	
4.5.6	All tutors receive formal training in both subject matter and effective pedagogy for the discipline.	
4.5.7	An academic support center provides diverse and active learning experiences such as workshops, study groups, self-paced instruction via video or software, and experiential learning.	

Suggested questions include:

1. Using the initial analysis of strategies as a basis, generally characterize the existence of this effective practice at your college.

2. What evidence exists to support the efficacy of this practice at your institution?

3. What barriers or limitations exist to implementing or enhancing this practice?

4. How might this practice be advanced or expanded upon in the future?

Reflective Assessment for Effective Practices and Strategies Related to Section 5: Professional Learning and Development

Effective Practice 5.1: Administrators support and encourage faculty development in basic skills, and the improvement of teaching and learning is connected to the institutional mission.

	Strategies Related to Effective Practice	Where Strategies Occur (Or Alternate Investigation Question(s))
5.1.1	Department, program, and/or institutional goals related to the improvement of developmental education are established.	
5.1.2	Professional development activities for developmental education faculty and staff are actively supported by senior administration.	

Suggested questions include:

1. Using the initial analysis of strategies as a basis, generally characterize the existence of this effective practice at your college.

2. What evidence exists to support the efficacy of this practice at your institution?

3. What barriers or limitations exist to implementing or enhancing this practice?

4. How might this practice be advanced or expanded upon in the future?

Effective Practice 5.2: The faculty play a primary role in needs assessment, planning, and implementation of staff development programs and activities in support of developmental education programs.

	Strategies Related to Effective Practice	Where Strategies Occur (Or Alternate Investigation Question(s))
5.2.1	Developmental education faculty are involved in the design, planning, and implementation of staff development activities related to developmental education.	
5.2.2	Developmental education staff development activities address both educational theory and practice.	
5.2.3	Staff development activities are widely attended and viewed as valuable by developmental education faculty and staff.	
5.2.4	The staff development program for developmental educators is regularly evaluated by participants, and data collected are used for continuous improvement.	
5.2.5	New faculty are provided staff development activities that assist them in transitioning into the community college academic environment.	
5.2.6	Staff development activities promote interactions among instructors.	

Suggested questions include:

1. Using the initial analysis of strategies as a basis, generally characterize the existence of this effective practice at your college.

2. What evidence exists to support the efficacy of this practice at your institution?

3. What barriers or limitations exist to implementing or enhancing this practice?

4. How might this practice be advanced or expanded upon in the future?

• • •

Effective Practice 5.3: Staff development programs are structured and appropriately supported to sustain them as ongoing efforts related to institutional goals for the improvement of teaching and learning.

	Strategies Related to Effective Practice	Where Strategies Occur (Or Alternate Investigation Question(s))
5.3.1	Developmental education staff development activities are clearly linked to department, program, and/or institutional goals.	
5.3.2	Developmental education staff development activities are not based around "one-shot" workshops; rather, staff development activities are comprehensive and ongoing.	
5.3.3	Staff development activities are adequately funded, funding is ongoing, and development activities are coordinated by specific designated staff as part of their core responsibilities.	

Suggested questions include:

1. Using the initial analysis of strategies as a basis, generally characterize the existence of this effective practice at your college.

2. What evidence exists to support the efficacy of this practice at your institution?

3. What barriers or limitations exist to implementing or enhancing this practice?

4. How might this practice be advanced or expanded upon in the future?

• • •

Effective Practice 5.4: Faculty development is connected to intrinsic and extrinsic faculty reward structures.

	Strategies Related to Effective Practice	Where Strategies Occur (Or Alternate Investigation Question(s))
5.4.1	A structure that provides faculty who participate in staff development with intrinsic rewards (e.g., praise, support, or peer recognition) is promoted.	
5.4.2	Opportunities exist for colleagues across disciplines to engage in interchanges that foster a "culture of teaching," which in turn develops a "community of scholars."	
5.4.3	The institution expresses value for staff development activities through provision of extrinsic rewards where appropriate (e.g., funding, time, salary advancement, or formal recognition of achievement).	

Suggested questions include:

1. Using the initial analysis of strategies as a basis, generally characterize the existence of this effective practice at your college.

2. What evidence exists to support the efficacy of this practice at your institution?

3. What barriers or limitations exist to implementing or enhancing this practice?

4. How might this practice be advanced or expanded upon in the future?

• • •

Effective Practice 5.5: Staff development opportunities are flexible, varied, and responsive to developmental needs of individual faculty, diverse student populations, and coordinated programs and services.

	Strategies Related to Effective Practice	Where Strategies Occur (Or Alternate Investigation Question(s))
5.5.1	Peer Mentoring	
5.5.2	Instructional Consultation	
5.5.3	Reflective Teaching	
5.5.4	Scholarship of Teaching & Learning	
5.5.5	Classroom Assessment Techniques	
5.5.6	Great Teacher Seminars	

	Strategies Related to Effective Practice	**Where Strategies Occur (Or Alternate Investigation Question(s))**
5.5.7	Academic Alliances (e.g., K-16 Inter-Segmental Partnerships)	
	Other (specify activity):	
	Other (specify activity):	
	Other (specify activity):	

Suggested questions include:

1. Using the initial analysis of strategies as a basis, generally characterize the existence of this effective practice at your college.

2. What evidence exists to support the efficacy of this practice at your institution?

3. What barriers or limitations exist to implementing or enhancing this practice?

4. How might this practice be advanced or expanded upon in the future?

Stage Three: Strategic Priorities—Identifying "Next Steps"

Presumably your institution engaged in the self-assessment process as a means of clarifying its current practices and determining how it might better serve students in developmental education courses and programs. Given what you have discovered and discussed, how can you best advance your institution's ability to serve underprepared students? What are the "next steps"? Remember to consider the interrelationships between the five broad sections as you complete this final stage of the self-assessment.

Strategic Priorities

Section One: Organizational and Administrative Practices

Institutional choices concerning program structure, organization, and management matter, and have been related to the overall effectiveness of development education programs. Review the Effective Practices Analyses related to Section One. Identify the logical next steps for strengthening and improving developmental education:

1. _____

_____

2. _____

_____

3. _____

_____

4. _____

_____

5. _____

_____

Section Two: Program Components

Program components such as mandatory orientation, counseling, and financial aid also matter, as does the regular evaluation of meaningful data to review and improve the delivery of developmental education. Review the Effective Practices Analyses related to Section Two. Identify the logical next steps for strengthening and improving developmental education:

1. _____

_____

2. _____

_____

3. _____

_____

4. _____

_____

5. _____

_____

Section Three: Instructional Practices

Certainly effective instructional practices are central to achieving desired student outcomes for developmental programs. Review the Effective Practices Analyses related to Section Three. Identify the logical next steps for strengthening and improving developmental education:

1. _____

_____

2. _____

_____

3. _____

_____

4. _____

_____

5. _____

_____

Section Four: Student Support Services and Strategies

The most successful developmental education programs provide an integrated approach to education, connecting academics and student services. Review the Effective Practices Analyses related to Section Four. Identify the logical next steps for strengthening and improving developmental education:

1. _____

_____

2. _____

_____

3. _____

_____

4. _____

_____

5. _____

_____

Section Five: Professional Learning and Development

This section asserts the importance of comprehensive training and professional development opportunities for faculty and staff. Review the Effective Practices Analyses related to Section Five. Identify the logical next steps for strengthening and improving developmental education:

1. _____

_____

2. _____

_____

3. _____

_____

4. _____

_____

5. _____

_____

Action Planning

Finally, we encourage you to translate the strategic priorities identified in the preceding five areas into a cohesive action plan. A sample is provided next. In doing so, you may wish to specify target dates for completion, leadership and oversight responsibilities, and associated measures to evaluate improvements. You may also wish to note where the successful implementation of a particular priority hinges on the implementation of other identified priorities.

• • •

Where additional resources are necessary, you may find it helpful to use the Investment-Revenue Model provided in Chapter Seven. As noted in that chapter, the perceived costs ascribed to many of these practices has limited their implementation. We urge you to use this model as a tool in helping the institution think differently about the cost of robust developmental education programs.

Sample Action Plan Matrix

Please state your college's Long-Term Goals (five years) for developmental education. Identify related Priority Actions for the next year (one year). Include actions that require new (or reallocated) funds as well those which can be accomplished without funding changes. Reference the related effective practice(s), identify targeted completion dates, and identify persons responsible for each activity.

Long-Term Goals (Five Years):

_____

_____

_____

Priority Actions

Academic Year _____ (*please specify year*)

Planned Action	Effective Practice and Strategy	Target Date for Completion	Responsible Person(s)/ Department(s)
Example: Refine academic support center program design to include recommended software in reading and to facilitate active learning, study groups, and workshops.	4.5.7 An academic support center provides diverse and active learning experiences such as workshops, study groups, self-paced instruction via video or software, and experiential learning.	May 30, _____	Reading Program Chair, Learning Center Director

Chapter 7

The Economics of Innovation in Developmental Education

Innovation in Developmental Education

As referenced in numerous places in this book, research has fairly consistently demonstrated that the historical "one instructor, one classroom, limited suite of support services" model of developmental education is not particularly effective. However, it is still the prevalent model offered to the vast majority of community college students. Many of the effective practices identified in this work can be found interspersed on campuses throughout the country, *most commonly with "boutique" programs that serve a mere fraction of the student population who participate in developmental education*. There are many reasons for the fairly restricted occurrence and scope of these programs, including:

- Limited awareness about the literature and its findings

- A need for paradigm shifts in the thinking of campus administrators, faculty, and staff

- A concomitant need for organizational change

- A lack of historically detailed institutional research to provide hard data evaluating program results

- A desire to pilot programs to determine effectiveness, often without sufficient institutional commitment to evaluate potential efficacy

On the flip side, as is noted in the literature review, a significant amount of data exists that suggests that these alternative approaches are successful. In California, where this work originated, the Center for Student Success summarizes a wide range of these programs, many of which have hard data indicating success. Furthermore, after noting the largely depressing data on the effectiveness of the traditional model of developmental education in seven California Community Colleges, Johnstone (2004) also summarized a number of innovative alternate approaches in place at the seven colleges, each of which had hard data indicating increased achievement of student outcomes.

In addition to the reasons cited previously for the relative dearth of scope of alternate approaches, arguably the most critical factor historically limiting the use of such programs has been their *perceived cost* to the campuses. Why are these programs considered to be more expensive than their traditional counterparts? Largely, it is because these programs devote additional up-front resources to change the "one instructor, one classroom, limited suite of support services" model in some fundamental way. Examples of such resources would include paying successful former students as tutors in a supplemental instruction model, dedicating counselors to participate in a learning community classroom, providing faculty release time to develop or maintain learning communities, carrying equipment and supply costs for a service learning model, or funding coordination time for faculty or classified staff to run a nontraditional program.

These and other costs of nontraditional programs are often seen as the primary barrier to their implementation. Against the backdrop of limited resources that exist in the community college system in an absolute sense and as relative to other segments of higher and secondary education, the cost of deviating from the traditional model of providing developmental education is a significant concern. However, the case will be made in the following sections that these costs can be seen as an *investment* that produces higher levels of student success, which will reap not only the attendant moral and ethical benefits but also a net financial gain to colleges.

Thus, as the literature and local data lead colleges to investigate the need to "do things differently" in terms of developmental education, discussions about the cost effectiveness of these alternate approaches for individual colleges can and should become somewhat more sophisticated. Otherwise colleges are left with a situation where society demands that they succeed in the mission of developmental education, but traditional funding models seem to suggest that it would be too expensive to systemically implement the innovative approaches that would lead to increased success.

The remainder of this chapter includes:

- An analysis of the societal impacts of developmental education programs
- A discussion of the logic behind the incremental revenue approach
- A description of how the theory can be applied in the real world using the provided Excel model

- An analysis of the model's application using empirical data collected from four community colleges in California

- A brief description of how the model works with non-California economic structures, based on colleges in five other states (Illinois, Kansas, New York, Ohio, and Texas)

The Logic Behind the Investment in Innovation's Incremental Revenue Approach

Aside from the numerous reasons to do things differently in order to truly fulfill the mission of the community college, there are college-level, economic reasons that alternate approaches to developmental education at the very least go a long way toward paying for themselves—and in many cases may very well result in a net economic benefit to the college. The goal of this section is to provide a different way of thinking about the cost to colleges of alternate developmental education programs. This approach is not without its parameters and caveats, but as colleges consider potentially expanding current small, boutique programs and systemically improving developmental student outcomes, this different perspective is potentially very important. *In the end, the model and the logic behind the approach were developed to support the case that colleges should seek to offer innovative, successful, nontraditional approaches at scale, to the entire range of students who are in dire need of their improved ability to lead to successful outcomes.*

First, it should be noted that colleges are most commonly set up to think in terms of fiscal periods—usually as fiscal years. Simplistically, this year's salaries, fixed costs, and variable costs need to be offset by revenues generated by apportionment, tuition, property tax, and other general fund sources. While there is a wide variety in funding models across the states, in nearly all of them the "variable funding" of state apportionment revenue, tuition, and fees—the funding that increases proportionately as enrollment increases—comprises at least 50% of the total general fund revenue. In California, variable funding is essentially the only source of general fund revenue—the percentage of funding contributed by apportionment is over 90% at most colleges. It is this variable funding that will be targeted in the approach described in the following section.

If innovative developmental education programs are successful, they have the following outcomes:

- Increased course retention

- Increased course success rates

- Increased persistence
- Increased progression to college-level work
- Increase in overall units attempted or earned

Clearly, these outcomes are desirable from the standpoint of the mission of the college and the entire system, but they are also associated with tangible economic benefits to be realized for the individual campuses. Specifically, as these students successfully progress through their developmental education work, persist in their studies, achieve college-level work, and graduate or achieve transfer readiness at higher rates, these more successful and persisting students produce a financial side benefit—an increase to the college in full-time equivalent students (FTES).

Here is the crux of the incremental revenue approach—this increase in FTES from newly successful students in the innovative programs generates additional apportionment and tuition or fee revenue to the college. Note that this incremental increase in FTES would not have been available under the "traditional" model of developmental education, with its lower levels of success and retention. Thus, this amount can be applied to offset much if not all of the incremental costs of the nontraditional programs. In the six states examined in this analysis, the total variable funding per FTES ranged from $3,100 to $5,500 per FTES. As will be demonstrated below with real-world data, quite often this additional funding would offset costs or even "turn a profit" for the college even when it is compared to the sometimes significant costs of doing things differently.

Consider the state of Ohio, where the combination of state apportionment funding and tuition results in roughly $4,000 of funding per FTES. If an innovative learning community program serves 200 students annually and, because it is extremely successful, it might produce an incremental gain of 50 FTES when compared to a traditional program, there is 50 × $4,000 = $200,000 available to offset the incremental costs associated with running the learning community program. We'll delve into the details in the next section, but you can see the picture—when these innovative programs are successful, a tangible, measurable economic gain accrues.

It should be noted that this approach to calculating apportionment revenue from successful developmental education students is not without its caveats. First, the revenue is not unencumbered—there will likely be additional instructional costs for students who are successfully retained and made ready for college-level courses. Although many of these students may very well fill classrooms that are not currently at capacity, there certainly will be the need to open some additional sections, which then incurs instructional cost. Certainly this is a good "problem" to have. Ironically, this cost will be relatively higher at more efficient schools, where a higher majority of classes are full or nearly full. Conversely, many of these successful developmental education students will likely funnel into highly productive programs in the general education sequence (such as large lecture courses), so the cost may not be as high as it would be in other domains of the curriculum.

Second, as with all revenue generated from FTES, there is an associated overhead cost. Estimating this overhead is very complex—especially for "incremental" FTES that may or may not increase a college's infrastructure. Different campuses would estimate this figure with quite different methods; as such, there is no methodology designated here to investigate this overhead cost. Discussions with various internal and external observers have led to a range of estimates for the percentage of this FTES revenue that can be referred to as "profit"—anywhere from 40% to 75%. Regardless of the specifics, however, it can be argued that a significant portion of this revenue would be available to offset the program costs (such as tutoring costs, faculty release time, coordination time, dedicated counselor support, supplies).

Third, this is not a sophisticated economic model, taking into account such concepts as the fact that money "recovered" in the future is often not worth as much as the money's current value. It would be fairly easy to include such concepts, but in the interest of parsimony and making the material easily attainable to practitioners, these concepts were not incorporated. Ultimately, this approach is designed to be an order-of-magnitude demonstration; specific decisions about strategies to expand and fund innovation in developmental education clearly need to be fleshed out by practitioner experts on individual college campuses.

Finally, there may be specific state-level idiosyncrasies that complicate matters. For example, in California, where apportionment funding is subject to an enrollment cap, a primary concern is that this approach becomes problematic if a college is near or above its enrollment cap. That is, if incremental FTES will not be funded by the state, then a college is actually de-incentivized to create additional FTES. While a good problem to have, as it would be caused by students being more successful and persisting to achieve their educational goals, the California system would need to account for this increase in FTES. In other states, the relative economics of the variable funding of apportionment and tuition or fee revenue versus the fixed funding provided from local property taxes or levies also could become complicated.

Complexities aside, the bottom line is that this investment in innovation approach suggests that the primary reason often cited for not doing things differently in developmental education—the cost of nontraditional programs—may not truly be the barrier that it is commonly perceived to be.

The Incremental Revenue Model in Action

To illustrate this line of thinking, we have created a model in Microsoft Excel that can be fairly easily applied to any innovative developmental education program. This section will draw upon nine models that are available in an Excel file that can be downloaded from the Research & Planning Group for the California Community College's Web site at www.rpgroup. org/publications/StudentSuccessBook.htm to illustrate the various pieces of the model. Further, these real-world examples of the models demonstrate how this framework can be implemented for different types of innovative developmental education approaches. The Excel file on the Web site also includes a blank template that readers can use to customize the model to their own campus.

Four of the models are based on real-world cost and revenue data from existing innovative developmental programs in California—Cerritos College's Learning Communities Program, Chaffey College's Service Learning Program, De Anza College's Math Performance Success Program (Dedicated Counselor, Increased Time on Task), and Foothill College's Pass the Torch Program (Supplemental Instruction). The samples are included to provide examples of the types of costs and incremental FTES that a campus might encounter in these types of programs—the experience on each campus with a given type of program could vary widely both in cost and its effect on students success. The ultimate value in this approach is to customize these models for the existing or proposed programs on each campus, with real costs and incremental contact hours and success rates.

We have also included five models based on the same hypothetical learning community model and the economic structures of five colleges from five states, to illustrate how the model can easily account for state-level differences in funding. These five colleges are Moraine Valley Community College in Illinois, Johnson County Community College in Kansas, Cuyahoga Community College in Ohio, Monroe Community College in New York, and Dallas County Community College District in Texas. We would like to thank these colleges and the four California colleges for agreeing to share their real-world data or funding structures with us to help illustrate how the model works.

An important note: Given that different colleges will have different methodologies for computing metrics and will have different approaches to estimating the various parameters in the model, these models should not be used to compare programs across colleges—especially with the hypothetical programs in the non-California schools! Ultimately, the value of this tool is that colleges can internally use it in a customized fashion to explore the cost-revenue relationships of the various programs within their college. In the end, these models can be utilized to help college decision makers understand the potential cost-benefit implications of expanding existing programs or developing new ones.

Preamble—The Foundation of the Model

For the purposes of this approach, we assume that the traditional model of one instructor in one classroom for a standard class time is the benchmark against which we can measure the costs and incremental revenue associated with alternate programs such as learning communities, supplemental instruction, structurally required tutoring, dedicated counseling support, and the like. The overall idea, then, is to estimate and account for the incremental or additional annual costs and revenue that are incurred with a given program because its approach is different from the traditional model. There tends not to be much controversy about associating costs to the alternate programs; it is really in associating revenue that there has been little attention devoted.

Examples of the Model

The model is divided into four basic parts:

Section 1 allows the reader to either input the *number of students* served annually by a current program they are modeling or a desired number of students that might be served if a current program is brought to scale or a new program is initiated. Here's an example from Cerritos College's Learning Community program, which at the time of the study served 150 students:

Section 1: Students Served in Program	150

Sections 2 through 4 accounts for the *incremental costs* associated with innovative developmental education programs—including incremental salaried personnel (Section 2), hourly personnel (Section 3), and incremental fixed costs such as equipment or supplies (Section 4).

Section 5 *summarizes* these incremental costs. Here's an example of the Section 5 summary from Chaffey College's Service Learning Program, which has no incremental salaried personnel costs but includes both hourly personnel and fixed costs:

Section 5: Incremental Cost Summary		
	A. Item	**B. Annual Cost/Budget**
1.	Salaried Personnel Costs	$0
2.	Hourly Personnel Costs	$15,532
3.	Fixed Costs	$32,431
	Total Program Costs:	$47,963

Section 6 provides the college's *FTES funding structure*, which will certainly vary state to state and can vary within a state. Here's an example from Johnson County Community College in Kansas, where apportionment funding and tuition-fees funding from an incremental FTES totals $4,215.

Section 6: FTES Funding Assumptions		
	Description	**Value**
1.	Apportionment Funding from State per FTES	$2,265
2.	Tuition/Fees Funding per FTES (30 units @ $65/unit)	$1,950
	Total Funding per FTES:	$4,215

Another example of Section 6 comes from De Anza College, which displays the model for a California Community College where tuition-fee revenue is not kept locally.

Section 6: FTES Funding Assumptions		
	Description	**Value**
1.	Apportionment Funding from State per FTES	$4,361
2.	Tuition Funding per FTES (N/A in California)	$0
	Total Funding per FTES:	$4,361

Section 7 accounts for the *incremental revenue* generated when the programs are successful. The data for Foothill College's Pass the Torch program are included. This is where the "magic" happens, and successful programs are translated into increased revenue through the incremental FTES that

are generated. In this case using real-world data, note that the program serves 110 students annually, and that as a result of the program's success, these 110 students produce 91.2 incremental FTES, which represents a 47% increase over the control or traditional group and generates nearly $400,000 in incremental revenue that can be used to offset the program costs. It should be noted that this is an expensive program, but it certainly seems less expensive when the incremental revenue is factored in.

It is also worth noting that obtaining the FTES data for both the innovative program cohorts as well as for a carefully selected control group is not a trivial task. However, it is quite attainable for practitioners working closely with a college's institutional research office. The model can also be used in a "what-if" fashion, where practitioners enter hypothetical program or control group sizes and FTE gains to estimate the amount of incremental revenue that would be generated.

Section 7: Incremental FTES from Program		
	Description	**Value**
1.	Students in Program Annually	110
2.	Subsequent FTES from Students in Program	283.7
3.	Students in Control Group	110
4.	Subsequent FTES from Students in Control Group	192.5
5.	Incremental FTES from Students in Program	91.2
	(N-adjusted to Program size)	
6.	Percentage Increase in FTES from Program	47%
7.	Potential Revenue from FTES @ $4,361/FTES	$397,574

Finally—to drive home the point about the economics of innovation—here are Sections 5 and 7 for the hypothetical learning community at Moraine Valley Community College in Rochester, New York. Note that this learning community program, which is hypothesized to serve 150 students, costs roughly $113,000 a year to run. However, with its hypothesized 32% increase in incremental FTES over the control group—a realistic figure given the gains noted with real-world data in California—the program would generate an additional $443,000 in revenue. Even if you were to discount this figure by 50% to account for a more extreme estimate of operational costs, the program would still generate a "profit" of ($443,000 × .50) = $221,500 − $113,000 = $108,500 from running the innovative program.

Section 5: Incremental Cost Summary		
	A. Item	**B. Annual Cost/Budget**
1.	Salaried Personnel Costs	$88,865
2.	Hourly Personnel Costs	$19,375
3.	Fixed Costs	$5,000
	Total Program Costs:	$113,240

• • •

Section 7: Incremental FTES from Program		
	Description	**Value**
1.	Students in Program Annually	150
2.	Subsequent FTES from Students in Program	324.5
3.	Students in Control Group	150
4.	Subsequent FTES from Students in Control Group	245.0
5.	Incremental FTES from Students in Program	79.5
	(N-adjusted to Program size)	
6.	Percentage Increase in FTES from Program	32%
7.	Potential Revenue from FTES @ $3,966/FTES	$443,213

Different Methods, Different Sizes—All Effective in Their Own Way

Armed with a firmer understanding of the model, let's go back and take a look at the four programs from the California Community Colleges. Although it was mentioned earlier that the model isn't designed to compare programs—especially across colleges—an investigation of the empirical data from these four programs illustrates that there are very different ways a college could experience a net financial benefit. The following table summarizes the costs, number of students, percentage increase in FTES, and potential revenue from the real-world data collected on the four California programs:

Description	Size	Total Costs	FTES % Increase	Potential Revenue
Cerritos College's Learning Community Model	424	$22,617	6%	$178,748
Chaffey College's Service Learning Model	416	$47,963	18%	$503,696
De Anza College's MPS Model	75	$81,990	36%	$213,357
Foothill College's Pass the Torch Model	110	$353,634	47%	$397,574

An examination of this table reveals a number of interesting observations. First, the programs serve populations of quite different size, from over 400 at both Cerritos and Chaffey to closer to 100 at De Anza and Foothill. The programs also differ quite notably in terms of the incremental cost, from $22,600 annually at Cerritos to $353,600 at Foothill. Perhaps not unrelated is the finding that the incremental increase in FTES over the control group ranged from 6% at Cerritos to 47% at Foothill. Finally, the potential revenue generated from the programs ranged from roughly $180,000 at Cerritos to over $500,000 at Chaffey.

These different approaches reveal that there are different levers that can be pushed to potentially adjust the different outcomes, depending on what is most valued to a college. From a strictly fiscal standpoint, it is clear that a "profit" can be turned in at least two clear ways. First, as in the Cerritos case, a relatively inexpensive program in terms of incremental costs can be applied to a relatively larger number of students—even with a modest 6% increase in incremental FTES, this program is clearly profitable financially no matter how much the potential revenue is discounted. Conversely, as in the De Anza model, a program could serve a relatively small number of students, with a higher level of incremental costs, provided that it produces a bigger net increase in FTES relative to a control group (36%, in this case).

Note that by far the most "profitable" program is Chaffey's, which serves a larger number of students (400+), with moderate incremental costs ($48,000), and produces a relatively robust increase in FTES (18%). Even if we discounted the potential incremental revenue of $504,000 by an extremely conservative 60%, it would still net the college over a return of more than four times its investment: $504,000 − $301,000 = $203,000 in revenue, compared to $48,000 in incremental costs. Clearly this program is ripe for further expansion; though a program serving over 400 students is large when compared to the average size of the "boutique" programs commonly observed at many colleges, it is still a mere fraction of the total population of students needing such approaches on Chaffey's campus—and of course on the rest of our campuses as well.

Although Foothill's program is clearly "expensive," it should be noted that it also produces the biggest jump in incremental FTES (47%); the program clearly works. As will be mentioned in the next section, this program clearly is a candidate for the economies of scale that a modestly larger number of students would produce. At the same time, it also is a program that a college might want to reserve for its most needy students, given its relatively high cost and extremely high rate of effectiveness.

A Quick Look at the Models from the Schools Outside California

As mentioned previously, real-world data was collected from the four California community colleges to illustrate the model in action (the model was originally designed in California). We also developed hypothetical models for five schools from different states to examine and illustrate the effects of their unique incremental funding structures. For each of these programs, the same hypothetical learning community was utilized—serving 150 students annually, with incremental costs of $113,000, and generating a 32% increase in incremental FTES—or about 80 incremental FTES. The only difference between the models at the five schools, then, was the FTES Funding Assumptions summarized in Section 6 of each of the models. This information was gathered from key personnel at each of the five colleges.

The key information from Section 6 is reproduced here for the five schools, as well as the potential revenue generated from Section 7 based on these different funding amounts.

College/State	Apportionment Funding	Tuition/Fees Funding	Total Funding/FTES	Potential Revenue
Cuyahoga CC, Ohio	$1,550	$2,416	$3,966	$315,313
Dallas County CCD, Texas	$2,054	$1,170	$3,224	$256,308
Johnson County CC, Kansas	$2,265	$1,950	$4,215	$335,093
Monroe CC, New York	$2,675	$2,900	$5,575	$443,213
Moraine Valley CC, Illinois	$750	$2,426	$3,176	$252,452

As the table clearly portrays, the different "Total Funding per FTES" amounts produce a range of potential revenue from just over $250,000 at Moraine Valley in Illinois to over $440,000 at Monroe in New York. Note that while the amount of funding per FTES varies considerably at these five schools, the incremental revenue approach still results in a "profitable" outcome for each of these schools—with hypothesized costs of $113,000, even the lowest potential revenue figure of $250,000 is still going to produce a profit when discounted by 50%.

It is also interesting to note that if California's economic structure were applied to this same hypothetical learning community, with its funding of $4,361 per FTES, the results would be very similar to Johnson County's in the preceding table. The big difference in the five non-California schools included here as well as for the rest of the country, however, is that these schools also have additional "fixed" funding sources that don't increase with the number of FTES generated—from sources such as property taxes and levies.

Some Final Thoughts in Summary

It should be noted that it is very likely that no single innovative approach or program will work for the entirety of the diverse student populations that exist both between and within community college campuses across the country. It is likely that a mix of nontraditional programs would optimize the benefits in student success. For example, a college might consider the highly successful "Pass the Torch" program from Foothill College, with its 47% increase in incremental FTES and fairly expensive cost structure, as an option for the students most needing such an intervention—and pair it with two or three more conservatively funded yet still successful programs such as Cerritos' Learning Communities model or Chaffey's Service Learning model. *In doing so, a college could reach "scale" with a suite of nontraditional programs that serve most or all students who are in the developmental education pathways.*

Further, as programs are expanded past their current small reach, they will likely experience some decrease in incremental success. This might occur for a couple of reasons—for example, the small size of the program may be contributing to its success, there might be an effect of students in the current programs being more motivated, and it is also possible that faculty currently in the program are more comfortable with the innovations they often helped create. The flip side is that costs do not scale up proportionally—and this usually is a good thing as economies of scale emerge. At the very least, these forces may very well balance each other—and it is more likely that the economies of scale would provide more of a benefit than the decreases associated with larger programs. It is, however, an open question; ideally, as more programs scale to become systemic approaches, more data will become available for further analysis of this issue.

In the end, the authors feel strongly that colleges should be looking to expand more successful nontraditional developmental education programs for moral, ethical, and societal reasons. The Incremental Revenue approach described here simply suggests that colleges also have a financial incentive for doing so. One can easily see a brighter future for our community colleges' developmental education students, where a suite of effective nontraditional programs serve the needs of the entire range of students needing them, rather than the handful currently receiving these successful interventions.

Given the increasing demands for an educated workforce at a time when legions of students are "stuck in neutral" in developmental education pathways, it is not too bold a prediction to state that our ability to significantly and systemically transform our approach to developmental education may very well be the most important lever we possess to meet this critical need.

Conclusion

The authors of this guide worked diligently to avoid including their own independent assessments or personal observations in the review of the research literature in Part One and the development of the tools in Part Two; their focus was to identify the practices for which there was clear independent evidence of effectiveness and to create user-friendly assessment protocols and budgetary tools that could be used to promote innovation. Nevertheless, the collaboration by this team of experienced professionals has led to a number of general conclusions and observations that deserve attention and should receive specific emphasis.

> *The research on basic skills education clearly establishes a series of effective practices that have been demonstrated to produce improvements in student outcomes.*

Although this point may seem self-evident as the reader goes through this guide, it is important to draw attention to this fact. There is clear evidence that certain practices work and that we have the tools to more effectively meet our mission for all students. This guide does not assume that *all* colleges will adopt *all* of these practices. Each college will need to rigorously review its programs and services and develop and implement action plans designed to improve outcomes within its own instructional, support services, and organizational structures. In fact, the active engagement of a broadly representative group of faculty and staff in the self-assessment, planning, and implementation process is probably the most crucial first step toward improving practices that are identified in this guide.

> *The improvement of basic skills education must be an institutional priority and is an institutional responsibility.*

Too frequently, basic skills development is viewed as the responsibility of a limited cohort of the college's faculty and staff. English (reading and composition), mathematics, and English as a second language departments, as well as educational support services and counseling, are commonly seen as "the people who work with *those* students." Sometimes this isolation extends to sub-units within each of those programs, segmenting the faculty who teach basic skills courses from those who teach "transfer-level" curriculum.

Although specialization is a crucial factor in the success of certain developmental education activities, basic skills students belong to the entire institution. They are registered in all types of classes, and the development of their academic skills is the responsibility of *all* faculty and staff. Many faculty and administrators share a broad-based concern about the erosion of academic standards based upon the inability of large segments of the student population to adequately perform basic reading, writing, and mathematical reasoning skills. It is the responsibility of all faculty, teaching in all disciplines at all levels, to communicate appropriate expectations and utilize effective methods for communicating information, support students' growth in reading and writing skills, develop critical-thinking processes, and evaluate student work to advance the overall state of our students' basic skills.

In spite of efforts to improve the preparation of students in the K–12 system, the number of students entering community colleges in need of developmental education is increasing. Though we cannot assume responsibility for the failures of other segments of our educational system, we must take responsibility for what happens to students within our academic environment. The identity of our students does not change, and many of their needs remain the same as they move from their basic skills classes into discipline-based courses.

Therefore, the approach to improving developmental outcomes must be directly connected to modifications across the curriculum. The effective practices identified in this study are not restricted to basic skills courses. Fundamentally, they are models for good practice in every aspect of the community college environment, and any effort to implement these practices should involve every component of the college's programs and services.

Although much of this study focuses on the responsibilities of the colleges, their faculty, and their staff, the practices advocated also address the responsibilities of students. They address the importance of developing the students' resources for functioning effectively in college-level studies and relying on a symbiotic relationship between student and institutional objectives and commitment. Just as the literature on effective practices advocates a holistic approach to meeting the needs of students, so too must the approach to improving developmental education be holistic. The transformation of developmental education must be an institutional activity in which every administrator, faculty member, support staff, and student participates and takes responsibility for improving outcomes.

> *Our charge in basic skills education is developmental, not remedial.*

There is significant controversy surrounding the name attached to these programs and services. The term "basic skills" is frequently perceived as demeaning, contributing to a negative self-concept for students assigned to these programs. Some colleges have adopted alternate designations such as "foundational skills." These distinctions may help students to better adjust to the results of placement tests and course requirements, although there is not much research on this topic. Practically speaking, students usually know that they are in some form of developmental education.

However, we believe the distinction between the terms "remedial" and "developmental" *is* significant. Remedial is defined as "intended to correct, to supply a remedy." This presumes that something is "wrong," and that the student must be held responsible for correcting it. Developmental education does not judge the student or even the educational experiences of the student prior to entering the new learning environment. Instead, it views the current educational process as transformational, taking the student from one state and developing his or her abilities into those of a more capable, self-confident, and resourceful learner. Similarly, the assessment of basic skills programs and services needs to be viewed as developmental. We are not correcting something that is wrong. We are trying to transform the way we provide programs and services to make them more effective in producing the desired outcomes for students.

> *Improvements in basic skills outcomes are likely to be incremental. Appropriate, realistic expectations for change should be established and communicated.*

Too frequently, efforts to identify effective practices in basic skills resemble the search for a "magic pill": a practice or set of practices that will completely change the outcomes of developmental education and instantly produce radically improved outcomes using standard measures of success, such as pass rates or subsequent course success rates. However, the research on successful practice suggests that, in general, changes in success rates are usually incremental. Studies commonly report increases of 5–15% as an indication of success. They advocate building on these incremental changes over a long period of time to improve the long-range success measures of program completion, degree attainment, and transfer. Therefore, it is not reasonable to expect that any combination of the effective practices described in this study will create large changes in success rates in a short period of time.

However, the literature does show that sustained efforts over extended periods of time do transform institutions, and student success rates do improve over time. It is crucial that colleges as well as governing bodies (such as trustees, outside evaluators, and legislators) see this work on improving basic skills outcomes as developmental, requiring a long-term investment of coordinated efforts and resources. The number of students coming to community colleges with developmental needs is large (and growing), and incremental improvements can produce significantly larger cohorts of individuals capable of succeeding in subsequent educational, vocational, and personal endeavors.

> *Continued research and documentation of effective practices in basic skills education is essential to facilitating improvements in practice.*

The literature review in this guide spans a broad array of studies conducted over the past thirty years. These studies include primary research, practitioner reports of effective practices, writings reflecting expert opinion, and the findings from prior large-scale meta-analyses of the literature. As noted above, the effective practices cited in this study had to meet the test of evidence of effectiveness based on sound research practice. However, this effort to distinguish the practices that *were* validated by sound research design and valid data from the practices that *were not* adequately supported by evidence has led the project team to develop some observations and caveats about the overall state of research and literature in this area.

A number of studies relied solely on participant surveys or anecdotal reports from practitioners, students, or other stakeholders with little or no outcomes-based measures of effectiveness. Other studies used data-based evidence but did not contain the rigorous scientific controls or strict methodologies that would allow for reasonable validation of the findings.

The project team found that the use of a true experimental research design is rare, largely because of the limitations that researchers and practitioners face conducting research in educational environments. The large body of "good" research reviewed for this project used broadly different methodologies and a wide variety of outcome measures to validate practices. There is not a common set of clearly defined metrics against which all practices can be judged. Therefore, developing a set of effective practices based on sound research and data-based evidence requires a careful analysis and assessment of diverse research methodologies and a variety of outcome measures.

In addition, the literature that attempts to synthesize the varied research and summarize the effective practices for developmental education is becoming dated. Though new studies are continually being produced in a variety of specific areas, more comprehensive efforts to draw summative conclusions about effective practice in the field are not keeping pace with the emerging methodologies, evolving research, and changes in the basic skills populations (the most notable exception being Hunter Boylan's *What Works in Developmental Education*, published in 2002).

Equally important, much of the most significant research happens at the institutional level and either goes unreported or is not readily duplicated to validate its application beyond an individual institution. We must continue to develop the collaboration within and among the community college systems across the United States to share examples of good practice and benefit from individual institutional research.

We must also continue to refine the way we evaluate successful outcomes. Good faith efforts to evaluate effectiveness of various interventions too often fall prey to errors in research design or faulty assumptions regarding the validity of outcome measures. For example, a lack of improvement in student grade point average or course success may result from variability in faculty grading rather than from a particular programmatic innovation's lack of effect. In every analysis, it is important to examine the entire system and any underlying variables that might affect our assessment results. The promotion of effective practices beyond individual colleges requires good research to support the adoption of these practices across institutions.

> *The principles contained in this research have the potential to transform institutional efforts not only in developmental education but also in transfer and occupational programs.*

Although this study focuses primarily upon research and practice in developmental education, the results of this analysis can be applied to a wider range of institutional efforts. The effective practices described in this guide include a broad range of approaches to classroom pedagogy that result in greater student success. As noted above, the students in our basic skills programs become the students in our transfer and occupational programs, and frequently those students are concurrently enrolled in developmental and college-level course work. Equally important, the students who enter our colleges with better preparation for college-level studies are no less in need of the effective instructional methodologies than students entering with weaker skills.

Common sense suggests that some—perhaps many—of the effective practices identified in this study would result in measurable improvements in the outcomes for students at all levels of community college instruction. There should not be artificial barriers between the practices used in developmental, occupational, and transfer education. Because research demonstrates that coordinated and focused faculty and staff development is an essential component in any endeavor to improve instruction, professional development activities related to these effective practices should be extended to include *all* faculty and staff.

Recently, there has been a renewed, vital, and significantly increased commitment to meeting the needs of basic skills students in community colleges. The California Basic Skills Initiative, the stimulus for this study, is part of a larger national recognition of the role that community colleges must play in ensuring not only access to higher education but also success for a broad range of the adult population in attaining educational goals and contributing to the economic and cultural growth of the United States.

This renewed commitment has fostered support at the state and federal levels for expanding the resources necessary for community colleges to meet the needs of all students entering two-year institutions. Community college systems and individual colleges recognize that the improvement of outcomes in developmental education is central to the overall effectiveness of their programs and services. Statewide, regional, and local efforts are bringing together faculty, administrators, and staff as well as statewide leaders within and outside of higher education in much more focused and potentially unified efforts to address effective innovation and improved outcomes. The level of interest and productive activity that this study provoked in California community colleges can and should be duplicated in other states and systems.

This study illustrates that we *can* identify "what works." We have the tools for assessing how well practices work and which students benefit from various innovations. We can even project the long-range fiscal benefits to the institution for putting extra resources "on the front end" to ensure that more students succeed and attain their educational goals. Though some lament the ever-decreasing level of preparation for college-level studies among increasing numbers of our student population, our society cannot afford to ignore the potential for success that we have in postsecondary education. This renewed commitment and concentrated activity marks the beginning of a new chapter in community colleges' efforts to provide a major effective pathway to higher education for *all* students.

Appendix

This brief overview of the California community college system is intended to give the reader a context for understanding the circumstances and conditions that influenced the development of this study and the implementation of the system's Basic Skills Initiative (BSI) at the local and statewide levels. Whole books have been written about the California community colleges, and this brief description is not intended as a complete introduction to the system. It is meant to provide a context so that the reader can adapt the discussion of the effective practices and self-assessment to other community college systems across the United States.

California Community College Mission

As one of the three segments of higher education, California community colleges serve a variety of missions. The primary educational missions are to provide (1) career and technology training to prepare the California workforce; (2) associate degrees with emphases in a broad spectrum of academic and vocational disciplines; (3) transfer preparation for students desiring to transfer to the CSU, UC, or private colleges and universities; (4) lifelong learning for the state's adult population. Whereas each of the other two segments of higher education provide opportunities in all but one of these areas (neither CSU or UC awards associate degrees), the community colleges are the only open-access institutions with a history of state-mandated and legislatively controlled low fees. The base undergraduate fee for full-time students at UC is currently $8,700; at CSU it is approximately $4,800; at CCCs it is $780. When combined with the ancillary costs of housing, transportation, and other related costs of living, the community colleges become the only higher education option that many California students can afford. Because any high school graduate or person over 18 years old can enroll in any California community college without any other form of admissions criteria, community colleges are the most accessible form of higher education in the state.

Local Organization

The California Community Colleges (CCC) is the largest higher educational system in the nation, comprised of 72 districts and 110 colleges serving almost 3 million students per year. Community colleges offer workforce training and basic skills education, prepare students for transfer to four-year institutions, and offer opportunities for personal enrichment and lifelong learning (CCC Chancellor's Office, 2009). Some community college districts are responsible for multiple colleges within a geographic area (with as many as nine colleges in a single district); others are single-college districts, although some single-college districts have multiple campuses. Each district has a publicly elected board of trustees with policy and fiduciary responsibility for all of the colleges within the district.

The district structure for CCCs evolved out of the K–12 school districts across the state. Over time, community colleges established independent status, and the system became an independent component under California's landmark Master Plan, initially adopted in 1960 and periodically reviewed and revised over the last five decades. Most individual colleges have a traditional administrative structure, with chief executive, instructional, student development, financial and administrative services officers, supported by academic and student services deans and/or department chairs. Most multi-college districts have a district organizational structure that mirrors the organizational structure of its colleges (for example, CEO, CIO, CFO, and so on). All of these administrative structures report to the district's board of trustees.

Institutional research is handled in a variety of ways and organized under a number of different offices depending on the nature of the college and the district. The capacity of colleges and districts to support institutional research varies considerably, frequently limited by the number and type of staff and financial resources available for research. Most, but not all, colleges have a research office, some with as few as one researcher, others with a much more robust research capacity supported by specialized staff. In some districts, institutional research is a centralized district responsibility. In other districts, each college has its own research office.

Statewide Organization

California community colleges are part of three independent systems of higher education established in "A Master Plan for Higher Education in California" that includes the California State University system (with 23 campuses currently serving 450,000 students) and the University of California system (with 10 campuses currently serving 220,000 students). The Master Plan stipulates that UC will serve the top 12.5% of students; CSU will serve the top one-third and CCCs will serve all students who are able to benefit regardless of previous academic experience or preparation.

CCCs are probably the most heavily regulated higher education institutions in the United States. Much of the regulation is part of the legislative education code that controls finances, the parameters of programs and services, and certain educational standards. The system is organized under a statewide board of governors, appointed by the state governor, and a chancellor, appointed by the board of governors and approved by the state governor. The board of governors is responsible for a statewide set of regulations, derived from the legislative education code. The chancellor's office (CCCCO) is primarily a regulatory and compliance agency responsible for ensuring that the colleges function within the parameters of the education code and regulations. The CCCCO also advocates for the system at the state and national levels and develops and coordinates various statewide initiatives (such as BSI, several educational technology initiatives, a statewide Management Information System that provides statewide data on CCCs). The organization of the CCCCO mirrors the organization of the districts and colleges with a CEO, CIO, CSSO (student services), and so forth.

Currently, the state funds approximately 90% of each district's operating budget through the annual state legislative budgeting process. Most of that state funding is based on the number of full-time student equivalencies (FTES) within the district using a formula based on "seat time" (known as Weekly Student Contact Hours, or WSCH). The state pays a base amount per (FTES), which varies somewhat by district based on a historical funding model implemented when California passed the landmark Proposition 13 in 1978. Prior to Prop. 13, most of the funding for CCCs came from local property tax assessments imposed by each district's board of trustees. A small portion of real estate taxes continues to support most districts' revenues, along with various state and federal categorical funding (for example, matriculation services, Disabled Students' Programs and Services, Extended Opportunity Programs and Services, and special programs such as the BSI, and so on). The basic apportionment of state funding is tied to another voter-approved proposition, Proposition 98, which mandates that 40% of California's annual general fund budget is allocated to K–14 education. The split between K–12 and CCCs and the total amount required to meet the mandate of Prop. 98 are central to annual budget deliberations in Sacramento. Therefore, CCC budgets are not only subject to the overall health of the state's economy, but also political negotiations within and outside of the CCC system. Funding for facilities is usually allocated through a combination of state funds, raised through statewide bond initiatives and appropriated by the chancellor's office and state department of finance, and local bond initiatives.

Governance

As noted above, the education code regulates many of the policies, procedures, and standards of CCCs, including a significant portion of academic policies. These regulations can be interdependent and have a substantial impact on programs and services as well as efforts toward educational reform. For example, the education code stipulates the level of math and English courses that can be awarded degree-applicable credit, although it also permits virtually unlimited nondegree applicable credit courses in developmental education. However, the education code also limits the total number of units a student may take in basic skills courses to 30 units and, in most cases, stipulates the number of times a student may repeat a course. A similar web of interrelated laws and regulations govern finance, personnel practices, curriculum, support services, and virtually every other aspect of community college operations across the state. Therefore, governance must always be viewed through the prism of these complex and generally restrictive regulations.

Until the passage of Prop. 13 in 1978, the board of governors had little influence over the regulations, programs, and services within the system. Local boards, within the parameters of the education code, exercised considerable authority over their institutions. However, since Prop. 13, the BOG is empowered to interpret the education code through the development of regulations, and much of the overall responsibility for the oversight of the system has been vested in the state chancellor's office under the guidance of the BOG. Though it has been 30 years since the passage of Prop. 13, there is still a tension between the efforts toward creating "a California Community College *system*" and the maintenance of local control by colleges and boards of trustees.

In 1988, the legislature passed a major reform of the CCC governance system designed to remove the historical vestiges of the K–12 system, known as AB 1725 (Assembly Bill 1725). Credentials were replaced with statewide "minimum qualifications" for faculty by discipline. AB 1725 established a "shared governance" system in which Academic Senates share responsibility for the governance of the institution and local boards are required to rely on the advice of faculty for specific academic and professional decision making, including curriculum and academic standards. Generally, Academic Senates represent faculty in institutional decision making with formal delineation of the domains of Senates and collective bargaining units.

A statewide Academic Senate for California Community Colleges (ASCCC), with representatives from each college, recommends policy to the BOG and assumes responsibility for the implementation of initiatives and academic standards. For example, the statewide Basic Skills Initiative grew out of an ASCCC effort to raise and standardize graduation requirements in mathematics and English. The ASCCC, in collaboration with the CCCCO and other statewide constituencies, developed the BSI to facilitate more students attaining the higher-level graduation standards. The ASCCC receives operational funding in the state budget through categorical allocations to the CCCCO.

Student Demographics

With 110 colleges spread out over one of the largest and most diverse states in the United States, California's student demographics vary considerably from college to college. California has many urban, suburban, and rural communities, each with its own population characteristics and educational resources. To illustrate the variance in student populations, Table A.1 shows the demographics for seven colleges, distributed throughout the state. Gender is the only demographic that is fairly similar across all seven colleges, and that demographic still has a 12% point spread among the sample colleges.

Precollegiate English and Mathematics

State regulations establish that the English graduation requirement will be a course equal to the CSU or UC freshman composition course and that any course *more* than one level below that course will be considered basic skills. However, the organization and sequencing of instruction in English varies considerably from college to college, and sometimes even differs among colleges within a single district. The number of developmental English courses ranges from none (for example, only one course below freshman composition) to as many as six courses. At some colleges, reading and writing are taught in separate courses; at others, reading and writing are integrated. At some colleges with separate reading and writing courses, students may completely avoid developmental reading because only the composition courses are required as prerequisites to freshman composition. There is

TABLE A.1

Comparative Demographics for Selected California Community Colleges

		System-Wide	Large Urban	Large Urban	Large Suburban	Medium Suburban	Small Suburban	Small Rural	Small Rural
Age	19 or less	25.2%	15.0%	23.5%	44.2%	23.3%	20.3%	20.4%	23.3%
	20–24	25.8%	26.6%	24.0%	23.6%	20.5%	22.8%	18.3%	20.4%
	25–49	36.7%	47.8%	41.0%	23.0%	37.3%	43.8%	36.2%	32.6%
	Over 49	11.7%	10.6%	11.2%	9.2%	18.9%	13.1%	24.8%	23.7%
	Unknown	0.5%	0.0%	0.0%	0.0%	0.0%	0.0%	0.3%	0.0%
Gender	Male	54.5%	55.1%	59.4%	53.9%	54.6%	62.5%	56.6%	50.6%
	Female	44.4%	44.6%	40.6%	45.5%	45.4%	34.7%	41.5%	48.9%
	Unknown	0.1%	0.3%	0.0%	0.5%	0.1%	2.7%	2.0%	0.5%
Ethnicity	African American	7.5%	8.1%	10.4%	4.5%	3.3%	3.4%	4.6%	3.3%
	American Indian/ Alaskan Native	0.8%	0.6%	0.4%	0.4%	0.4%	0.3%	0.8%	1.9%
	Asian	12.0%	29.5%	14.0%	19.4%	24.9%	7.8%	2.8%	1.0%
	Filipino	3.4%	7.0%	5.4%	4.3%	2.6%	3.9%	7.9%	0.4%
	Hispanic	29.6%	15.2%	42.8%	38.8%	10.9%	40.4%	20.0%	8.7%
	Other Non-White	2.2%	3.0%	1.9%	13.1%	1.9%	1.5%	0.9%	0.4%
	Pacific Islander	0.7%	0.9%	0.3%	0.6%	0.8%	1.6%	0.7%	28.5%
	Unknown/Non-Respondent	9.4%	8.1%	6.2%	4.2%	15.2%	7.9%	14.9%	28.5%
	White Non-Hispanic	34.4%	27.5%	18.6%	14.7%	40.1%	33.1%	47.3%	55.8%

Source: Data Mart and ARCC Report 2009: CCCCO

no clearly established common standard for the freshman composition course, although over time, the individual college's articulation agreements with CSU and UC have created a certain level of common expectations for freshman composition.

However, since these articulation agreements have been developed individually by each college, there is considerable variation in the anticipated outcomes for freshman composition across the system. In addition, there are considerable differences in the methodology and content of both the college-level and precollegiate English sequences. Some colleges maintain a commitment to a traditional literature-based approach to reading, writing, and critical analysis whereas others focus their curriculum on college-success skills with nonfiction reading, analysis, and cross-disciplinary academic writing assignments. Many colleges blend the two approaches.

English as a second language (ESL) is another factor in developmental English programs. Many CCCs have large second language populations—at some institutions as many as 40–50% of the students come from non- or limited-English speaking backgrounds. There is also considerable variation in the organization and sequencing of ESL programs. Some colleges have both credit and noncredit ESL courses. Others offer ESL solely as credit or noncredit. The number of ESL courses in the sequence varies considerably at each college as does the course content. Although there are some statewide and national standards used to compare ESL programs, the actual organization of those programs at each college varies considerably. Some colleges have designated transition points at which students can move into the English reading and writing sequence. Others use their placement testing or some other criteria for determining the student's readiness for English classes. A few colleges have parallel English and ESL sequences including an ESL freshman composition course.

The sequencing of mathematics courses is a little less chaotic than English but still far from standardized. As with freshman composition, the articulation of college-level algebra with UC and CSU has produced a fairly standardized set of expectations for that course. However, the courses leading up to that level vary considerably, especially in the area of computation and basic mathematical reasoning. Not only are there differences in the number of basic computation courses, there is also considerable variation in the instructional methodologies, ranging from entirely self-paced learning with progression to the next level based on competency-based testing to traditional lecture-based course sequencing—and everything in between those two extremes. The course sequence leading up to college algebra also varies from college to college.

Matriculation policies also differ among colleges. State regulations govern the basic elements of matriculation (for example, assessment, counseling, and the like). However, the regulations allow colleges latitude in the application of matriculation rules, and frequently students can easily maneuver around the college's policies and procedures, especially if they avoid taking the courses in the English and mathematics sequences. Though the matriculation procedures provide for counseling and academic planning, there is no required accountability for tracking students' progress through their academic plan and no forced intervention for students who are not making adequate progress, short of state-mandated academic probation based on GPA or the proportion of courses from which a student has withdrawn after registering. The ratios of students to counselors (sometimes as high as 1,400 to 1) shifts the responsibility for accountability almost entirely to the student, many of whom are ill-prepared for that responsibility. Since most colleges do not have prerequisites on discipline-based courses and enrollment in courses is open to any student, students can continue to matriculate without ever addressing their developmental skills needs. Although a relatively small percentage of these students eventually do take and progress through the developmental course sequences to complete the college-level math and English, many more get caught in a pattern of failure or find they cannot balance their academic responsibilities with their personal circumstances (such as family, work, and so on); they drop out. Some of these students become "stop-outs," leaving college for a period and returning, but still avoiding the developmental curriculum when they reenroll.

Going Forward

Increasing calls for accountability, challenging budgetary times, and a growing recognition of the role that community colleges play in the state's social and economic health continue to focus on improving developmental education and the relationship between basic skills and educational goal attainment. Recently there have been calls for restricting the access that "underprepared" students have to college-level courses and programs. These calls range from requiring every student to demonstrate college-level English and mathematics competencies *before* taking any college-level course to establishing some type of "basic skills floor" for certain college-level courses to ensure the academic rigor of those courses. There is an emerging recognition that open-access and educational opportunity must be balanced with the expectation that students in college-level courses and programs are required to use college-level reading, writing, mathematical, and critical-thinking skills. It is not clear whether this will lead to a great integration of basic and college-level skills across the curriculum and support services or a greater segregation of students in developmental education from students in degree-applicable programs and services. Equally important, the state is focusing seriously on the role of basic skills in career and technical education and the impact that these skills have on students' long-range career and economic attainment.

References

Abdal-Haqq, I. (1994). Culturally responsive curriculum. *ERIC Digest.* (ERIC Document Reproduction Service No. ED370936).

Academic Senate for California Community Colleges. (2000, April). *The state of basic skills instruction in California Community Colleges.* (ERIC Document Reproduction Service No. ED447876).

Academic Senate for California Community Colleges. (2000, Spring). *Faculty development: A senate issue.* (ERIC Document Reproduction Service No. ED445755).

Academic Senate for California Community Colleges. (2003). *A survey of effective practices in basic skills.* (ERIC Document Reproduction Service No. ED479522).

Academic Senate for California Community Colleges. (2004, Fall). *Issues in basic skills assessment and placement in the California Community Colleges.*

Adelman, C. (2004). *Principal indicators of student academic histories in postsecondary education, 1972–2000.* Washington, DC: U.S. Department of Education, Institute of Educational Sciences. (ERIC Document Reproduction Service No. ED483154).

American Educational Research Association. (2004, Winter). English language learners: Boosting academic achievement. *Research Points: Essential Information for Education Policy, 2*(1), 1–4.

American Educational Research Association. (2006, July 1). *Review of Educational Research—Submissions Update.* Retrieved December 19, 2006, from www.aera .net/publications/?id=505.

American Mathematical Association of Two-Year Colleges (AMATYC). (2006). *Beyond crossroads: Implementing mathematics standards in the first two years of college.* Memphis, TN. Retrieved December 20, 2006, from www.bc.amatyc.org/index.html.

Anderson, J. (1988). Cognitive styles and multicultural populations. *Journal of Teacher Education, 39*(1), 2–9. (ERIC Document Reproduction Service No. EJ374357).

Angelo, T. A. (1991, Summer). Classroom research: Early lessons for success. Introduction and overview: From classroom assessment to classroom research. *New Directions for Teaching and Learning, 46,* 7–16.

Angelo, T A. (1994, June). From faculty development to academic development. *AAHE Bulletin.*

Angelo, T. A., & Cross, K. P. (1993). *Classroom assessment techniques: A handbook for college teachers.* San Francisco: Jossey-Bass.

Arendale, D. (1997a). *Bridging the gap of teaching and learning.* Speech given at the annual conference of the National Association for Developmental Education.

Arendale, D. (1997b). Supplemental instruction (SI): Review of research concerning the effectiveness of SI from the University of Missouri-Kansas City and other institutions from across the United States. *Proceedings of the 17th and 18th Annual Institutes for Learning Assistance Professionals: 1996 and 1997* (pp. 1–25). Tucson, AZ: University Learning Center. Retrieved December 20, 2006, from www.pvc.maricopa.edu/%7Elsche/proceedings/967_proc_arendale.htm.

Armington, T. C. (2003). Environmental barriers to student success. In T. Armington (Ed.), *Best practices in developmental mathematics* (2nd ed.). NADE Mathematics Special Professional Interest Network. Retrieved December 20, 2006, from www.etsu.edu/devstudy/spin/bestpractices.htm.

Ashwin, P. (2003). Peer support: Relations between the context, process, and outcomes for the students who are supported. *Instructional Science, 31,* 159–173.

Astin, A. W. (1985). Involvement: The cornerstone of excellence. *Change 17*(4), 35–39.

Bailey, T. (2003, January). *Community colleges in the 21st century: Challenges and opportunities.* (CCRC Brief). New York: Community College Research Center, Teachers College, Columbia University.

Bailey, T., Alfonso, M., Calcagno, J., Jenkins, D., Keigl, G., & Leinbach, T. (2004). *Improving student attainment in community colleges: Institutional characteristics and policies.* New York: Community College Research Center, Teachers College, Columbia University.

Baker, E. D., Hope, L., & Karandjeff, K. (2009). *Contextualized teaching & learning: A faculty primer.* Sacramento, CA: Statewide Academic Senate.

Baker, L. (1989). Metacognition, comprehension monitoring, and the adult reader. *Educational Psychology Review, 1,* 3–38.

Bandura, A. (1989). Regulation of cognitive processes through perceived self-efficacy. *Developmental Psychology, 25*(5), 729–35.

Banks, J. A. (ed.). (2004). *Handbook of research on multicultural education* (2nd ed.). San Francisco: Jossey-Bass.

Banks, J. A., McGee, B., & Cherry, A. (2001). *Multicultural education and perspectives* (4th ed.). New York: Wiley.

Barkley, E. F., Cross, K. P., & Major, C. H. (2005). *Collaborative learning techniques: A handbook for college faculty.* San Francisco: Jossey-Bass.

Baron, W. (1997). *The problem of student retention: The Bronx Community College solution—the freshman year initiative program.* New York: Bronx Community College of the City University of New York. (ERIC Document Reproduction Service No. ED409971).

Beatty-Guenter, P. (1994, March/April). Sorting, supporting, connecting, and transforming: Retention strategies at community colleges. *Community College Journal of Research and Practice, 18*(2), 113–29. (ERIC Document Reproduction Service No. EJ479903).

Belcher, J., & Glyer-Culver, B. (1998). *Trends in teaching and learning innovation.* Sacramento, CA: Los Rios Community College District. (ERIC Document Reproduction Service No. 414988).

Beno, B., Smith, C., DeVol, M., & Stetson, N. (2003). *Evaluating staff and organization development.* Sacramento, CA: California Community Council for Staff & Organizational Development and Community College League of California.

Berlin, L. N. (2005). *Contextualizing college ESL praxis: A participatory approach to effective instruction.* Mahwah, NJ: Erlbaum.

Berns, R., & Erickson, P. (2001). *Contextual Teaching and Learning: Preparing Students for the New Economy. The Highlight Zone: Research @ Work No. 5.* National Dissemination Center for Career and Technical Education. Retrieved from ERIC database.

Berquist, W. H., & Philips, S. R. (1975). Components of an effective faculty development program. *Journal of Higher Education, 46,* 177–211.

Bettinger, E. (2004). How financial aid affects persistence (Working paper #10242). Cambridge, MA: National Bureau of Economic Research.

Bettinger, E. P., & Long, B. T. (2005). Remediation at the community college: Student participation and outcomes. *New Directions for Community Colleges, 129,* 17–26.

Biggs, J. (1994). Student learning research and theory: Where do we currently stand? In G. Gibbs (Ed.), *Improving student learning: Theory and practice.* Oxford: Oxford Centre for Staff Development. Retrieved October 15, 2006, from www .city.londonmet.ac.uk/deliberations/ocsd-pubs/isltp-biggs.html.

Blackburn, R. T., Boberg, A., O'Connel, C., & Pellino, G. (1980). *Project for faculty development program evaluation: Final report.* Ann Arbor: Center for the Study of Higher Education, University of Michigan. (ERIC Document Reproduction Service No. ED208767).

Bland, R. G., & Schmitz, C. C. (1990). An overview of research on faculty and institutional vitality. In J. H. Schuster, D. W. Wheeler, & Associates, *Enhancing faculty careers: Strategies for development and renewal.* San Francisco: Jossey-Bass.

Bloom, D., & Sommo, C. (2005). *Building learning communities: Early results from the opening doors demonstration at Kingsborough Community College.* New York: Manpower Demonstration Research Corporation.

Boaler, J. (1998). Alternative approaches to teaching, learning and assessing mathematics. *Evaluation and Program Planning, 21*(2), 129–141.

Board of Governors of the California Community Colleges. (2008). Report of the System's Current Programs in English as a Second Language (ESL) and Basic Skills. Retrieved December 3, 2009, from http://www.cccco.edu/Portals/4/Executive/Board/2008_agendas/january/7-1_Basic%20skills%20report%2012-19-07%20%283%29.pdf

Bond, L. (2004). Using contextual instruction to make abstract learning concrete. *Techniques: Connecting Education and Careers, 79*(1), 30–33.

Borko, H. (2005). Professional development and teacher learning: Mapping the terrain. *Educational Researcher, 33*(8), 3–15.

Boroch, D., Fillpot, J., Gabriner, R., Hope, L., Johnstone, R., Mery, P., et al. (2007). *Basic skills as a foundation for student success in California Community Colleges.* Berkeley, CA: Research and Planning Group Center for Student Success.

Bosworth, K. (1994). Developing collaborative skills in college students. In K. Bosworth & S. Hamilton (Eds.), *Collaborative learning: Underlying processes and effective techniques.* San Francisco: Jossey-Bass.

Bothern, T. S., & Wambach, C. A. (Winter, 2004). Refocusing developmental education. *Journal of Developmental Education, 28*, 2.

Bottoms, G., & Young, M. (2008). *Lost in transition: Building a better path from school to college and careers.* Atlanta: Southern Regional Education Board.

Bourdon, C., & Carducci, R. (2002). *What works in the community colleges: A synthesis of literature on best practices.* Los Angeles: UCLA Graduate School of Education. (ERIC Document Reproduction Service No. ED471397).

Bowles, T. J., & Jones, J. (2003). An analysis of the effectiveness of supplemental instruction: The problem of selection bias and limited dependent variables. *Journal of College Student Retention 5*(2), 235–243.

Boyer, E. L. (1990). *Scholarship reconsidered: Priorities of the professoriate.* Princeton, NJ: Carnegie Foundation for the Advancement of Teaching.

Boylan, H. (1983, January). *Is developmental education working? An analysis of research.* (Rep. No. 2). Chicago: National Association for Remedial-Developmental Studies in Postsecondary Education. (ERIC Document Reproduction Service No. ED238471).

Boylan, H. (2002). *What works: Research-based best practices in developmental education.* Boone, NC: Appalachian State University, Continuous Quality Improvement Network with the National Center for Developmental Education.

Boylan, H., Bliss, L., & Bonham, B. (1997). Program components and their relationship to student performance. *Journal of Developmental Education, 20*(3).

Boylan, H., Bonham, B., Claxton, C., & Bliss, L. (1992, November). *The state of the art in developmental education: Report of a national study.* Paper presented at the First National Conference on Research in Developmental Education, Charlotte, NC.

Boylan, H., Bonham, B., & Rodriguez, L. (2000, March). What are remedial courses and do they work: Results of national and local studies. *Learning Assistance Review, 5*(1), 5–14. (ERIC Document Reproduction Service No. EJ608522).

Boylan, H., Bonham, B., White, R., & George, A. (2000). Evaluation of college reading and study strategies programs. In R. Flippo & D. Caverly (Eds.), *Handbook of college reading and study strategy research* (pp. 365–402). Mahwah, NJ: Erlbaum.

Boylan, H., & Saxon, D. (1998). *An evaluation of developmental education in Texas public colleges and universities.* Austin: Texas Higher Education Coordinating Board.

Boylan, H., & Saxon, D. (2002). *What works in remediation: Lessons from 30 years of research.* Prepared for the League for Innovation in the Community College.

Boylan, H., Sutton, E., & Anderson, J. (2003, Fall). Diversity as a resource in developmental education. *Journal of Developmental Education, 27*(1), 12.

Bransford, J., & Brown, A. L. (2000). *How people learn: Brain, mind, experience, and school: Expanded edition.* Washington, DC: National Research Council, Committee on Learning Research and Educational Practice.

Brawer, F. B. (1990, Summer). Faculty development: The literature. *Community College Review, 18*(1).

Braxton, J. M. (2006, June). *Faculty professional choices in teaching that foster student success.* Paper presented at the annual meeting of National Postsecondary Education Cooperative, Washington, DC.

Braxton, J. M., Sullivan, A. S., & Johnson, R. T. (1997). Appraising Tinto's theory of college student departure. In J. C. Smart (Ed.), *Higher Education: Handbook of Theory and Research,* Vol. 12, pp. 107–158. New York: Agathon.

Bray, C. (1985). Early identification of dropout prone students and early intervention strategies to improve student retention at a private university. *Dissertation Abstracts International 45*(07A), 1990.

Brock, T., Jenkins, D., Ellwein, T., Miller, J., Gooden, S., Martin, K., et al. (2007, May). *Building a culture of evidence for community college student success: Early progress in the Achieving the Dream Initiative.* New York: Manpower Demonstration Research Corporation. (ERIC Document Reproduction Service No. ED496977).

Brock, T., & Richburg-Hayes, L. (2006, May). *Paying for persistence: Early results of a Louisiana scholarship program for low-income parents attending community college.* New York: Manpower Demonstration Research Corporation. (ERIC Document Reproduction Service No. ED491719).

Brookfield, S. D. (2002, Summer). Using the lenses of critically reflective teaching in the community college classroom. *New Directions for Community Colleges, 118,* 31–38.

Brothen, T., & Wambach, C. A. (2004). Refocusing developmental education, *Journal of Developmental Education, 28*(2).

Burdman, P. (2001, December 6). Fulfilling their potential: Faced with demanding course work and a competitive campus climate, wise students see need to utilize academic support services. *Black Issues in Higher Education.* Retrieved September 30, 2009, from http://findarticles.com/p/articles/mi_m0DXK/is_21_18/ai_81105665/.

Burns, M. (1994). A study to formulate a learning assistance model for the California Community College. In S. Mioduski & G. Enright (Eds.), *Proceedings of the 13th and 14th Annual Institutes for Learning Assistance Professionals: 1992 AND 1993* (pp. 20–23). Tucson: University Learning Center, University of Arizona. Retrieved October 3, 2006, from www.pvc.maricopa.edu/~lsche/proceedings/923_proc/923proc_burns.htm.

California Community College Board of Governors (September 2002). *Basic Skills: A Report 6.2.*

California State Postsecondary Education Commission. (1988, March). *State policy for faculty development in higher education: A report to the governor and legislature in response to supplemental language in the 1986 Budget Act.* (Rep. 88–17). Sacramento, CA. (ERIC Document Reproduction Service No. ED297655).

Carino, P. (1995). What do we talk about when we talk about our metaphors: A cultural critique of clinic, lab, and center. In C. Murphy and J. Law (Eds.), *Landmark essays on writing centers* (pp. 37–46). Davis, CA: Hermagoras.

Carnegie Foundation for the Advancement of Teaching. (2008). *Basic skills for complex lives: Designs for learning in the community college.* Stanford, CA: Strengthening Pre-collegiate Education in Community Colleges (SPECC).

Carnevale, A., & Desrochers, D. (1999, March). Getting down to business: Matching welfare recipients' skills to jobs that train. *Policy & Practice of Public Human Services, 57*(1), 18.

Cartnal, R., & Hagen, P. (1999, June). *Evaluation of the Early Alert Program, Spring 1999.* San Luis Obispo, CA: Cuesta College. (ERIC Document Reproduction Service No. ED441541).

Casazza, M. E. (1996). Confirming a professional identity and a philosophy for practice. *Research and Teaching in Developmental Education, 12*(2).

Casazza, M. E., & Silverman, S. (1996). *Learning assistance and developmental education: A guide for effective practice.* San Francisco: Jossey-Bass.

Castator, M. M., & Tollefson, N. (1996). Underprepared students and the college curriculum: Identifying high-risk courses. *Journal of Applied Research in Community College, 3*(2), 179–200.

Caverly, D. C. (1994). Technology and the learning assistance center. In S. Mioduski and G. Enright (Eds.), *Proceedings of the 15th and 16th Annual Institutes for Learning Assistance Professionals*. Tucson: University Learning Center, University of Arizona. Retrieved January 12, 2007, from www.pvc.maricopa.edu/~lsche/proceedings/945_proce/945proc_caverly.htm.

Centra, J. (1975, January). Colleagues as raters of classroom instruction. *Journal of Higher Education*. (ERIC Document Reproduction Service No. EJ117807).

Centra, J. (1978, January). Types of faculty development programs. *Journal of Higher Education*. (ERIC Document Reproduction Service No. EJ178030).

Chaffee, J. (1992). Teaching critical thinking across the curriculum. *New Directions for Community College, 77,* 25–35. San Francisco: Jossey-Bass.

Chickering, A. W., & Gamson, Z. (Eds.). (1991). *Applying the seven principles for good practice in undergraduate education*. San Francisco: Jossey-Bass.

Choitz, V., & Widom, R. (2003, July). *Money matters: How financial aid affects nontraditional students in community colleges*. New York: Manpower Demonstration Research Corporation. Retrieved December 16, 2006, from www.mdrc.org/publications/348/abstract.html.

Chung, C. J. (2005, Spring). Theory, practice, and the future of developmental education. *Journal of Developmental Education. 28*(3), 2–33.

Clark, S. M., Corcoran, M. E., & Lewis, D. R. (1989). Faculty renewal and change. In G. G. Lozier & M. J. Dooris (Eds.), Managing faculty resources. *New Directions for Institutional Research, 16,* 19–32. San Francisco: Jossey-Bass.

Clegg, S., Bradley, S., & Smith, K. (2006, May). I've had to swallow my pride: Help seeking and self-esteem. *Higher Education Research and Development, 25(2),* 101–113. (ERIC Document Reproduction Service No. EJ736206).

Cohen, D., & Hill, H. C. (2001). *Learning policy: When state education reform works*. New Haven: Yale University Press.

Collay, M., Dunlap, D., Enloe, W., & Gagnon, G. W. (1998). *Learning circles: Creating conditions for professional development*. Thousand Oaks, CA: Corwin Press.

Community College Survey of Student Engagement (CCSSE). (2006). *Act on fact: Using data to improve student success. National report of results*. Austin: The University of Texas at Austin, Community College Leadership Program. Retrieved January 2, 2007, from www.ccsse.org.

Community College Survey of Student Engagement (CCSSE). (2007). *Committing to student engagement: Reflections on CCSSE's first five years*. Austin: The University of Texas at Austin, Community College Leadership Program. Retrieved September 29, 2009, from www.ccsse.org/publications/2007NatlRpt-final.pdf.

Community College Survey of Student Engagement (CCSSE). (2008). High expectations and high support. Austin: The University of Texas at Austin, Community

College Leadership Program. Retrieved September 29, 2009, from www.ccsse.org./publications/2008_National_Report.pdf.

Condelli, L. (2004). *Effective instruction for adult ESL literacy students: Findings from the What Works Study.* Washington, DC: American Institute for Research. Retrieved January 2007, from www.nrdc.org.uk/uploads/documents/doc_54.pdf.

Condelli, L., & Wrigley, H. S. (2004). *Instruction, language and literacy: What Works Study for adult ESL literacy students.* Washington, DC: American Institute for Research.

Condravy, J. C. (1995). Learning together: An interactive approach to tutor training. In M. Maxwell (Ed.), *From access to success: A book of readings on college developmental education and learning assistance programs* (pp. 77–79). Clearwater, FL: H & H.

Cooper, L. (1979). An Interview with Terry O'Banion. *Journal of Developmental & Remedial Education, 3*(2): 14–15.

Craven, G. (1987, January). Science and developmental education. *New Directions for Community Colleges.* (ERIC Document Reproduction Service No. EJ352937).

Cronen, S., Silver-Pacuilla, H., & Condelli, L. (2004). *Conducting large-scale research in adult ESL: Challenges and approaches for the explicit literacy impact study.* Washington, DC: American Institutes for Research.

Cross, K. P. (1976). *Accent on learning.* San Francisco: Jossey-Bass.

Cross. K. P. (2001). *Motivation: Er . . . will that be on the test?* (The Cross Papers 5). Phoenix, AZ: League for Innovation in the Community College.

Cross, K. P. (2005). *What do we know about students' learning and how do we know it?* Berkeley, CA: Center for Studies in Higher Education. Retrieved November 19, 2006, from http://respositories.cdlib.org/cshe/CSHE-7–05.

Cross, K. P., & Steadman, M. H. (1996). *Classroom research: Implementing the scholarship of teaching.* San Francisco: Jossey-Bass.

Damashek, R. (1999, Winter). Reflections on the future of developmental education part II. *Journal of Developmental Education.* Retrieved October 12, 2006, from www.ncde.appstate.edu/reserve_reading/V23dmashek_reflections.htm.

Damasio, A. R. (1994). *Descartes' error: Emotion, reason, and the human brain.* New York: Grosset/Putnam.

DePree, J. (1998). Small-group instruction: Impact on basic algebra students. *Journal of Developmental Education 22*(1), 2–4.

Desimone, L. M., Porter, A. C., Garet, M. S., Yoon, K. S., & Birman, B. F. (2002). Effects of professional development on teachers' instruction: Results from a three-year longitudinal study. *Education Evaluation and Policy Analysis, 24*(2), 81–112.

Dorlac, A. (1994, March). Implementing holistic approaches in the community college reading center. *Proceedings of the Fountains of Opportunity, National Association for Developmental Education Annual Conference, Kansas City, MO,* (pp. 6–8).

Duranczyk, I., Goff, E., & Opitz, D. (2006, March). Students' experiences in learning centers: Socioeconomic factors, grades, and perceptions of the math center. *Journal of College Reading and Learning, 36*(2), 39–49. (ERIC Document Reproduction Service No. EJ742213).

Dvorak, J. (2001). The college tutoring experience: A qualitative study. *Learning Assistance Review, 6*(2), 33–46.

Eble, K. (1985, January). Educating Ritas: A different kind of competence. *Educational Horizons.* (ERIC Document Reproduction Service No. EJ319482).

Eble, K. (1985, September). Reaching out: A positive source of faculty morale. *Change, 17*(4), 44. (ERIC Document Reproduction Service No. EJ325456).

Eble, K., & McKeachie, W. (1985, January). Improving undergraduate education through faculty development: An analysis of effective programs and practices. (ERIC Document Reproduction Service No. ED266746).

Eimers, M. (2000, May). Assessing the impact of the Early Alert Program. *AIR 2000 Annual Forum Paper.* (ERIC Document Reproduction Service No. ED446511).

Elbow, P. (1999). Using the collage for collaborative writing. In J. Bernstein (Ed.), *Teaching developmental writing* (pp. 250–257). New York: St. Martin's Press.

Elbow, P. (2004) Writing, first! Putting writing before reading is an effective approach to teaching and learning. *Educational Leadership, 62*(2), 8–13.

Evans, R. (2001). *The human side of school change,* San Francisco: Jossey Bass.

Ferren, A. S. (1996). Achieving effectiveness and efficiency. In J. G. Gaff, J. L. Ratcliff, & Associates, *Handbook of undergraduate curriculum* (pp. 533–557). San Francisco: Jossey-Bass.

Fink, L. (2003). *Creating significant learning experiences.* San Francisco: Jossey Bass.

Fink, L. (2005, June). Creating significant learning experiences: An integrated approach to designing college courses. *Journal of Chemical Education, 82*(6), 819.

Florida Department of Education. (2006, November). *Taking student life skills courses increases academic success.* (Data Trend #31). Tallahassee: Office of the Chancellor, Florida Community Colleges and Workforce Education.

Forget, M., Lyle, N., Spear, M., & Reinhart-Clark, K. (2003, May). *Getting all teachers to use reading/writing to help students learn subject matter.* (ERIC Document Reproduction Service No. ED479376).

Gaff, J. G. (1975). *Toward faculty renewal.* San Francisco: Jossey-Bass.

Gale, C. (2001, May/June). *Going it alone: Supporting Writing Across the Curriculum (WAC) when there is no WAC program.* Presented at the National Writing Across the Curriculum Conference, Bloomington, IN.

Garet, M., Porter, A. C., Desimone, L., Birman, B., & Yoon, K. (2001) What makes professional development effective? Analysis of a national sample of teachers. *American Educational Research Journal 38,* 915–945.

Gay, G. (2000, January). Culturally responsive teaching: Theory, research, and practice. *Multicultural Education Series.* (ERIC Document Reproduction Service No. ED441932).

Gerlach, J. (1994, Fall). Is this collaboration? *New Directions for Teaching & Learning,*

Gerlaugh, K., Thompson, L., Boylan, H., & Davis, H. (2007). National study of developmental education II: Baseline data for community colleges. *Research in Developmental Education, 20*(4), 1–4.

Gier, T., & Hancock, K. (2006). Tutor Training: An examination of community college programs in the United States. In S. Mioduski & G. Enright (Eds.), *Proceedings of the 13th and 14th Annual Institutes for Learning Assistance Professionals: 1992 AND 1993.* Tucson: University Learning Center, University of Arizona. Retrieved October 15, 2006, from www.pvc.maricopa.edu/%7Elsche/proceedings/923 _proc/proc/923_gier.htm.

Glenn, D. (2007). Study finds mix of academic and financial aid improves student retention, *Chronicle of Higher Education, (53)*19.

Glennen, R. E., & Baxley, D. M. (1985). Reduction of attrition through intrusive advising, *NASPA Journal, (22)*3, 10 -14.

Goldstein, M., & Perin, D. (2008). Predicting performance in a community college-area course from academic skill level. *Community College Review, 36*(2), 89–115.

Goolsby, C. B., Dwinell, P. L., Higbee, J. L., & Bretscher, A. S. (1994). Factors affecting mathematics achievement in high risk college students. In M. Maxwell (Ed.), *From access to success: What works best in college learning assistance* (pp. 253–259). Clearwater, FL: H & H.

Gottshall, D. B. (1993). *The history and nature of the national great teachers movement.* Glen Ellyn, IL: College of DuPage.

Gourgey, A. (1994). Tutoring Practices that Promote Cognitive and Affective Development. In M. Maxwell (Ed.), *From access to success: A book of readings on college developmental education and learning assistance programs.* Clearwater, FL: H & H.

Goswami, U. (2008). *Neuroscience and education. Jossey-Bass reader on the brain and learning.* San Francisco: Jossey-Bass.

Grant, M., & Keim, M. (2002, December). Faculty development in publicly supported two-year colleges. *Community College Journal of Research & Practice, 26*(10), 793–807.

Greenleaf, C., Schoenbach, R., Cziko, C., & Mueller, F. (2001, Spring). Apprenticing adolescent readers to academic literacy. *Harvard Educational Review, 71*(1), 79.

Grodsky E., & Gamoran, A. (2003). The relationship between professional development and professional community in American schools. *School Effectiveness and School Improvement 14*(1), 1–29

Grossman, P., Schoenfeld, A. & Lee, C. (2005). Teaching subject matter. In L. Darling-Hammond & J. Bransford, *Preparing teachers for a changing world* (pp. 201–231). San Francisco: Jossey-Bass.

Grosso de Leon, A. (2002). *The urban high school's challenge: Ensuring literacy for every child.* New York: Carnegie Corporation of New York. (www.carnegie.org)

Grubb, W. N. (1999). *Honored but invisible: An inside look at teaching community colleges.* New York: Routledge.

Grubb, W. N. (2001). *Basic principles for basic skills: Criteria for exemplary approaches in community colleges.* Berkeley: University of California, Community College Cooperative.

Gusky, T. R. (1994, April). *Outcome-based education and mastery learning: Clarifying the differences.* Paper presented at the annual meeting of the American Educational Research Association, New Orleans, LA.

Haehl, M. (2003). Reading? In a math class? In T. Armington (Ed.), *Best practices in developmental mathematics* (2nd ed., pp. 31–33). NADE Mathematics Special Professional Interest Network. Retrieved December 20, 2006, from www.etsu.edu/devstudy/spin/bestpractices.htm.

Hallinan, M. (2003). Ability grouping and student learning. *Brookings Papers on Education Policy*, 95–124. Retrieved October 27, 2006, from http://muse.jhu.edu/journals/brookings_papers_on_education_policy/v2003/2003.1hallinan.html.

Harnish, C. A., & Creamer. D. G. (1986). Faculty stagnation and diminished job involvement. *Community College Review, 13*(3), 33–39.

Hartman, H. J. (1993). *Intelligent tutoring.* Clearwater, FL: H & H.

Haviland, C. P., Frye, C., & Colby, R. (2001). The politics of administrative and physical location. In J. Nelson & K. Evertz (Eds.), *The politics of writing centers* (pp. 15–22). Portsmouth, NH: Boynton/Cook.

Haycock, K. (2006, August). Promise abandoned: How policy choices and institutional practices restrict college opportunities. *The Education Trust.* Retrieved September 29, 2009, from www.education.ky.gov/users/otl/sec_res_cd/national%20research/PromiseAbandonedHigherEd.pdf.

Heisserer, D., & Parette, P. (2002, March). Advising at-risk students in college and university settings. *College Student Journal, 36*(1), 69–84.

Hennessey, J. (1990). At-risk community college students and a reading improvement course: A longitudinal study. *Journal of Reading, 34*(2), 114–20.

Hensen, K. A., & Shelley, M. C. (2003). The impact of supplemental instruction: Results from a large, public, Midwestern University. *Journal of College Student Development, 44*, 250–259.

Higbee, J. L. (1995). Misplaced priorities or alternative developmental opportunities: A case study. *Research & Teaching in Developmental Education, 11*(2), 79–84.

Higbee, J. L., & Thomas, P. V. (1999). Affective and cognitive factors related to mathematics achievement. *Journal of Developmental Education 23*(1), 8–14.

Hirshfield, C. (1984). The classroom quality circle: A widening role for students. *Innovation Abstracts. 6*(12), 1–2. (ERIC Document Reproduction Service No. ED 256383).

Huber, M T., & Sherwyn, P. M. (Eds.) (2002). *Disciplinary styles in the scholarship of teaching and learning: Exploring common ground.* Washington, DC: American Association for Higher Education and The Carnegie Foundation for the Advancement of Teaching.

Husain, S. P. (2008). Sense member profile: Broward Community College Fort Lauderdale, Florida [Special issue]. *Talking Sense* (pp. 1–2). Retrieved September 30, 2009, from www.ccsse.org/sense/aboutSENSE/Talking_SENSE/Broward %20CC%20Talking%20SENSE%20Profile.pdf.

Hutchings, P., & Shulman, L. S. (1999). The scholarship of teaching: New elaborations, new developments. *Change, 31,* 10–15.

Hutchings, P. (Ed.) (2000). *Opening lines: Approaches to the scholarship of teaching and learning.* Menlo Park, CA: The Carnegie Foundation for the Advancement of Teaching.

Illowsky, B. (2008, Winter). The California Basic Skills Initiative. In P. Schuetz & J. Barr (Eds.), *New directions for community colleges: Are community colleges underprepared for underprepared students?* San Francisco: Jossey-Bass.

Intersegmental Committee of the Academic Senates (ICAS). (2002, Spring). *Academic literacy: A statement of competencies expected of students entering California's public colleges and universities.* Sacramento: California Community Colleges, the California State University System, and the University of California. Retrieved on September 27, 2009, from www.asccc.org/Publications/Papers/ AcademicLiteracy/main.htm.

Inverson, L., Meirs, M., & Beavis, A., (2005). Factors affecting the impact of professional development programs on teachers' knowledge, practice and student outcomes & efficacy. *Education Policy Analysis 13*(10).

Irwin, D. E. (1980). Effects on peer tutoring on academic achievement and affective adjustment. In G. Enright (Ed.), *Proceedings of the Thirteenth Annual Conference of the Western College Reading Association* (pp. 42–45).

Jacoby, D. (2006). Effects of part-time faculty employment on community college graduation rates. *The Journal of Higher Education 77*(6), 1081–1103.

Jenkins, D. (2006). *What community college management practices are effective in promoting student success? A study of high- and low-impact institutions.* New York: Community College Research Center, Teachers College, Columbia University.

Jensen, E. (2005). *Teaching with the brain in mind* (2nd ed.). Alexandria, VA: Association for Supervision & Curriculum Development.

Johnstone, R. (2004, Fall). Community college research across California: Findings, implications, and the future. *IJournal: Insight into Student Services, 9.*

Jonassen, D., & Grabowski, B. (1993). *Handbook of individual differences, learning, and instruction.* Hillsdale, NJ: Erlbaum.

Jordan, M., & Schoenbach, R. (2003, December). Breaking through the literacy ceiling. *Leadership,* pp. 8–13.

Kane, M., & Henderson, F. (2006). Hartnell College's academic learning center: Recommitting to underrepresented student access and success. *Community College Journal of Research & Practice, 30*(2), 133–134.

Karabenick, S. (2004, September). Perceived achievement goal structure and college student help seeking. *Journal of Educational Psychology, 96*(3), 569–581. (ERIC Document Reproduction Service No. EJ685016).

Kennedy, M. (1998). Education reform and subject matter knowledge. *Journal of Research in Science Teaching, 35*(3), 249–263.

Kennedy, M. (2002). Knowledge and teaching. *Teachers & Teaching, 8*(3/4), 355–370.

Kiemig, R. (1983). *Raising academic standards: A guide to learning improvement,* (ASHE/ERIC Research Report #1). Washington, DC: Association for the Study of Higher Education.

King, P. M., & VanHecke, J. R. (2006). Making connections: Using skill theory to recognize how students build and rebuild understanding. *About Campus 11*(1), 10–16.

Kisker, C., & Outcalt, C. (2005, January). Community college honors and developmental faculty: Characteristics, practices, and implications for access and educational equity. *Community College Review, 33*(2), 1–21. (ERIC Document Reproduction Service No. EJ751691).

Kleinbeck, U., Quast, H., & Schwarz, R. (1989). Volitional effects on performance: Conceptual considerations and results from dual-task studies. In P. Kanfer, L. Ackerman, & R. Cudeck (Eds.), *Abilities, motivation, and methodology: The Minnesota symposium on learning and individual differences.* Hillsdale, NJ: Erlbaum.

Knowledgeloom. (2006). *Culturally responsive teaching.* Providence, RI: Brown University, The Education Alliance. Retrieved September 29, 2009, from http://knowledgeloom.org/crt/index.jsp.

Koeler, L. (1987). Helping students to succeed: A report on tutoring and attrition at the University of Cincinnati. (ERIC Document Reproduction No. ED290370).

Kozeracki, C. A. (2002). ERIC Review: Issues in developmental education. *Community College Review, 29*(4), 83–100.

Kozeracki, C. A. (2005). Preparing faculty to meet the needs of developmental students. *New Directions for Community Colleges, 129,* 39–49.

Kozeracki, C., & Brooks, J. (2006). Emerging institutional support for developmental education. *New Directions for Community Colleges, 136,* 63–73.

Kuh, G. D., Kinzie, J., Buckley, J., Bridges, B., & Hayek, J. (2006a). What matters to student success: A review of literature. *Commissioned Report for the National Symposium on Postsecondary Student Success.* National Postsecondary Education Cooperative. Retrieved January 2, 2007, from http://nces.ed.gov/npec/papers.asp.

Kuh, G. D., Kinzie, J., Cruce, T., Shoup, R., & Gonyea, R. M. (2006b). *Connecting the dots: Multi-faceted analysis of the relationships between student engagement results from the NSSE, and the institutional practices and conditions that foster students success.* (Lumina Foundation for Education Grant #2518). Bloomington, IN: Center for Postsecondary Research.

Kuh, G., Kinzie, J., Shuch, J., & Whitt, E. (2005). *Student success in college: Creating conditions that matter.* San Francisco: Jossey-Bass.

Kulik, C. C., & Kulik, J. A. (1991). Effectiveness of computer-based instruction: An updated analysis. *Computers in Human Behavior, 7,* 75–94.

Kulik, C. C., Kulik, J. A., & Schwalb, B. J. (1983). College programs for high-risk and disadvantaged students: A meta-analysis of findings. *Review of Educational Research, 53*(3), 397–414.

Laine, M. (1997). A qualitative study of college developmental students' perceptions of the reading and writing relationships in a co-taught paired reading course. In E. Paulson, S. Biggs, M. Laine, & T. Bullock (Eds.), *College reading research and practice: Articles from the Journal of College Literacy and Learning.* Newark, DE: International Reading Association.

Lenze, L. F. (1996, August). Instructional development: What works. *NEA Update, 2*(4).

Levinson-Rose, J., & Menges, R. J. (1981). Improving college teaching: A critical review of research. *Review of Educational Research, 51,* 403–434.

Levitz, R., Noel, L., & Richter, B. (1999). Strategic moves for retention success. *New Directions for Higher Education, 108,* 31.

Lipsky, M. (1980). *Street-level bureaucracy: Dilemmas of the individual in public services.* New York: Russell Sage.

Little, J. W. (2006). *Professional community and professional development in the learning-centered school.* Best Practices Working Paper. Washington, DC: National Education Association.

Long, B. T. (2005, Fall). *The remediation debate: Are we serving the needs of underprepared college students?* (National Cross Talk). San Jose, CA: The National Center for Public Policy and Higher Education. Retrieved on February 1, 2007, from www.highereducation.org/crosstalk/ct0405/voices0405-long.shtml.

Louis, K. S., & Kruse, S. D. (1995). *Professionalism and community: Perspectives on reforming urban schools.* Thousand Oaks, CA: Corwin Press.

Lumina Foundation, Achieving the Dream. (2006, July / August). Data notes: Keeping informed about Achieving the Dream data, 1(6). Retrieved on September 29, 2009, from www.achievingthedream.org.

MacGregor, J. (1990). Collaborative learning: Shared inquiry as a process of reform. In M. D. Svinicki (Ed.), *The changing face of college teaching*. San Francisco: Jossey-Bass.

Maitland, L. (2000). Ideas in practice: Self-regulation and metacognition in the reading lab. *Journal of Developmental Education 24*(2), 26–36.

Martin, D. C., & Blanc, R. A. (1994). VSI: A pathway to mastery and persistence. In D. C. Martin & D. R. Arendale (Eds.), *Supplemental instruction: Increasing achievement and retention* (pp. 83–93). San Francisco: Jossey-Bass.

Maxwell, M. (1995). Does tutoring help? In M. Maxwell (Ed.), *From access to success: A book of readings on college developmental education and learning assistance programs* (pp. 109–117). Clearwater, FL: H & H.

Maxwell, M. (1997a). What are the functions of a college learning assistance center? (ERIC Document Reproduction No. ED413031).

Maxwell, M. (1997b). The role of counseling in a comprehensive developmental program for post-secondary students. (ERIC Document Reproduction No. ED415932).

Maxwell, M. (1997c). Improving student learning skills. Clearwater, FL: H & H.

Maxwell, W. E., & Kazlauskas, E. J. (1992). Which faculty development methods really work in community college?: A review of research. *Community/Junior College Quarterly, 16*, 351–360.

McArthur, R. (1999). A comparison of grading patterns between full and part time humanities faculty: a preliminary study. *Community College Review, 27*(3), 65–76.

McCabe, R. (2003). *Yes we can! A community college guide for developing America's underprepared*. Phoenix, AZ: American Association of Community Colleges and League for Innovation in the Community College. (ERIC Document Reproduction Service No. ED475435).

McCabe, R. H. (2000). *No one to waste: A report to public decision-makers and community college leaders*. The National Study of Community College Remedial Education, Community College Press.

McCabe, R. H., & Day, P. R. (Eds.). (1998). *Developmental education: A twenty-first century social and economic imperative*. Phoenix, AZ: League for Innovation in the Community College and The College Board. (ERIC Document Reproduction Service No. ED421176).

McCarty, T. L., Lynch, R. H., Wallace, S., & Benally, A. (1991). Classroom inquiry and Navajo learning styles: A call for reassessment. *Anthropology & Education Quarterly, 22*(1), 42–59.

McCusker, M. (1999). ERIC Review: Effective elements of developmental reading and writing programs. *Community College Review, 27*(2), 93–105.

McKinsey & Company. (2007). How the world's best performing school systems come out on top. Retrieved September 29, 2009, from www.mckinsey.com/clientservice/socialsector/resources/pdf/Worlds_School_systems_final.pdf.

McLaughlin, M. W., & Talbert, J. E. (2001). *Professional communities and the work of high school teaching.* Chicago: University of Chicago Press.

McQueeny, P. (2001). What's in a name? In J. Nelson & K. Evertz (Eds.), *The politics of writing centers* (pp. 15–22). Portsmouth, NH: Boynton/Cook.

Medrich, E., Calderon, S., & Hoachlander, G. (2002). *Contextual teaching and learning strategies in high schools: Developing a vision for support and evaluation.* Berkeley, CA: MPR Associates.

Merriam, S., Caffarella, R., & Baumgartner, L. (2006, October). *Learning in adulthood: A comprehensive guide* (3rd ed). Jossey-Bass, An Imprint of Wiley. (ERIC Document Reproduction Service No. ED499592).

Mezirow, J. (2000). Learning to think like an adult. In J. Mezirow (Ed.), *Learning as transformation.* San Francisco: Jossey-Bass.

Miller, H., & Spence, S. (2007). Places—and faces—that foster student success. *Lumina Foundation Lessons.* Lumina Foundation. (ERIC Document Reproduction Service No. ED497034).

Moore, C., & Shulock, N. (2007). *Beyond the open door: Increasing student success in California Community Colleges.* Sacramento: Institute for Higher Education Leadership and Policy, California State University, Sacramento.

Moss, D., & Ross-Feldman, L. (2003). *Second language acquisition in adults: From research to practice.* Washington, DC: Center for Applied Linguistics. Retrieved January 6, 2007, from www.cal.org/Caela/esl_resources/digests/SLA.html.

Moyer, P., & Jones, M. (2004). Controlling Choice: Teachers, Students, and Manipulatives in Mathematics Classrooms. *School Science and Mathematics, 104*(1), 16–31.

Muraskin, L. (1997). *"Best practices" in student support services: A study of five exemplary sites. Follow-up study of student support services programs.* Washington, DC: Department of Education, Office of Planning, Budget, & Evaluation.

Muraskin, L., & Lee, J. (2004). *Raising the graduation rates of low-income college students.* Washington, DC: The Pell Institute for the Study of Opportunity in Higher Education.

Murray, J. P. (1999, Winter). Faculty development in a national sample of community colleges. *Community College Review, 27*(3), 47–65.

Murray, J. P. (2001). Faculty development in publicly supported 2-year colleges. *Community College Journal of Research and Practice, 25,* 487–502.

Murray, J. P. (2002a, Spring). Faculty development in SACS accredited community colleges. *Community College Review, 29*(4).

Murray, J. P. (2002b). The current state of faculty development in two-year colleges. *New Directions for Community Colleges, 118,* 89–97.

National Literacy Act. (1991, July 25). Public Law 102–73, section 3. Retrieved November 10, 2006, from www.nifl.gov/public-law.html.

National Writing Project. (2008). *Research Brief: Writing project professional development for teachers yields gains in student writing achievement.* Berkeley, CA: National Writing Project. Retrieved on September 29, 2009, from www.nwp.org/cs/public/download/nwp_file/10683/NWP_Research_Brief_2008.pdf?x-r=pcfile_d.

Neuberger, J. (1999). Executive board position paper: Research recommendations for developmental education and/or learning assistance programs in the State of New York. *Research and Teaching in Developmental Education, 16*(1), 5–22.

Nichols, R. (1986). Effects of intensive, intrusive faculty advising on college freshmen. *Dissertation Abstracts International 06A, 2048.*

Nist, S., & Hynd, C. (1985, January) The college reading lab: An old story with a new twist. In M. Maxwell (Ed.), *From access to success: A book of readings on college developmental education and learning assistance programs* (pp. 171–173). Clearwater, FL: H & H.

Noel, L., Levitz, R., & Kaufman, J. (1982). *Organizing the campus for retention.* Iowa City: American College Testing Program & National Center for the Academic Advancement of Educational Practices.

Nwagwu, E. C. (1998). How community college administrators can improve teaching effectiveness. *Community College Journal of Research and Practice, 22,* 11–19.

O'Banion, T. (1997). *A Learning College for the 21st Century.* Phoenix, AZ: Oryx Press.

Ogden, P., Thompson, D., Russell, A., & Simons, C. (2003). Supplemental instruction: Short and long-term impact. *Journal of Developmental Education, 26*(3), 2–8.

Ohio State University. (1999). Contextual Teaching and Learning Project. Retrieved January 13, 2007, from www.ed.gov/inits/teachers/exemplarypractices/c-3.html.

Palinscar, A. S., & Brown, A. L. (1984). Reciprocal teaching of comprehension-fostering and comprehension-monitoring activities. *Cognition and Instruction, 1*(2), 117–172.

Palinscar, A. S., & Brown, A. L. (1985). Reciprocal teaching: Activities to promote reading with your mind. In T. L Harris and E. J. Cooper (Eds.), *Reading, thinking and concept development: Strategies for the classroom.* New York: The College Board.

Paris, K., & Huske, L. (1998). *Critical issue: Developing an applied and integrated curriculum.* Naperville, IL: North Central Regional Educational Laboratory. Retrieved January 13, 2007 from www.ncrel.org/sdrs/areas/issues/envrnmnt/stw/sw100.htm.

Pascarella, E. T., & Terenzini, P. T. (1991). *How college affects students.* San Francisco: Jossey Bass.

Paulson, M. B., & Feldman, K. A. (2006). Exploring the dimensions of scholarship of teaching and learning: Analytics for an emerging literature. *New Directions for Institutional Research, 129,* 21–36.

Perin, D. (2002, April). The organization of developmental education: In or out of academic departments? (No. 14). New York: Community College Research Center, Teachers College, Columbia University.

Perin, D. (2005, Spring). Institutional decision making for increasing academic preparedness in community colleges. *New Directions for Community Colleges, 129,* 27–38.

Perin, D. (2006). Can community colleges protect both access and standards?: The problem of remediation. *Teacher's College Record, 108*(3).

Perin, D., & Charron, K., (2003). *Trends in community college assessment and placement approaches: Implications for educational policy.* New York: Community College Research Center, Teachers College, Columbia University. (ERIC Document Reproduction Service No. ED478367).

Perin, D., Keselman, A., & Monopoli, M. (2003). The academic writing of community college remedial students: Text and learner variables. *Higher Education, 45*(1), 19.

Person, A., Rosenbaum, J., & Deil-Amen, R. (2006). Student planning and information problems in different college structures. *Teachers College Record, 108*(3), 374–396.

Pintrich, P. R. (1995). *Understanding self-regulated learning.* San Francisco: Jossey-Bass.

Prince, D., & Jenkins, D. (2005). *Building pathways to success for low-skill adult students: Lessons from community college policy and practice from a longitudinal student tracking study.* (CCRC Brief No. 25.) New York: Community College Research Center, Teachers College, Columbia University.

Prince, H. (2005, April). *Standardization vs. flexibility: State policy options on placement testing for development education in community colleges.* (Achieving the Dream Project Policy Brief). Indianapolis, IN: Lumina Foundation. Retrieved on September 29, 2009, from www.achievingthedream.org/_images/_index03/Policy_brief-StandardFlex.pdf.

Raftery, S. (2005). Developmental learning communities at Metropolitan Community College. *New Directions for Community Colleges, 129,* 63–72.

Richardson, R. C., & Wolverton, M. (1994). Leadership Strategies. In A. M. Cohen & F. B. Brawer (Eds.), *Managing community colleges: A handbook for effective practice.* San Francisco: Jossey-Bass.

Rinehart, S., & Platt, J. (1984). Metacognitive awareness and monitoring in adult and college readers. *Forum for Reading, 15*(2), 54–62.

Ritze, N. (2005). The evolution of developmental education at the City University of New York and Bronx Community College. *New Directions for Community Colleges, 129,* 73–81.

Rossini, C. (2002, March). *My place or yours: Theorizing eclectic writing centers.* Paper presented at the Annual Meeting of the Conference on College Composition and Communication, Chicago, IL.

Roueche, J. (1973). *A modest proposal: Students can learn.* San Francisco: Jossey-Bass.

Roueche, J., & Baker, G. (1985). The success connection: Toward equality with excellence. *Community and Junior College Journal, 55*(7), 18–22.

Roueche, J., & Baker, G. (1987). *Access and excellence.* Washington, DC: Community College Press.

Roueche, J. E., Baker, G. A., & Roueche, S. D. (1985). Access with excellence: Toward academic success in college, *Community College Review, 12,* 4–9.

Roueche, J., Ely, E., & Roueche, S. (2001). *In pursuit of excellence: The Community College of Denver.* Washington, DC: Community College Press.

Roueche, J., & Roueche, S. (1977). *Developmental education: A primer for program development and evaluation.* Atlanta: Southern Regional Education Board.

Roueche, J., & Roueche, S. (1999). *High stakes, high performance: Making remedial education work.* Washington, DC: Community College Press.

Roueche, J., & Snow, J. (1977). *Overcoming learning problems.* San Francisco: Jossey-Bass.

Ryder, P. (1994). Giving or taking authority: Exploring the ideologies of collaborative learning. (ERIC Document Reproduction Service No. ED373363).

Sanchez, I. (2000). Motivating and maximizing learning in minority classrooms. *New Directions for Community Colleges, 2000*(112), 35.

Schmidt, W., Houang, R., & Cogan, L. (2004). A coherent curriculum: The case of mathematics. *Journal of Direct Instruction, 4*(1), 13–28.

Schoenbach, R., Greenleaf, C. L., Cziko, C., & Hurwitz L. (2000). *Reading for understanding: A guide to improving reading in middle and high school classrooms.* San Francisco: Jossey-Bass.

Schultz, R. (1989). Differences between academically successful and unsuccessful students in an intrusive academic advising program. *Dissertation Abstracts International, 51*(02A), 417.

Scrivener, S., Sommo, C., & Collado, H. (2009). *Getting back on track: Effects of a community college program for probationary students.* New York: Manpower Demonstration Research Corporation.

Sheldon, C. Q. (2002). Building an instructional framework for effective community college developmental education. *Eric Digest.* (ERIC Document Reproduction Service No. ED477909).

Shults, C. (2000). *Remedial education: Practices and policies in community colleges.* (Research Brief AACC-RB-00–2). Washington, DC: American Association of Community Colleges.

Silverman, S., & Casazza, M. (2000, January). Learning and development: Making connections to enhance teaching. *Higher and Adult Education Series.* (ERIC Document Reproduction Service No. ED435698).

Singer, S. R. (2002, Fall). Learning and teaching center: Hubs of educational reform. *New Directions for Higher Education, 119,* 59–64.

Smith, P., & Simmons, B. (1978). Evaluating learning centers. *Education, 98*(4).

Smreker, C., Guthrie, J. W., Owens, D. E., & Sims, P. G. (2001, September). *March toward excellence: School success and minority student achievement in department of defense schools.* Washington, DC: National Education Goals Panel. Retrieved September 29, 2009, from http://govinfo.library.unt.edu/negp/.

Snow, R. (1977, June). *Individual differences, instructional theory, and instructional design.* (Tech. Rep. No. 4.). Arlington, VA: Office of Naval Research, Personnel and Training Research Programs Office. (ERIC Document Reproduction Service No. ED151698).

Spears, M. (1990). A study of the effects of academic intervention on performance, satisfaction, and retention of business administration students in a public comprehensive college. *Dissertation Abstracts International, 51(08A),* 2656.

Sternberg, R. (2008). *The balance theory of wisdom. The Jossey-Bass reader on the brain and learning.* San Francisco: Jossey-Bass.

Stoik, J. H. (2001). Technology's role in collaboration. *Community College Journal of Research and Practice, 25,* 37–46.

Stout, B., & Magnotto, J. (1991). Building on realities: WAC programs at community colleges. *New Directions for Community Colleges, 73,* 9–13.

Stromei, L. K. (2000). Increasing retention and success through mentoring. In S. R. Aragon (Ed.), *Beyond access: Methods and models for increasing retention and learning among minority students* (pp. 55–62; 112). San Francisco: Jossey-Bass.

Svinicki, M. (Ed.). (1990). The changing face of college teaching. *New Directions for Teaching and Learning, 42.*

Svinicki, M. (1999). New directions in learning and motivation. In M. D. Svinicki (Ed.), *Teaching and learning on the edge of the millennium: Building on what we have learned.* San Francisco: Jossey-Bass.

Svinicki, M. (2004). *Learning and motivation in the postsecondary classroom.* Austin, TX: Anker.

Sydow, D. (2000). Long-term investment in professional development: Real dividends in teaching and learning. *Community College Journal of Research and Practice, 24,* 383–397.

Teachers of English to Speakers of Other Languages (TESOL). (2000, October). *Adult ESL language and literacy instruction: A vision and action agenda for the 21st century*. Washington, DC: National Center for ESL Literacy Education. Retrieved September 29, 2009, from www.cal.org/caela/esl_resources/vision.pdf.

Tei, E., & Stewart, O. (1985). Effective studying from text: Applying metacognitive strategies. *Forum for Reading, 16*(2), 46–55.

Tierney, W. G., Ahern, B., & Kidwell, C. S. (1996, Winter). Enhancing faculty development at tribal colleges. *Tribal Colleges Journal,* 36–39.

Tinto, V. (1993). *Leaving college: Rethinking the causes and cures of student attrition* (2nd ed.). Chicago: University of Chicago Press.

Tinto, V. (1997). Classrooms as communities: Exploring the educational character of student persistence. *Journal of Higher Education, 68*(6), 599–623.

Tinto, V. (2000a). What have we learned about the impact of learning communities on students? *Assessment Update, 12*(2), 1.

Tinto, V. (2000b). Looking at the university through different lenses. *About Campus, 4*(6), 2.

Tobias, S. (1995). *Overcoming math anxiety.* New York: Norton.

Torgerson, C., Brooks, G., Porthouse, J., Burton, M., Robinson, A., Wright, K., et al. (2004). *Adult literacy and numeracy interventions and outcomes: A review of controlled trials.* London: National Research and Development Center for Adult Literacy and Numeracy.

Travis, J. E. (1995). *Models for improving college teaching: A faculty resource.* (ASHE-ERIC: Higher education report No. 6). Washington, DC: Office of Educational Research and Improvement. (ERIC Document Reproduction No. ED403811).

Trawick, L., & Corno, L. (1995). Expanding the volitional resources of urban community college students. In P. R. Pintrich (Ed.), *Understanding self-regulated learning.* San Francisco: Jossey-Bass.

United States Department of Education. (2005). *Strengthening mathematics skills at the postsecondary level: Literature review and analysis.* Washington, DC: Office of Vocational and Adult Education, Division of Adult Education and Literacy.

Venezia, A., Kirst, M., & Antonio, A. (2003). *Betraying the college dream: How disconnected K–12 and postsecondary education system undermine student aspirations.* Stanford, CA: Stanford Institute for Higher Education Research.

Vincent, V. C. (1983). Impact of a college learning assistance center on the achievement and retention of disadvantaged students. (ERIC Document Reproduction Service No. ED283438).

Vineyard, E. E. (1994). The administrator's role in staff management. In A. M. Cohen and F. Brawer (Eds.). *Managing community colleges: A handbook of effective practice.* San Francisco: Jossey-Bass.

Washington State Board for Community and Technical Colleges. (2005, December). *Integrated Basic Education and Skills Training Program (I-BEST) Executive Summary.* (Research Report 05–2). Olympia, WA.

Waycaster, P. (2001a, March). *Community college collaborative on developmental mathematics.* Presented at the NADE 25th Annual Conference, Louisville, KY.

Waycaster, P. (2001b). Factors impacting success in community college developmental mathematics courses and subsequent courses. *Community College Journal of Research and Practice, 25,* 5–6.

Weimer, M. (1990). *Improving college teaching: Strategies for developing instructional effectiveness.* San Francisco: Jossey-Bass.

Weinbaum, A., & Rogers, A. M. (1995). *Contextual learning: A critical aspect of school-to-work transition programs.* Washington, DC: Office of Educational Research and Improvement. (ERIC Document Reproduction Service No. ED381666.)

Weinstein, C. E., & Meyer, D. (1991). Cognitive strategies and college teaching. In R. J. Menges and M. D. Svinicki (Eds.), *College teaching: From theory to practice.* San Francisco: Jossey-Bass.

Weissman, J., Bulakowski, C., & Jumisko, M. (1997). Using research to evaluate developmental education programs and policies. *New Directions for Community Colleges 100,* 73–80. (ERIC Document Reproduction Service No. EJ558593).

WestEd (2004a). *1997–2000: A study of teacher learning and student reading outcomes in SLI professional development network.* San Francisco: WestEd, Strategic Learning Initiative. Retrieved September 29, 2009, from www.wested.org/sli/linked_page_4_final.pdf.

WestEd (2004b). *2001–2004: Reading Apprenticeship classroom student linking professional development for teachers to outcomes for students in diverse subject-area classrooms.* San Francisco: WestEd, Strategic Learning Initiative. Retrieved September 29, 2009, from www.wested.org/sli/linked_page_6_final.pdf.

Wilcox, P., Winn, S., & Fyvie-Gauld, M. (2005, December). It was nothing to do with the university, it was just the people: The role of social support in the first-year experience of higher education. *Studies in Higher Education, 30*(6), 707–722. (ERIC Document Reproduction Service No. EJ721313).

Williams, W., & Sternberg, R. (1988, October). Group intelligence: Why some groups are better than others. *Intelligence, 12*(4), 351–77. (ERIC Document Reproduction Service No. EJ388098).

Wilson, S. M., & Berne, J. (1999). Teacher learning and the acquisition of professional knowledge: An examination of research on contemporary professional development. *Review of Research in Education. 24,* 173–209.

Wolfe, P. (2001). Brain Research and Education: Fad or Foundation? Retrieved December 6, 2006 from www.brainconnection.com/content/160_1.

Wyckoff, S. (1999, January). The academic advising process in higher education: History, research and improvement. *Recruitment and Retention in Higher Education, 13*(1), 1–3.

Zeidenberg, M., Jenkins, D., & Calcagno, J. (2007, June). *Do student success courses actually help community college students succeed?* (CCRC Brief. No. 36.) New York: Community College Research Center, Teachers College, Columbia University. (ERIC Document Reproduction Service No. ED499357).

Zhang, J. (2000). In defense of college developmental reading education. In E. Paulson, S. Biggs, M. Laine, & Bullock, T. (Eds.), *College reading research and practice: Articles from the journal of college literacy and learning* (pp. 43–49). Newark, DE: International Reading Association.

Zull, J. (2004). The art of changing the brain. *Educational Leadership, 62*(1), 68–72.

Index